Social Justice and International Education
RESEARCH, PRACTICE, AND PERSPECTIVES

Social Justice and International Education

RESEARCH, PRACTICE, AND PERSPECTIVES

EDITED BY
LaNitra M. Berger, PhD

Social Justice and International Education: Research, Practice, and Perspectives

Edited by LaNitra M. Berger

NAFSA: Association of International Educators
1307 New York Avenue, NW
8th Floor
Washington, DC 20005-4715

NAFSA is the largest and most comprehensive association of professionals committed to advancing international higher education. Based in the United States, we provide programs, products, services, and a physical and virtual meeting space for the worldwide community of international educators. The association provides leadership to its varied constituencies through establishing principles of good practice and providing professional development opportunities. NAFSA encourages networking among professionals, convenes conferences and collaborative dialogues, and promotes research and knowledge creation to strengthen and serve the field. We lead the way in advocating for a better world through international education.

Library of Congress Cataloging-in-Publication Data

Names: Berger, LaNitra M., editor.
Title: Social justice and international education : research, practice, and perspectives / edited by LaNitra M. Berger.
Description: Washington, DC : NAFSA, [2020] | Includes bibliographical references. | Summary: "Social Justice and International Education: Research, Practice, and Perspectives brings together a group of educators, scholars, and practitioners in the field of international education who are doing important and innovative work promoting social justice, confronting inequality, and fostering social responsibility in a global context. The book does not operate on a singular definition of social justice; rather, the authors describe their own working definition and how it has guided their international education work. Divided into three parts, the book explores social justice research, social justice in practice, and different perspectives from practitioners across the field"—Provided by publisher.
Identifiers: LCCN 2020031773 (print) | LCCN 2020031774 (ebook) | ISBN 9781942719342 (paperback) | ISBN 9781942719397 (ebook)
Subjects: LCSH: International education. | Social justice—Study and teaching.
Classification: LCC LC1090 .S63 2020 (print) | LCC LC1090 (ebook) | DDC 370.116—dc23
LC record available at https://lccn.loc.gov/2020031773
LC ebook record available at https://lccn.loc.gov/2020031774

Design and Layout by Kathleen Dyson

Copyright © 2020 by NAFSA: Association of International Educators. No part of this publication may be reproduced, stored in a retrieval system, or transmitted in any form or by any means, electronic, mechanical, photocopying, recording, scanning, or otherwise, except as permitted under Section 107 or 108 of the United States Copyright Act, without the prior written permission of the publisher. Requests to the publisher for permission should be addressed to Publications@nafsa.org. Printed in the United States.

Publisher's Note: The opinions expressed in this book reflect those of the individual authors and may or may not reflect the opinions or official positions of NAFSA: Association of International Educators. We respect the rights of these authors to state their personal opinions, and we are providing this forum in the spirit of academic freedom.

BULK PURCHASES
Quantity discounts are available for workshops and staff development.
Call 1.866.538.1927 to order.

First edition, 2020

10 9 8 7 6 5 4 3 2

Contents

Acknowledgments... ix

Introduction | LaNITRA M. BERGER, PhD 1

Part I. Social Justice Research 9

1   International Education's Potential for Advancing Social Justice
    DAVID WICK, EdD, AND TASHA WILLIS, EdD 11

2   Equity Education in a Time of Rising Nationalism: Challenges
    and Complexities
    SUPRIYA BAILY, PhD 43

3   The Evolution of Social Justice in International Higher Education
    AARON CLEVENGER, EdD 63

4   Being "Black" in a U.S. Context: Racialized Experiences of African
    and Caribbean International Students
    SHONTAY DELALUE, PhD 83

5   "Rebeldes en Acción": A Case Study in English Teaching in a
    Marginalized Colombian High School
    YECID ORTEGA, MA 111

Part II. Social Justice in Practice 135

6   View, Voice, and Visibility: A Liberating Framework for
    Social Justice in Education Abroad
    EDUARDO CONTRERAS JR., EdD 137

7   Social Justice-Centered Education Abroad Programming:
    Navigating Social Identities and Fostering Conversations
    MALAIKA MARABLE SERRANO, MA 155

8   Social Justice and Study Abroad at Historically Black Colleges and Universities: A Case Study of Howard University
TONIJA HOPE NAVAS, MA 173

9   Supporting Deaf Students in Education Abroad
BECCA ABURAKIA-EINHORN, MPA 191

10   Integrating Refugees into U.S. Higher Education
BRYCE LOO, MA 215

11   Exploring the Intersection of Transnationalism and Critical Race Theory: A Critical Race Analysis of International Students' Experiences in the United States
CHRISTINA W. YAO, PhD; CHRYSTAL A. GEORGE MWANGI, PhD; AND VICTORIA K. MALANEY BROWN, PhD 247

Part III. Perspectives from the Field 269

Building a Movement for Justice: Short-Term Programs Abroad
SHOSHANNA SUMKA, MAA 271

Study Abroad: The Power of Finding Your Place in the World
SALLY SCHWARTZ, MA 275

Toward Family Diplomacy for a More Caring World
PAUL LaCHELIER, PhD 279

Embracing Our Greater Purpose: The Role of International Education in Advancing Educational Equity
ANDREW J. GORDON 283

Afrophobia and International Education
KESHIA ABRAHAM, PhD 287

Street Law: Using the Law to Effect Social Justice
SEÁN ARTHURS, EdLD, AND JOHN LUNNEY, MSc 293

Perspectives on the Intersections of Social Justice and International Education
JESSICA BLACK SANDBERG, MA 297

Social Justice Through the Eyes of an International Educator
RODOLFO "RUDIE" ALTAMIRANO, PhD 301

Social Justice and International Education: Where Are the Voices of International Students and Scholars?
LING G. LeBEAU, PhD 305

The Sustainable Development Goals, Social Justice, and Global Learning
JOE WARREN, MPHIL 309

The Fight for Refugee Children's Education
ZAMA NEFF, JD 313

over&over
PÁDRAIG Ó TUAMA, MTH 317

About the Authors.. 321

Acknowledgments

I have been privileged to be uplifted and mentored by many people who have contributed to and shaped the direction of this book.

First, I would like to thank NAFSA's senior leadership and staff for giving shape and life to this book. Dr. Esther Brimmer has led a stellar team of professionals who guided this publication: Dorothea Antonio, Michael Kulma, Caroline Donovan White, and Joann Ng Hartmann have been insightful and careful reviewers and supporters. This book would not have been possible without the hard work and assistance of the NAFSA publications team: Martha Hawley-Bertsch and Natalie Ngo helped me come up with the original book concept, handled many of the tedious editorial details, and kept the project on schedule. Joe Vallina and Wendy Rubin later joined the publications team and dove right into the project, providing invaluable editorial guidance and support.

Thank you to all of the authors, who enthusiastically responded to my invitation to contribute to this book. I am thrilled to be able to share your innovative thoughts, ideas, and recommendations with a wider audience through this publication.

My career in international education began at the National Association for Equal Opportunity in Higher Education (NAFEO), a trade association for the presidents of historically and predominantly Black colleges and universities. Learning about campus internationalization through the lens of social justice-oriented institutions has fundamentally shaped the way I view the role international education plays in promoting justice and equality. I am grateful to NAFEO President Lezli Baskerville and my supervisor, Selena Mendy Singleton, for providing me with the opportunity to organize three national dialogues on international education at HBCUs, which laid the early foundations for my ideas about this book. My first connection to NAFSA began in 2005, when I became the liaison between NAFEO and NAFSA to contribute ideas on how to shape the Commission on the Abraham Lincoln Study Abroad Fellowship Program. This work was critical in developing my ability to serve as an advocate for underrepresented students in international education, and it continues to inform my work as a scholar and administrator today.

I would like to thank my colleagues at George Mason University for giving me the time and the space to work on such an important book project. Former President Ángel Cabrera supported my efforts to build a fellowships office centered in social justice principles. My supervisors, Zofia Burr in the Honors College and Bethany Usher in the Office of Undergraduate Education, believed that this book was consistent with George Mason University's commitment to social justice and inclusive excellence in international education.

I would also like to thank Rachel Zelizer, my wonderful research assistant. Rachel has worked with me on this project from the very beginning. She kept me organized as I corresponded with authors, edited chapters, and worked to meet deadlines.

Finally, my husband, Matthew Berger, is my best editor: critical in the most loving of ways. I am committed to social justice and international education work for my two sons, Nathan and Luke, and their generation. May they be inspired to travel the world and devote their energy to social change.

Introduction

LaNITRA M. BERGER, PhD

During the 1930s and 1940s, German-Jewish scholars were expelled from their academic posts in German universities by the Nazi regime. Becoming refugees and in danger of being deported to concentration camps, many academics pleaded for asylum in the United States and requested teaching appointments in American colleges and universities. Many universities did not offer these scholars positions, and the scholars were denied entry into the United States (Edgcomb 1993).

The exception was a group of historically Black colleges and universities (HBCUs), institutions that were founded to educate the sons and daughters of American slaves. HBCUs offered teaching positions to approximately 50 German-Jewish refugee scholars in fields ranging from mathematics to visual art (Edgcomb 1993). Part of the core educational missions of these institutions was to address social inequality and to work toward racial justice. Administrators at HBCUs saw an opportunity to extend this commitment by welcoming refugee scholars to their campuses. Merging international education and social justice ideals led to extraordinary results. The Jewish scholars provided HBCU students with a high-quality education, which the students could not have accessed elsewhere in the United States. Shocked by the segregation and racial violence in the South, many refugee scholars observed chilling parallels to the anti-Semitism they had left behind in Europe. Some were compelled to encourage students to resist racism by protesting segregation laws and participating in the civil rights movement. In this case, HBCUs set an example by providing refuge to German-Jewish scholars, who in turn taught Black students to use their critical thinking skills to challenge white supremacy.

This is just one example of how international education can be both a catalyst and an incubator for transformational work in communities at home and abroad. *Social Justice and International Education: Research, Practice, and Perspectives* features the perspectives of contemporary scholars and practitioners from around the world who are doing innovative work at the intersection of these two areas. The authors bring a depth of experience to their integration of social justice theories and concepts in international education. They are research scholars, education abroad professionals, teachers, university administrators, poets, and community activists who are using international education to work for social equality. Designed to reach a wide audience, the chapters address critical issues in the fields of international education and social justice. Young professionals, graduate students, activists, K–12 teachers and administrators, senior university leadership, and citizens who wish to take action in their communities, among others, will gain valuable insight into the ways in which international education can apply a social justice perspective to cultivate and support global citizenship.

Key Themes

This book illuminates the ways in which the field of international education uses social justice pedagogy, curriculum design, and community engagement practices to address inequality and systems of oppression in various forms around the world. Its aims are twofold. First, this book provides multiple frameworks for defining and thinking about social justice in international education, as there is no singular approach or method for this work. Authors draw from a variety of academic disciplines and theories for their work, such as Kimberlé Crenshaw and colleagues' *Critical Race Theory* (1995); Paulo Freire's *Pedagogy of the Oppressed* (1972); and Sara Lawrence-Lightfoot's theorization of view, voice, and visibility (2017). Second, the book is a call to action, prompting readers to be introspective and think critically about what steps they can take to initiate or amplify the global dimensions of their social justice work. The authors discuss how to guide students in the classroom and in communities in thinking about their dual roles as learners and as social justice advocates. International educators acknowledge that issues such as equalizing access, addressing implicit bias, promoting inclusive excellence, and supporting peacebuilding are shared goals in both social justice and international education (Womack-Wynne 2018). However, what can we do now to take more decisive action on these issues and assess the outcomes? How can we bring more voices and perspectives together in constructive dialogue about social justice and how it shapes internationalization (Olson, Evans, and Schoenberg 2007)? To help readers with this second aim, a number of the authors present recommendations and questions for the reader to consider as they think about integrating social justice principles into their work and the work of their institutions.

Throughout the book, the authors find different ways to articulate the concept of a social justice mindset in international education. This mindset includes a framework for, and an approach to thinking about, social issues and institutional barriers in a global context that address three important themes: (1) identifying and challenging institutional structures that perpetuate social inequality using a critical theoretical lens; (2) embracing a "bottom up" approach to thinking about how specific marginalized groups are affected by their relationships to power and privilege; and (3) developing processes and exercises that seek to analyze and interrogate individual and group biases. Throughout the book, the authors present concrete examples of how these themes inform research, practice, and perspectives on social justice and international education.

Overview of the Book

This book is divided into three sections: Social Justice Research (part I), Social Justice in Practice (part II), and Perspectives from the Field (part III). In part I, academic researchers share their findings from conducting social justice-oriented research in international education. These chapters demonstrate how to ask scholarly questions with a social justice mindset. David Wick and Tasha Willis open this section with an overview of the scholarly social justice questions that impact the field of international education, arguing that all international educators should approach their work with a social justice lens because peacebuilding and mutual understanding are shared goals of international educators and social justice advocates. Yecid Ortega uses a similar argument in his study of a social justice curriculum for English language learners in Colombia, reiterating the claim that together, peacebuilding and social justice work can promote social transformation and racial healing. Aaron Clevenger offers alternative ways to think about the history and evolution of the term "social justice" and how to design international social justice programs for students who are underrepresented in education abroad but considered privileged in almost every other context (e.g., male students in STEM fields). Supriya Baily's chapter looks at the problems that nationalist political ideologies present for international education and how social justice advocacy can help counteract nationalist tendencies. Shontay Delalue analyzes the challenges that Black African international students face in being racialized in the U.S. higher education context and marginalized as racial minorities; for many of these students, it is the first time in their lives they have this experience.

The chapters in part II are written by practitioners in international education who provide examples and recommendations for how readers can use social justice principles in their own work. Eduardo Contreras urges education abroad professionals to discontinue the "deficit mindset" approach to advising students and warns against the "prejudice of invisibility" in overlooking underrepresented students or assuming they have little to contribute to shaping education abroad experiences. In her chapter on developing an education abroad program specifically for HBCU students interested in social justice, Tonija Hope Navas underscores the importance of foreign language fluency in supporting students' cross-cultural social justice learning. Malaika Marable Serrano brings the concepts of intersectionality and multiple identities to the center of social justice teaching in education abroad. Helping students understand how their identities relate to their academic content abroad, she argues, creates opportunities for conversation about empathy and engaging across differences. Becca AbuRakia-Einhorn writes about her work with students who are deaf and hard of hearing in the education abroad office at Gallaudet University, the only university in the United States specifically for people who are deaf and hard of hearing. Advocating for deaf students to have the resources needed for equal access to study abroad opportunities, AbuRakia-Einhorn raises awareness of the difficulties and additional costs that these students incur to study abroad. Bryce Loo argues that from a social justice perspective, refugee students at U.S. higher education institutions need to be supported academically but also fully integrated into campus life so that their intellectual interests and life experiences become part of an inclusive campus culture. Finally, Christina W. Yao, Chrystal A. George Mwangi, and Victoria K. Malaney Brown use Critical Race Theory to consider how international students are racialized on U.S. college campuses and how this racialization negatively affects their learning and co-curricular experiences. In the process of developing their argument, the authors call for an expansion of the Critical Race Theory into a transnational framework.

Part III includes 11 short essays and a poem, or "Perspectives from the Field," from authors' direct experiences working on social justice issues in international education. Authors in this section come from a variety of sectors, including human rights, secondary schools, nonprofits, universities, peacebuilding, and community activism. The essays provide specific examples of how each author challenges the prevailing assumptions in their sectors to expand opportunities and access to marginalized groups. As a collection, the essays complement the book's earlier chapters by describing examples of what the authors' theories and practical recommendations look like "on the ground."

The COVID-19 Pandemic and the Response to Systemic Racial Injustice

This book was published in the midst of the COVID-19 pandemic and a movement across the United States and around the world to confront systemic racial injustice. These issues and the global responses to them—as well as their economic, social, and political consequences—have dramatically impacted higher education broadly, with consequences specifically for international education. Those working in international education should approach these global challenges with a social justice lens.

The coronavirus has unequal outcomes, disproportionately affecting communities of color around the world, those living in environmentally degraded areas, and people who have fewer financial means or lack access to quality healthcare. In addition, the first cases of the virus were diagnosed in Wuhan, China, which has provoked racist acts against people of Asian descent around the world and sparked xenophobic policies targeted toward foreigners and immigrants.

The United States and many other countries have also been forced to reckon with systemic racial injustice that is manifested through white supremacy, police violence, health disparities, social and economic inequality, and other forms of oppression. The collective outrage about these issues has started a global conversation about the international dimensions of white privilege and the specific need to name, confront, and end anti-Black racism by unequivocally asserting that Black Lives Matter.

As the pandemic and the response to systemic racial injustice continue, one thing is clear: The international education community is entering a new and critical phase in which the work of those in the field can make a direct contribution to fostering social change. International education professionals must think critically about how the social justice principles and themes in this book can inform international education more broadly, reaching more disciplines, faculty, programs, and research collaborations.

A Note on Capitalization

Readers may notice some variation in capitalization throughout the book, specifically with regard to "Black"/"black," "white"/"White," and "people or students of color"/"people or students of Color." Recognizing ethnic identity is an important aspect of social justice scholarship, practice, and pedagogy. In some chapters, authors capitalize or lowercase terms such as "Black," "white," or "people/students of Color" to recognize and affirm people from marginalized groups and identities. To support the authors in this work and to respect their perspectives, NAFSA has diverged a bit from its style guidelines that would typically treat these terms in the same way throughout the book.

Conclusion

Social Justice and International Education: Research, Practice, and Perspectives aims to educate, challenge long-held assumptions, and inspire action. Leading scholars and practitioners from around the world are working to imagine new ways of thinking about how to broaden and deepen widespread engagement in social issues and communicate their global significance. Now, more than ever before, the intersection of social justice and international education is relevant, urgent, and consequential.

References

Crenshaw, Kimberlé, Neil Gotanda, Gary Peller, and Kendall Thomas, eds. 1995. *Critical Race Theory: The Key Writings That Formed the Movement*. New York, NY: The New Press.

Edgcomb, Gabrielle Simon, and Mazal Holocaust Collection. 1993. *From Swastika to Jim Crow: Refugee Scholars at Black Colleges* (Original Edition). Malabar, Florida: Krieger Publishing Company.

Freire, Paulo. 1972. *Pedagogy of the Oppressed* (M. B. Ramos, Trans.; Reprint edition). New York, NY: Herder and Herder.

Lawrence-Lightfoot, Sara. 2017. "Let the Great Brown River Smile." https://www.youtube.com/watch?v=0qbGoo0N0lU.

Olson, Christa L., Rhodri Evans, and Robert Shoenberg. 2007. *At Home in the World: Bridging the Gap Between Internationalization and Multicultural Education*. Washington, DC: American Council on Education.

Womack-Wynne, Carly. 2018. "Global Citizenship 2.0." *International Educator*, May/June 2018, 20–26.

Part I
Social Justice Research

1
International Education's Potential for Advancing Social Justice

DAVID WICK, EdD, AND TASHA WILLIS, EdD

> *International education exchange is the most significant current project designed to continue the process of humanizing mankind to the point, we would hope that nations can learn to live in peace.*
> —J. WILLIAM FULBRIGHT (FULBRIGHT N.D.)

> *Authentic liberation—the process of humanization—is not another deposit to be made in men. Liberation is a praxis: the action and reflection of men and women upon their world in order to transform it.*
> —PAULO FREIRE (2009, 79)

There are several profound connections between J. William Fulbright's commitment to international education and Paulo Freire's perspective on liberation. In these quotes and their other work, both Fulbright and Freire identify humanization as one of education's key ideals and propose models for achieving these goals. Yet, few international educators—coming from a field that, in the United States, aligns strongly with Fulbright's ideas—consider the connection between international education's promotion of peace and understanding and Freire's goals of reducing oppression and inequity. Social justice educators aligned with Freire, on the other hand, can appear rooted in local communities. Clearly, there is room for international and social justice educators to learn from and with one another to imagine educational activities that address global systems and structures that reproduce inequity.

Giroux's (2010) statements about Freire connect these two ways of thinking about education and humanization. Giroux (2010, 719) writes, "Although

Freire was a theoretician of radical contextualism, he also acknowledged the importance of understanding the particular and the local in relation to larger, global and cross-national forces. For Freire, literacy as a way of reading and changing the world had to be reconceived within a broader understanding of citizenship, democracy and justice that was global and transnational." This chapter explores these connections that make the examination of social justice and international education activities essential for all international educators.

Connections Between International Education and Social Justice

We, as international educators, believe that our field has the potential for advancing social justice. At the same time, we challenge the notion that international education activities, including but not limited to global student mobility, automatically or inherently lead to critical self-reflection, intercultural competence, critical empathy, and the betterment of humanity—all of which we see as components of socially just international education. The fundamental change that we propose is to make social justice the purpose and goal of international education activities, instead of framing it as an ancillary benefit. In this chapter, we approach our examination of international education's potential for advancing social justice with a critical lens, a lens that is informed by our review of the literature, professional experiences, and emerging research.

From our perspectives, in education and social work, we define "social justice in international education" as a redistribution of resources that is designed to foster critical consciousness, develop critical interculturality, and work toward equitable impacts on individuals and their communities. Our review of the literature suggests that a critical examination of the rhetoric and practices related to the internationalization of higher education and of international education activities can help us to recognize the impacts of structural inequity on our work and thus develop transformative practices. Through our own professional experience, we have noted some promising practices that can lead to socially just outcomes for all involved in the experiences. We have also become more aware of many of the challenges and difficulties through our own missteps.

From all these sources, we believe that international education activities are potentially powerful opportunities for socially just transformations at the individual, institutional, community, and maybe even global levels. In order to achieve these aims, we propose a critical pedagogy for international education—one that can apply to education abroad activities, work with international students and scholars, and internationalization at home. This critical pedagogy offers all of us in the field a way to critically reimagine international education activities and thus make them more likely to consistently promote social justice at home and abroad.

Education's Role in Fostering Critical Consciousness

Numerous scholars have argued that education should be a dominant force for social change, using language such as democratization (Dewey 1916), humanization and liberation (Freire 2009), and social justice (Ladson-Billings 1998; Ladson-Billings and Tate 1995). Freire's (2009) concept of critical consciousness is an objective that many critical educators strive to develop among students as a pathway toward social justice education. "Critical consciousness" can be defined as the achievement of the awareness of the social and political structures that oppress certain groups and the agency to resist these forces through action (Freire 2009). A more recent derivative of the concept of critical consciousness includes the construct of "transformative potential" (Jemal 2017), which both encompasses and moves beyond critical consciousness to include "transformative action" as an implicit and urgent purpose of education.

Critical thought can inform the work of international educators and stimulate critical consciousness and transformative potential. We look to multiple critical theoretical frameworks for ways of thinking about how systemic inequity functions and how scholars and educators can disrupt these systems. Frameworks we have used include Critical Race Theory (Ladson-Billings and Tate 1995), Black Feminist Thought (Collins 2015), Intersectionality (Crenshaw 1989), and Chicana Feminist Epistemology (Bernal 1998), though many other critical theories exist, such as Latina/o Critical Theory (Kiehne 2016) and Critical Disability Studies (Meekosha, Shuttleworth, and Soldatic 2013), among others. Taken together, these frameworks provide multiple analytic lenses through which we can critically examine the ways that systems of privilege and power serve to perpetuate marginalization and oppression.

As it has developed, Critical Race Theory has come to refer to five central tenets: (1) centrality of race; (2) challenge to dominant ideology; (3) commitment to social justice; (4) centrality of experiential knowledge; and (5) an interdisciplinary perspective (Ladson-Billings and Tate 1995). The primary argument is that race and racism are central to understanding the systems and structures that oppress people of color and maintain hegemony (Ladson-Billings and Tate 1995). The intersections between race and other aspects of identity such as socioeconomic status, age, gender, and sexuality are also included in this critical perspective.

Critical theories generally took root in U.S. contexts and have primarily been applied in domestic educational spaces. However, we believe that critical theories must also be used to interrogate and critique the profession of international education and the process of internationalization (Knight 2004). As critical international educators committed to equity, inclusion, diversity, and justice in the field, we must call for approaches that are informed by critical thought and designed to advance social justice in content, form, and outcomes. We encourage international educators to learn from critical theories, especially those related to their identities and those of their students, coworkers, and surrounding communities. Each of these theories can challenge our inherent biases and help us to critically reflect on ourselves and others as we develop empathy for the rich and complex perspectives and life experiences of those around us.

Critical Approaches to Internationalization

We recognize that internationalization and international education are complex and distinct terms. For the purposes of this chapter, we differentiate between the two. We have adopted Knight's (2004, 11) definition of "internationalization" as "the process of integrating an international, intercultural or global dimension into the purpose, functions or delivery of post-secondary education." And we use the term "international education" to reference the work that international educators do to design, manage, facilitate, and assess programs and activities. Thus, international education activities are programs designed to result in student growth and development related to international, intercultural, and, we propose, social justice objectives.

Multiple scholars have sought to explain the rationales for international education programming and internationalization of higher education institutions. These rationales often suggest that integrating global, international, and intercultural dimensions into higher education is equally beneficial to all involved. The arguments for internationalization from governments, corporations, and educational institutions also emphasize the importance of international education exchange for employability.

However, critical analysis of the underlying rhetoric for the internationalization of higher education reflects neoliberal agendas that are inherently colonial and contrary to the espoused values. For example, critical scholars have analyzed internationalization rhetoric and have noted an avoidance of ethical and political dimensions, especially in relationship to unequal privilege and power dynamics (Buckner and Stein 2019). Others have highlighted the ways that a policy brief issued by 32 international education organizations communicates a commodification of international students and scholars (Yao and Viggiano 2019). Moreover, Yao and Viggiano (2019) note that the brief focuses almost exclusively on the benefits that international students and scholars bring to U.S. soft power, knowledge production, and economy, with almost no mention of the benefits to the students and scholars or their home communities.

Critical analysis of the governmental, corporate, and educational arguments for internationalization suggests that the purpose and goals of international education activities actually reproduce structural inequities. Most governments, corporations, and institutions promote vastly different opportunities to students coming from the global north than they do for students coming from the global south. As Vavrus and Pekol (2015, 8) state, "In contrast to much of the theory that has informed the field of international education in general, and the design of study abroad programs in particular, critical social theory insists on attention to relations of power that shape the encounter between the self and the cultural Other, and between institutions with different degrees of prestige and financial resources."

A Critical Analysis

The following analysis of the theories that drive internationalization serves to challenge their failure to recognize and critique systems of injustice. By failing to critically examine systemic inequity, current international education activities are likely to be reproducing inequity. Other scholars have expressed a similar critique of the stated goals for global student mobility: "[T]hough presented with an appealing veneer of multicultural understanding and progressive global responsibility, the current discourse of study abroad is nationalistic, imperialist, and political in nature" (Zemach-Bersin 2007, 17).

An analysis of the global flows of students also reflects divergent beliefs about the purpose and value of global student mobility to participants and home countries. The flows of students to and from the United States (Institute of International Education Center for Academic Mobility Research and Impact 2018; Institute of International Education 2018) illustrate the inequitable distribution of educational opportunity. In reviewing these flows, we notice that the number of international students coming to the United States has always been many times higher than the number of U.S. students studying abroad. Furthermore, the activities that students are undertaking are dramatically different.

The U.S. study abroad data from 2016–17 presented by the Institute of International Education (IIE) reflect students who participate in short-term study abroad programs (up to 1 year, with 65 percent participating for 8 weeks or less and 2.3 percent participating for an academic or calendar year) (IIE 2018) as part of their studies at U.S. institutions. On the other hand, most of the international students (75.4 percent in 2017–18) in the United States are pursuing full degrees (IIE 2018). This distinction reflects what some people see as the minimal value that the United States places on international education experiences, which are only beneficial if they are part of the process of earning a degree in the United States. This is in stark contrast to the perceived value of a degree in the United States that compels international students to leave their home countries and regions to pursue full degrees in the United States. This is one of the ways that the international education activities involving global student mobility reinforce current power systems and support the status quo (Buckner and Stein 2019; Yao and Viggiano 2019).

Taken together, these critiques of internationalization suggest a need for reimagining this process in order to align more fully with the espoused values. In addition to rethinking the process of internationalization, we recommend examining international education activities.

Critical International Education Activities

As with the process of internationalization, international education activities, such as education abroad, have often been critiqued for ignoring the larger, unjust contexts in which they operate and thus failing to promote social justice. For example, Zemach-Bersin (2007, 17) states:

> Proponents of international education identify study abroad as a remedy for widespread cross-cultural misunderstanding, prejudice, global ignorance, and failed international policy. Such enthusiasm, however, overlooks the many ways in which the discourse of study abroad surreptitiously reproduces the logic of colonialism, legitimizes American imperialist desires, and allows for the interests of U.S. foreign policy to be articulated through the specious rhetoric of global universality.

This critique suggests that international educators need to explicitly teach students to recognize and critique systems of inequity. Some scholars have proposed ways to reimagine international education activities that can create socially just learning spaces. Fiedler (2007, 51–52) states:

> Approaches like development education (DE) and intercultural education (ICE) have already paved the way for the opening up of sites of enquiry where assumptions and perceptions can be challenged and critiqued from a global and social justice perspective. In general, both concepts can be seen as educational responses to the need to empower young people to think critically, independently and systemically about the (often unequal) state of our world and the society we live in. Both concepts are, therefore, intrinsically linked to historical processes like imperialism and colonialism that have shaped the world we live in

today. With their strong emphasis upon values and perceptions DE and ICE also prepare learners to participate effectively in society, both locally and globally, so as to bring about positive change for a more just and equal world.

Many of the concepts embedded in the educational approaches cited by Fiedler lead to specific critiques of some underlying assumptions about international education. For example, Fiedler (2007, 55) challenges the adjective "intercultural":

> the adjective "intercultural" carries the danger of reintroducing essentialist concepts that conceive cultures as fixed or sphere-like entities. In other words, considering the concept of intercultural space as a place that provides an encounter between two distinct cultures would obscure the fundamentals of postcolonial theory and its critical assessment of traditional European concepts of culture.

Fiedler's final understanding of intercultural spaces echoes some of what Wick (2011) found in his research, namely that international education exchange can become a uniquely powerful context for critical self-reflection. Fiedler (2007, 55) writes, "[S]imilar to what Homi Bhabha has called the 'Third Space' (Bhabha, 1988: 208) [intercultural spaces] should not be primarily perceived as a place of encounter but of negotiation and discussion." The elements of critical pedagogy, combined with these ways of thinking about international education, can lead us to some essential elements for socially just international education. We propose a critical pedagogy for international education that can help to better create and sustain learning spaces that function in these ways.

Critical Pedagogy for International Education

We see the integration of critical pedagogy into all international education activities as an essential way to reimagine the work of international educators in order to consistently advance social justice. Critical pedagogy allows us to re-envision international education activities ranging from international student and scholar support to education abroad and internationalization at home as opportunities to advance social justice.

The concept of critical pedagogy emerged from Paulo Freire's (2009) work and has led to many recommendations related to the content and form of social justice education. At its core, critical pedagogy is about practicing social justice in educational settings, which involves collaborating with students and communities to transform the systems that perpetuate injustice.

We have found many rich and useful models for social justice education in the literature on critical pedagogy (Ladson-Billings and Tate 1995; Tatum 1992). These sources are generally more developed than those we find in the literature on international education, so we have drawn out key critical pedagogy concepts that inform our work to provide models for others who seek to advance social justice through international education activities. Three key concepts we note include (a) recognizing and rewarding students' strengths; (b) teaching critical self-reflection and identity negotiation; and (c) naming and confronting systems of oppression.

Recognizing and Rewarding Students' Strengths

Critical pedagogies include a few key elements that we see as essential to the development of socially just internationalization and international education activities. A critical pedagogy for international education must begin by recognizing the strengths of student backgrounds. Throughout the process, critical international education activities must name privilege and power and must question the forces that reproduce inequity at home and abroad by leveraging students' voices and stories. A critical approach to international education means supporting the negotiation of identity. Together, these first elements of critical pedagogy provide support for the ultimate goal of developing agency for social justice action at home and abroad for U.S. and international students.

Critical pedagogy recognizes and rewards the knowledge and experience that all students bring to their educational endeavors. Instead of viewing students as empty vessels who need to be taught, or as people with limitations, critical pedagogies acknowledge that students bring rich life experiences and perspectives. Thus, instead of attributing the academic challenges of international students or students of color as a logical outcome of cultural deficiencies, critical pedagogies focus on what students bring to their educational experiences and for ways that teachers can amplify those students' assets throughout the curriculum and pedagogy.

The concepts of funds of knowledge and community cultural wealth are two ways that educators can shift to assets-based thinking about students. Moll et al. (1992) suggest that all students enter education with social, linguistic, and cultural resources that can help them succeed in the school environment. Yosso (2005) proposes that communities of color possess six types of community cultural wealth: (a) aspirational; (b) familial; (c) social; (d) linguistic; (e) resistant; and (f) navigational.

Rather than seeing issues with families that do not recognize the importance of international education, Yosso would recognize the support structures and connections that families can have in communities of color and how those provide a foundation from which students can thrive. Under her concept of aspirational capital, instead of suggesting that families of students of color need to be convinced of the value of education or international education, Yosso (2005) explains that families of color are often very positively disposed toward education. We have seen aspirational capital among international students and scholars, especially those from the developing world or from marginalized communities in their home countries.

Similarly, rather than seeing language as a limitation, Yosso (2005) proposes that students of color (and we would add international students) are often practiced at navigating multiple languages and discourses. Examining each of the types of community cultural wealth that Yosso (2005) describes has led to many promising approaches to designing international education activities for and with historically underrepresented U.S. students and international students and their families in ways that allow them to leverage and reinforce their many strengths.

Teaching Critical Self-Reflection and Identity Negotiation

For many students, international experiences present powerful opportunities to critically reflect on their privilege in ways that are difficult to see in the home context (Wick 2011). Thus, international exchange provides a powerful context for identity negotiation, an essential element of this critical pedagogy for international education. We see identity development as the foundation that will sustain students in their work to challenge the inequitable structures that they have named as they develop, or further develop, their critical consciousness.

The social construct of identity is central to understanding how people make sense of who they are in relation to ethnicity, race, sexuality, gender, religion, ability, and other social locations. Developmental frameworks for identity, such as the Reconceptualized Model of Multiple Dimensions of Identity (Abes, Jones, and McEwan 2007), which we will discuss later, offer insights into the lived experiences of students. Many developmental theories, such as those explored by Helms (1993), present stages of identity development. These theories also examine how structural inequity and systems of oppression impact each individual's capacity to develop a positive and productive relationship with each aspect of his or her identity.

Tatum (1992) and Helms (1993) both argue that identity development can lead to empowerment. The internalization-commitment stage in Cross's (as cited in Helms 1993) model of Black Racial Identity Development and the autonomy phase in Helms's White Racial Identity model both include a comfort with self and a commitment to confront race-based injustice. These two identity stages bear a strong resemblance to transformational resistance, which includes a "critique of oppression and a desire for social justice" (Solórzano and Bernal 2001, 329). Connecting these two ideas suggests that facilitating identity negotiation and development in relationship with students' assets can create the foundation that students need to work toward social justice.

Naming and Confronting Systems of Oppression

Critical international education activities must also include an examination of how social, political, and cultural structures serve to reinforce inequity in the United States and abroad. Naming oppression and oppressive structures is a central aspect of Freire's (2009) work and has informed many approaches to critical pedagogy. It builds on the previous concepts about students' strengths and the importance of teaching critical self-reflection by suggesting that it is not enough to simply celebrate the knowledge and experiences in communities of color and international students, or to guide them to examine their social locations. As Donaldo Macedo (2009, 17) writes in his introduction to Freire's *Pedagogy of the Oppressed*, identity and experience must be connected to the "problematics of power, agency, and history."

Naming the structures of power, privilege, and authority has been linked to the importance of counter-narratives and voice in critical pedagogy. Ladson-Billings and Tate (1995) discuss the importance of voice and naming one's own reality as central to Critical Race Theory and critical pedagogy. They describe three key benefits to naming one's own reality: (a) this approach acknowledges that reality is socially constructed; (b) these stories can provide a vehicle for psychic self-preservation; and (c) stories challenge preconceptions and stereotypes for both the teller and the receiver (Ladson-Billings and Tate 1995).

Building on these ideas, critical international education can only have an emancipatory function if race, racism, power, authority, privilege, and hegemony are named, discussed, and confronted throughout the process. Discussions must also include examinations of intersections between race, class, gender, sexuality, socioeconomic status, ability, and other subjectivities at home and abroad for U.S. and international students. Integrating students' voices throughout all international education activities and facilitating discussions around the problematics that Macedo (2009) describes empower students to confront systems in ways that are, ideally, personally, academically, and professionally potent.

Designed with social justice at the fore, international education activities can provide a foundation for critical praxis by helping students develop their identities, learn to critique and confront structural inequities, and discover ways to leverage the strengths they possess to challenge injustice and change the status quo at home and abroad.

Supporting Intersecting Identities

As noted earlier in our discussion on critical pedagogy, social justice educators recognize the importance of social identities in students' experiences as learners conceptualizing not only individual identities, but the ways that identities interact with each other and within social and societal structures. This is essential in considering how to create learning environments that are productive for all students and will allow everyone to build awareness toward actions related to social justice and transformation.

Kimberlé Crenshaw (1989) first articulated the concept of intersectional identities in her legal practice, where she noted that multiple social identities, such as gender and race, had salience and relevance simultaneously in people's lived experiences and in their treatment by the legal system. Intersectionality is also relevant in educational settings (Bhopal and Preston 2012) and can help us to better recognize the many external forces that influence learning spaces and how students come to those spaces. Moreover, scholars have noted the importance of recognizing the differing impacts of aspects of identity as they relate to structural inequity (Murphy-Erby et al. 2009).

Making sense of intersecting identities in educational settings presents certain challenges. Through their research, Jones and McEwan (2000) developed the Model of Multiple Dimensions of Identity, which makes it possible to see how each person's sense of self is created by the interplay between core aspects of self (e.g., race, gender, and sexuality) and contextual factors (e.g., peers, family, cultural norms, stereotypes, sociopolitical conditions, and physical location). As underscored by Crenshaw's (1989) work on intersectionality, the salience and interplay of these elements must be examined in relationship to historical and contemporary systems of oppression and injustice. To build international education activities that promote social justice, we must recognize not only how systemic inequity functions in the home context but also how it functions in the host context for U.S. and international students. Furthermore, we must guide all students to examine and critique these systems and take action for social justice.

In further research, Abes, Jones, and McEwan (2007) integrated external factors into their model and developed their Reconceptualized Model of

Multiple Dimensions of Identity. This model places the contextual forces outside of the individual and can serve as an effective metaphor for what happens when students are learning in a new context (Abes, Jones, and McEwan 2007). In effect, all of a person's contextual influences change when they shift to a new learning environment, as is the case when students participate in study abroad.

The mediating factor in their model is the "meaning-making filter," which is the student's capacity to respond to the contextual factors (Abes, Jones, and McEwan 2007). When preparing students for international experiences, international educators often focus on issues of health and safety and emphasize cross-cultural differences. Abes, Jones, and McEwan's (2007) model, however, stresses preparing students for the many ways in which they will experience all aspects of their identity differently in the international context. To move toward social justice, educators must recognize and describe how systems of privilege and power function and influence students' negotiation of intersecting identities in the home and host cultures (Fiedler 2007; Vavrus and Pekol 2015).

As noted by Fiedler (2007), intercultural constructs have often been presented as an essentialization of the "other" as fixed and separate, rather than as entities that have been and are impacted by inequitable systems and structures. Fielder (2007, 54) suggests that "based on the postcolonial notion of writing back, education should dare to create such sites of enquiry and design them as postcolonial learning spaces where identities and difference are constantly negotiated and re-written." By actively teaching critical self-reflection as part of international education activities, we prepare all students to contribute to social justice.

Capacity for Engagement with Difference

In order to shift the focus of international education activities to social justice, we believe that it is essential to teach students to value others, which can apply to people in any cultural context. Many international educators have focused on developing students' intercultural competency (Deardorff 2009) or intercultural sensitivity (Bennett 2013) as essential learning outcomes for international experiences. However, coupling this focus on intercultural growth with critical consciousness (Freire 2009) of inequities of social structures is crucial to the formula if social justice is to be an outcome of international education activities at home and abroad for U.S. and international students.

Chavez, Guido-DiBrito, and Mallory (2003) propose a framework of individual diversity development that illustrates how each of us must go through a developmental process in relationship to each aspect of human difference. They visualize this as wedges in a circle, with Unawareness/Lack of Exposure in the middle and Integration/Validation on the outside (Chavez, Guido-DiBrito, and Mallory 2003). Each wedge represents an aspect of identity such as race, ethnicity, sexuality, ability, or nationality. The intermediary stages of Dualistic Awareness, Questioning/Self Exploration, and Risk Taking/Exploration of Otherness all require exposure to people holding those identities, for each aspect of human difference (Chavez, Guido-DiBrito, and Mallory 2003). Many people will move back and forth in these stages as they learn about different human realities and experiences. For each stage, Chavez, Guido-DiBrito, and Mallory (2003) describe cognitive, affective, and behavioral skills in relation to other people. The authors also stress that movement toward Integration/Validation does not happen automatically and is not unidirectional (Chavez, Guido-DiBrito, and Mallory 2003). This model provides us as international educators with a more nuanced way to look at human differences and to consider how we can help U.S. and international students develop their capacity for building new connections and navigating new environments.

In the context of international education activities, students enter into unfamiliar situations in which they may be confronted with new ways of being themselves and different ways of performing many aspects of identity and intersecting identities. Chavez, Guido-DiBrito, and Mallory's (2003) model of individual diversity development suggests that educators seeking to promote students' critical self-reflection must guide students to (a) gain awareness of others; (b) challenge their perceptions of other people; and (c) learn to make complex choices about validating others. Along with the intrapersonal awareness that comes from examinations of intersectional identities and salience at home and abroad, this work on interpersonal differences can serve as the building blocks for a critical approach to intercultural competency, which can contribute to social justice orientations. As educators, we can support this process by establishing identity exploration as an explicit student learning outcome to be valued and pursued in addition to the disciplinary academic student learning outcomes for U.S. and international students.

Intergroup Dynamics for Community Growth

Many researchers suggest that intergroup contact itself does not lead to intergroup harmony or friendships, intercultural gains, or the dismantling of structural inequities. Bowman and Park's (2014) large-scale study identifies the need for intentional institutional programming to facilitate interracial friendships, which do not automatically emerge from cross-racial interaction. Haslerig et al. (2013) argue that without intentional facilitation by faculty, the benefits of diverse classrooms will not be gained. They call for faculty training and propose that "activating" diversity is not an innate skill (Haslerig et al. 2013).

Moreover, Hikido and Murray (2016) suggest that without institutional intervention—even at multiracial campuses with "positive" racial climates where diversity and inclusion are promoted and celebrated—White supremacy will be maintained. This need for everyone in a learning environment to develop knowledge and skills related to human difference is underscored by Chavez, Guido-DiBrito, and Mallory's (2003) work related to individual diversity development, as discussed earlier.

It stands to reason that if the campus climate and students' experiences with it are influenced by dynamics related to their social identities and institutional intervention, or lack thereof, these dynamics may be replicated or even exacerbated abroad, albeit in new cultural contexts. As such, research has begun to reveal examples of intergroup dynamic challenges for students studying abroad as well. For example, Chang (2017) highlights the frustration that many U.S. Latina students experienced in Guatemala in response to some of their White peers' cultural insensitivity and lack of awareness of privilege. In another study, Willis (2015) notes that Black women studying abroad experienced microaggressions from their U.S. peers and host country nationals alike, while Sweeney (2014) documents a range of alienating experiences among both male and female African American students abroad.

Host Community Impact

The goal of enhancing students' global perspectives and other dimensions of development can lead us to overlook or underexamine the impact of student mobility on host communities. This is highly problematic if we are committed to socially just exchanges of experience, knowledge, and skills between students and faculty from partner institutions. Research has also suggested that it is possible to reify stereotypes, misconceptions, and power imbalances through intercultural exchanges. For example, Landau and Moore's (2001) article sheds light on complex dynamics at play on a Ghanaian campus, from the perspective of Ghanaian students, faculty, and staff, as well as Black and White U.S. students. Among many other nuances, the study reveals privileged treatment of U.S. students, tension from economic disparities between U.S. and Ghanaian students, and unchallenged stereotypes that stymied the building of intercultural friendships (Landau and Moore 2001).

Multiple authors call for reverse mission approaches to international experiential education (Abram and Cruce 2007; Abram, Shufeldt, and Rose 2004; Abram, Slosar, and Walls 2005), partially in an attempt to intentionally counter "benevolent imperialism" (Razack 2002). In their article in *Social Work Education*, Abram and Cruce (2007, 163) define a "reverse mission approach" as one that draws "upon ecumenical efforts of global mission education" and emphasizes "learning, consciousness-raising, and advocating for changes in one's home country that can impact poverty and injustice in the world" rather than "teaching, preaching, and trying to convert others."

Beyond the concept of reverse mission, Appadurai (1999, 10–11) argues that although greater reciprocity of student mobility between countries of the global south and north would "not level the global international education playing field, [it] would be a significant step toward the development of experiences that represent the U.S. and help to repair relations of disjuncture." For example, rather than stopping at U.S. students studying genocide in Rwanda with Rwandan students, it would be appropriate and reparative to, in turn, have Rwandan students study the history of genocide and contemporary issues faced by Native Americans in the United States with U.S. students.

In short, to engage in socially just international education activities, we must consider and assess the impacts on host communities at least as much as we assess impacts on individual students. We cannot focus solely on the question, "Did the student learn?"—lest we risk an extractive relationship with our host partner communities or the home communities of international students (Yao and Viggiano 2019; Zemach-Bersin 2007).

Challenges, Opportunities, and Recommendations

In striving to develop international education activities that center on social justice, critical consciousness, and global stewardship for all participants involved, we recognize that there are myriad considerations to keep in mind. These include both pitfalls and opportunities, many of which we as authors have learned during and after the process. As scholar-practitioners, we continuously seek to critically reflect on and evaluate our practices to improve upon them. It is with these considerations that we share several candid examples of lessons learned that we hope will assist readers in their process of developing or refining their international education activities.

Navigating the Imbalance of Gains

As we noted in the work we shared from Zemach-Bersin (2007) and Yao and Viggiano (2019), international educators often consider the impacts of education abroad on U.S. students and the benefits for U.S. institutions from international students and scholars. This overlooks the impact and experiences of our partners—be they the host communities receiving U.S. students or the international students living in the United States.

IMBALANCE OF GAINS: *Having a mutually beneficial, continuing, six-week summer internship program for eight Spanish/English bilingual, master's-level social work (MSW) students in Costa Rica under our belts, I (Tasha) was eager to build upon our institutional relationships to develop a two-week service-learning course for 17 undergraduates the following summer. Both sides of the partnership had expressed deep satisfaction with the gains experienced from the program, which had been designed with reciprocity in mind. Our MSW students had benefited greatly from the experiential learning, and the host project staff were pleased as our students brought linguistic and social work practice skills to the communities they served. Our host partner university seemed up for this new opportunity, so we developed a new undergraduate service-learning course.*

The 17 undergraduate students had positive experiences overall and expressed excitement over their learning. However, we discovered in our postprogram debrief with the host country staff that developing meaningful learning opportunities that also benefited our local partners' projects was challenging as their staff struggled to find useful assignments for such short-term involvement and for such a large group. Further, several local staff felt taxed by the additional responsibility of supervising our students on top of their already full plates—though my coleader and I provided what support we could. It turned out that the added responsibility had been foisted upon staff by their administrators, who were trying to fulfill our request to accommodate such a large group. These issues led us to reconsider the sustainability of the undergraduate course, given our intention to create programs that were as beneficial to the host community as they were to students.

LESSON LEARNED: *In hindsight, I believe that part of the problem of the undergraduate program actually may have resulted from the positive relationship that had emerged from the MSW program. On our end, several challenges were at play. In my attempt to increase access through* *the undergraduate program, I focused on a short duration based on a common campus narrative that many students on our campus faced time and financial constraints. However, if I had polled the students before finalizing the dates, I might have learned that they could have stayed longer than 2 weeks. I also felt pressure to recruit a large group of students to defray salary costs, as this was a for-credit experience involving two faculty members. I should have considered other options for program leadership rather than increase the number of students to 17. For example, a graduate student traveled with us to conduct her thesis on the program outcomes. With a smaller group, I think the two of us, along with one of our hosts, could have been a strong enough team to support students in their placements. On our partner's side, perhaps the desire to accommodate our initial request and to protect the mutually beneficial MSW program—and considering the underlying power imbalance inherent in south-north relationships—may have led them to overextend themselves and not share their concerns in advance of our arrival.*

Developing Mutually Beneficial Partnerships

COLLABORATIONS FOR MUTUAL BENEFITS: *At our large, urban, public, and largely commuter campus, international students have not been thoroughly integrated into the fabric of our institution and curricular integration is uneven across disciplines. In speaking with my international student services colleagues, I (Tasha) learned that many international students might appreciate the opportunity to get to know domestic students outside of their classes but that this generally does not happen easily. Many opportunities exist, such as through linking them to our cross-cultural centers, other student organizations, or at the academic department level. However, in our school of social work, we do not host many international students. In my cross-cultural social work practice class, students are expected to complete an ethnographic interview with someone who is culturally different from them in three major ways. So, I worked with* *the international student and scholar office to seek volunteers from their rosters who would be interested in the opportunity to be interviewed by my students. Students from both groups expressed some initial nervousness but also great interest and excitement about participating. Many social work students realized that their interviewee might want to ask them questions as well "to be fair," and I have heard from several after the fact that they formed new friendships with each other.*

LESSONS LEARNED: *Partnerships, whether with different institutions or different offices within the same campus, can facilitate enhanced gains for all involved. Working across campus and international boundaries to think of ways to benefit both international and domestic students may take extra effort but can also yield rich rewards. By ensuring we keep everyone's needs in mind, rather than focusing solely on the students immediately in front of us, we can find a path toward reciprocal gains.*

With every partnership, I (David) strive to find ways to work toward mutual benefit. This means that I ask each partner about their current efforts and challenges. I then collaborate with the partners to design student projects in which students work with partners abroad before and during the program to prepare possible solutions to their current challenges. These project-based elements enhance student learning and give something back to the partners abroad for their participation and contributions to the program. With each program, I have had to shift my approach accordingly to make it more likely that we find mutual benefit in our collaborations.

Navigating the Threat of a Neocolonial Mentality

A key critique of education abroad, particularly models that emphasize learning about local social justice issues, is that faculty and, by extension, students may assume a neocolonial stance. Such a stance often frames the U.S. perspective as more advanced, virtuous, or right in relationship to people of local communities (Chang 2017; Zemach-Bersin 2007). The risk of this is heightened when a program is designed to include volunteerism, service-learning, and/or internships, which can reproduce power imbalances and assumptions common in global south-north relations.

> **NEOCOLONIAL THREAT:** As a social work faculty member, I (Tasha) know that many social work students desire to assist people and communities by being of "direct" service to individuals. Many students come into our field full of idealism and a desire to see the tangible results, with some even unconsciously anticipating gratitude from the people they set out to "help." So, when a group of students invited me to join them for a tour run by an educational travel organization billed as an "anti-human trafficking delegation in Thailand," I was pleased to hear directly from the provider that it was a "reality tour." The intent was raising awareness rather than providing on-site service.
>
> The organization's aim was that we would all become cognizant of the issues and bring this knowledge home to share with others in our own communities and hopefully inspire interest and local action. This made sense to me: We all had a lot to learn about the topic in general, and especially in a Thai cultural context. None of us had been to Thailand, none of us spoke Thai, nor had any of us had any social work experience with human trafficking victims or Thai clients, even in the United States, so we were not in a position to be of assistance, let alone culturally responsive.
>
> Most students appreciated this approach and, upon return, engaged in several meaningful local actions to spread awareness and counter human trafficking in Los Angeles, California, and in Thailand. Nearly all the students participated in a local walk-a-thon to raise funds for proposed anti-human trafficking legislation in our state. The whole group also initiated its own fundraiser for the legislation and for an organization we visited in Thailand.
>
> Nonetheless, during the travel portion of the experience in Thailand, two students were frustrated and had difficulty accepting our intent of raising awareness. They had wanted to serve the Thai people directly in some way and expressed disappointment in the experience, even though

this would have gone against what the local organizations sought from their engagement with us. The two students had also imagined that they would hear directly from victims/survivors rather than the organizations that served them, even though this could have placed survivors in the uncomfortable and potentially harmful position of having to relive their trauma by recounting it yet again to strangers.

LESSON LEARNED: *I now view this as part of the reality of working with different learners who are at different stages of their developmental process, particularly in light of the powerful, neocolonial, deficit-based narrative that features U.S. Americans (and frankly, social workers) as saviors. Though our predeparture preparation included discussion about the stance our group would take and the establishment of learning goals, I realized in hindsight that different activities might have been more effective at ensuring that students managed their expectations and set appropriate learning goals. Rather than the large group discussion exploring participants' "hopes and fears" about the experience, it may have been a more constructive and consciousness-raising approach to assign a written reflection on our discussion about the program's aim to engage at home rather than provide service in-country. Reviewing and discussing the students' learning goals privately before departure may have also helped to manage expectations.*

Striving to Subvert Neocolonialism

DIFFERENT APPROACHES TO GOALS: *In meeting a new potential university partner from an Afro-Colombian region, we (I, Tasha, and a faculty colleague from my campus) initially had high hopes for a balanced south-north student mobility program. We wanted to avoid creating a learning experience that would disproportionately benefit students from our U.S. campus and/or reify economic, political, and social power imbalances* *between our campuses. However, our host contact explained that mobility for her students was not a likely possibility given the myriad structural obstacles (socioeconomic, racial, political, etc.) they faced, even with potential grant funding. Instead, she impressed upon us that, from their vantage point, hosting our students would present their campus with the most significant intercultural and international learning opportunity for the largest group of their students and was, therefore, what they were most interested in pursuing with us.*

So we worked collaboratively to develop goals and objectives for the program over the course of 18 months. We also preintroduced students to each other through a Facebook group and assigned "buddies" several weeks prior to our students' arrival. Our primary intention was to help both groups of students explore intercultural communication and structural inequities through their interactions with each other, so we built in sustained contact through academic lectures, site visits, and social activities; conducted multiple reflection sessions that included program participants and their local buddies; and incorporated self-reflective journals to complement the homestays and other learning activities. We also designed a formal research project related to student learning outcomes for both groups that provided ongoing reflection opportunities even after the program ended. This "high intervention" (Bathurst and La Brack 2012) approach was at the heart of the experience for both groups of students and led to powerful outcomes.

LESSON LEARNED: *The program's setting in an Afro-Colombian region provided a meaningful opportunity to challenge our 12 U.S. students' (four identified as Black/African American and eight identified as Latinx, though not of African descent) assumptions about Latinx identity, culture, and communication. Similarly, students from our host community had their stereotypes about "Americans" and people from Los Angeles ("Hollywood") pleasantly debunked through exposure to our students' diversity in terms of* *racial, socioeconomic, and other identities. Our high intervention approach seems to have facilitated the raising of both groups' consciousness of varying forms of oppression across national boundaries. In addition, many host students reported that they felt motivated to continue their academic studies, to dive more deeply into learning English, and even to find ways to overcome obstacles to studying abroad as a result of their involvement with the exchange. The U.S. Latinx students articulated greater awareness of anti-Black racism, and the U.S. Black students were empowered through their connection to the vastness of the African diaspora. This experience highlighted for us the value of the experience (just as our partner predicted), despite the lack of south-north mobility, and helped us become more flexible in our planning for future programs where economic imbalances make bilateral mobility difficult.*

Navigating Structural Barriers

International education activities often present staff and faculty with challenges to surmount, whether they stem from institutional structures, informal practices, campus culture, or a combination of these. If these institutional elements are recognized from the outset, however, they can be more easily navigated and overcome to enhance outcomes and increase access for students.

BARRIERS TO INTERNATIONAL STUDENT INTEGRATION: *The student body at my (David) institution, the Middlebury Institute of International Studies, is composed of around 30 percent international students. This, and our commitment to language learning and intercultural competency development, led us to believe that integration would automatically happen. However, in focus groups on equity and inclusion on campus, we learned that there are many barriers to integration. For example, international students' contributions to group projects may be thwarted because they are not native speakers of English, thus often leaving them left out of efforts related to diversity, equity, and inclusion.*

> **LESSONS LEARNED:** *Through focus groups, we realized that from their arrival on campus, we were separating international students in ways that created community divides. In response, we developed a session on navigating our diverse community for all students that is conducted in small groups with faculty, staff, and peer facilitators. In this session, we share examples of implicit bias, marginalization, and oppression and we guide small groups that include U.S. and international students to work together to develop inclusive practices.*

Program Design for Social Justice

In general, social justice-oriented educators and international educators often believe that social justice work must include service or take place in the Global South. We argue instead that all programs can, and should, be designed and run in ways that promote diversity, equity, inclusion, and social justice regardless of content and location.

Just as public policy may be used to promote equitable behavior, we recommend that policies be evaluated from a social justice lens. This may include critical policy analysis (Iverson 2007). By critically examining the ways that injustice is built into policies and then refining policies to disrupt that reproduction of inequity, educators can make social justice part of the fabric of their work rather than an optional add-on that can be chosen when convenient.

Program Objectives and Learning Outcomes

From our review of the literature and professional practice resources related to program design, we find that most focus on the benefits derived by U.S. student participants, with a strong emphasis on the benefits to employability. As other authors have noted (Buckner and Stein 2019; Fiedler 2007; Vavrus and Pekol 2015; Yao and Viggiano 2019; Zemach-Bersin 2007), this emphasis on the benefits to U.S. students, on U.S. interests, and on human capital development is deeply rooted in neoliberal ideals and is directly at odds with a social justice orientation.

Instead, we propose that designing for social justice requires that we begin with program objectives that are social justice–oriented for everyone involved, throughout the process. With these clear goals in mind, it is also important to incorporate, from the very beginning, a plan to assess and evaluate program efficacy in guiding students to these outcomes. This is a crucial aspect of critical praxis that requires reflection and refinement.

Program Content

All programs must include content that allows U.S. and international students to critically examine how privilege and power function at home and abroad and pushes them to examine their roles in confronting and dismantling structural inequity. This may require programs to use both culturally relevant content (Ladson-Billings 1995) and a problem-posing approach (Freire 2009). Additionally, programs that seek to advance social justice will need to decolonize the sources of knowledge, the ways that knowledge is created on the program, and the ways that the learning is distributed. Content should be informed by diverse voices in the local community and be based on scholarship, narratives, live history, conversations, observation, self-inquiry, and other sources.

Program Pedagogy

As we discussed in the section on critical pedagogy, teaching methodologies also need to be designed to foster social justice for U.S. and international students. Not only do program leaders and faculty need to critically engage with the program content, they also need to examine their teaching methods to deliver a critical pedagogy (Ladson-Billings and Tate 1995) that builds on the strengths of students, supports them in critically self-reflecting and examining their identities, and exposes and confronts systems of oppression. Critical pedagogies can be applied to internationalization at home, work with international students, and education abroad program design.

Conclusion

As we began this chapter, we asserted that internationalization and international education activities have the potential to foster social justice for all involved. From this review of theory, research, and practice, we have sought to show that achieving this goal will take more than reconsiderations of recruitment strategies, program locations, costs, and student demographics. Instead, we believe that we must critically examine the underlying mission and values of internationalization and international education activities. From this perspective, we can begin to define policies, design programs, articulate practices, utilize critical pedagogies, and assess our work based on how it contributes to social justice and humanization at home and abroad for U.S. and international students and their communities.

We believe that it is only by framing all of our work with the explicit intent of dismantling systems of inequity that we can begin to move our field toward realizing international education's full potential for positive and meaningful global change. This will require all of us in our roles as international educators to critically self-reflect. We must take stock of our own levels of awareness, our own identities, and our own relationships to power and privilege in order to confront the systems of inequity within which we work. We must ourselves engage in this challenging yet liberating process in order to support students in doing the same through their international education activities.

References

Abes, Elisa S., Susan R. Jones, and Marylu K. McEwen. 2007. "Reconceptualizing the Model of Multiple Dimensions of Identity: The Role of Meaning-Making Capacity in the Construction of Multiple Identities." *Journal of College Student Development* 48, 1:1–22.

Abram, Faye Y., and Ashley Cruce. 2007. "A Re-Conceptualization of 'Reverse Mission' for International Social Work Education and Practice." *Social Work Education* 26, 1:3–19.

Abram, Faye Y., Gregory Shufeldt, and Kelle Rose. 2004. "Can Reverse Mission Internationalize Social Work Without the Hegemony of Religious, Social, or Intellectual Conversion?" *Social Work & Christianity* 31, 2:136–161.

Abram, Faye Y., John A. Slosar, and Rose Walls. 2005. "Reverse Mission: A Model for International Social Work Education and Transformative Intra-National Practice." *International Social Work* 48, 2:161–176.

Appadurai, Arjun. 1999. "Globalization and the Research Imagination." *International Social Science Journal* 51, 160:229–238.

Bathurst, Laura, and Bruce La Brack. 2012. "Shifting the Locus of Intercultural Learning: Intervening Prior to and After Student Experiences Abroad." In *Student Learning Abroad: What Our Students Are Learning, What They're Not, and What We Can Do About It*, eds. Michael Vande Berg, R. Michael Paige, and Kris Hemming Lou. Sterling, VA: Stylus Publishing.

Bennett, Martin. 2013. *Basic Concepts of Intercultural Communication: Paradigms, Principles, & Practices*. Boston, MA: Intercultural Press.

Bernal, Dolores Delgado. 1998. "Using a Chicana Feminist Epistemology in Educational Research." *Harvard Educational Review* 68, 4:555–583.

Bhopal, Kalwant, and John Preston, eds. 2012. *Intersectionality and Race in Education*. New York, NY: Routledge.

Bowman, Nicholas A., and Julie J. Park. 2014. "Interracial Contact on College Campuses: Comparing and Contrasting Predictors of Cross-Racial Interaction and Interracial Friendship." *Journal of Higher Education* 85, 5:660–690.

Buckner, Elizabeth, and Sharon Stein. 2019. "What Counts as Internationalization? Deconstructing the Internationalization Imperative." *Journal of Studies in International Education*. Published electronically February 15, 2019.

Chang, Aurora. 2017. "'Call Me a Little Critical If You Will': Counterstories of Latinas Studying Abroad in Guatemala." *Journal of Hispanic Higher Education* 16, 1:3–23.

Chavez, Alicia Fedelina, Florence Guido-DiBrito, and Sherry L. Mallory. 2003. "Learning to Value the 'Other': A Framework of Individual Diversity Development." *Journal of College Student Development* 44, 4:453–469.

Collins, Patricia Hill. 2015. "No Guarantees: Symposium on Black Feminist Thought." *Ethnic and Racial Studies* 38, 13:2349–2354.

Crenshaw, Kimberlé. 1989. "Demarginalizing the Intersection of Race and Sex: A Black Feminist Critique of Antidiscrimination Doctrine, Feminist Theory and Antiracist Politics." *University of Chicago Legal Forum* 1989, Article 8.

Deardorff, Darla K. 2009. *The SAGE Handbook of Intercultural Competence*. Thousand Oaks, CA: SAGE Publications.

Dewey, John. 1916. *Democracy and Education: An Introduction to the Philosophy of Education*. New York, NY: Macmillan.

Fiedler, Matthias. 2007. "Postcolonial Learning Spaces for Global Citizenship." *Critical Literacy: Theories and Practices* 1, 2:50–57.

Freire, Paulo. 2009. *Pedagogy of the Oppressed*. Translated by Donald Mitchell. New York, NY: Continuum.

Fulbright, J. William. n.d. "J. William Fulbright Quotes." Washington, DC: U.S. Department of State Bureau of Educational and Cultural Affairs. https://eca.state.gov/fulbright/about-fulbright/history/j-william-fulbright/j-william-fulbright-quotes.

Giroux, Henry A. 2010. "Rethinking Education as the Practice of Freedom: Paulo Freire and the Promise of Critical Pedagogy." *Policy Futures in Education* 8, 6:715–721.

Haslerig, Siduri, Laura M. Bernhard, Marcia V. Fuentes, A. T. Panter, Charles E. Daye, and Walter R. Allen. 2013. "A Compelling Interest: Activating the Benefits of Classroom-Level Diversity." *Journal of Diversity in Higher Education* 6, 3:158–173.

Helms, Janet E. 1993. *Black and White Racial Identity: Theory, Research, and Practice.* Westport, CT: Praeger Publishers.

Hikido, Annie, and Susan B. Murray. 2016. "Whitened Rainbows: How White College Students Protect Whiteness Through Diversity Discourses." *Race Ethnicity and Education* 19, 2:389–411.

Institute of International Education (IIE). 2018. *Open Doors Report on International Educational Exchange.* Institute of International Education. http://www.iie.org/opendoors.

Institute of International Education Center for Academic Mobility Research and Impact. 2018. *A World on the Move: Trends in Global Student Mobility, Issue 2.* New York, NY: Institute of International Education. https://www.iie.org/Research-and-Insights/Publications/A-World-on-the-Move.

Iverson, Susan VanDeventer. 2007. "Camouflaging Power and Privilege: A Critical Race Analysis of University Diversity Policies." *Educational Administration Quarterly* 43, 5:586–611.

Jemal, Alexis. 2017. "Critical Consciousness: A Critique and Critical Analysis of the Literature." *Urban Review* 49, 4:602–626.

Jones, Susan R., and Marylu K. McEwen. 2000. "A Conceptual Model of Multiple Dimensions of Identity." *Journal of College Student Development* 41, 4:405–414.

Kiehne, Elizabeth. 2016. "Latino Critical Perspective in Social Work." *Social Work* 61, 2:119–126.

Knight, Jane. 2004. "Internationalization Remodeled: Definition, Approaches, and Rationales." *Journal of Studies in International Education* 8, 1:5–31.

Ladson-Billings, Gloria. 1995. "But That's Just Good Teaching! The Case for Culturally Relevant Pedagogy." *Theory Into Practice* 34, 3:159–165.

Ladson-Billings, Gloria. 1998. "Just What Is Critical Race Theory and What's It Doing in a Nice Field like Education?" *International Journal of Qualitative Studies in Education* 11, 1:7–24.

Ladson-Billings, Gloria, and William F. Tate IV. 1995. "Toward a Critical Race Theory of Education." *Teachers College Record* 97, 1:47–68.

Landau, Jennifer, and David Chioni Moore. 2001. "Towards Reconciliation in the Motherland: Race, Class, Nationality, Gender, and the Complexities of American Student Presence at the University of Ghana, Legon." *Frontiers: The Interdisciplinary Journal of Study Abroad* VII: Fall 2001.

Macedo, Donaldo. 2009. "Introduction to the Anniversary Edition." In *Pedagogy of the Oppressed*, by Paulo Freire. New York, NY: Continuum International Publishing Group Inc.

Meekosha, Helen, Russell Shuttleworth, and Karen Soldatic. 2013. "Disability and Critical Sociology: Expanding the Boundaries of Critical Social Inquiry." *Critical Sociology* 39, 3:319–323.

Moll, Luis C., Cathy Amanti, Deborah Neff, and Norma Gonzalez. 1992. "Funds of Knowledge for Teaching: Using a Qualitative Approach to Connect Homes and Classrooms." *Theory Into Practice* 31, 2:132–141.

Murphy-Erby, Yvette, Valerie Hunt, Anna Zajicek, Adele Norris, and Leah Hamilton. 2009. *Incorporating Intersectionality in Social Work Practice, Research, Policy, and Education*. Washington, DC: National Association of Social Workers.

Razack, Narda. 2002. "A Critical Examination of International Student Exchanges." *International Social Work* 45, 2:251–265.

Solórzano, Daniel G., and Dolores Delgado Bernal. 2001. "Examining Transformational Resistance Through a Critical Race and Latcrit Theory Framework: Chicana and Chicano Students in an Urban Context." *Urban Education* 36, 3:308–342.

Sweeney, Karyn L. 2014. "Race Matters: An Examination of the Study Abroad Experiences of African American Undergraduates." Doctoral dissertation, University of Denver.

Tatum, Beverly D. 1992. "Talking About Race, Learning About Racism: The Application of Racial Identity Development Theory in the Classroom." *Harvard Educational Review* 62, 1:1–24.

Vavrus, Frances, and Amy Pekol. 2015. "Critical Internationalization: Moving from Theory to Practice." *FIRE: Forum for International Research in Education* 2, 2:5–21.

Wick, David. 2011. "Study Abroad For Students Of Color: A Third Space For Negotiating Agency And Identity." Dissertation, San Francisco State University. http://sfsu-dspace.calstate.edu/handle/10211.3/99358.

Willis, Tasha Y. 2015. "'And Still We Rise…': Microaggressions and Intersectionality in the Study Abroad Experiences of Black Women." *Frontiers: The Interdisciplinary Journal of Study Abroad* 26:209–30.

Yao, Christina W., and Tiffany Viggiano. 2019. "Interest Convergence and the Commodification of International Students and Scholars in the United States." *Journal Committed to Social Change on Race and Ethnicity* 5, 1:82–109.

Yosso, Tara J. 2005. "Whose Culture Has Capital? A Critical Race Theory Discussion of Community Cultural Wealth." *Race Ethnicity and Education* 8, 1:69–91.

Zemach-Bersin, Talya. 2007. "Global Citizenship and Study Abroad: It's All About US." *Critical Literacy: Theories and Practices* 1, 2:16–28.

2

Equity Education in a Time of Rising Nationalism
Challenges and Complexities

SUPRIYA BAILY, PhD

> *Today's nationalists decry the "globalist" liberalism of international institutions. They attack liberal elites as sellouts who care more about foreigners than their fellow citizens. And they promise to put national, rather than global, interests first. (Snyder 2019)*

At this current time, it is clear to even casual followers of global politics that nationalism, xenophobia, and a nativist approach to the nation-state have become global norms rather than fringe elements of politics in the post-World War II era. What might have been seen as a quiet rise of populist rhetoric over the past decade has now clearly manifested into a global nationalist ideology. From India to the United States, and from Brazil to the Philippines, political leaders have sought to tap into people's fears of the "other," identifying foreigners of all sorts—from ethnic to religious to skin color differences—as reasons to marginalize and isolate. On this stage, voters have determined that the narrative of safety and security requires strong action against whoever is deemed the "other" by those leaders hungry to move their ideologies forward. All of this has worked together to undermine decades of effort made through international education to foster internationalism and, by extension, negates any work around building socially cohesive and just communities.

Within this tense global space, a number of questions are raised, especially for those who have looked at internationalization as a positive, forward-thinking, and progressive hope for the future. How did the shift to demonize internationalism become so popular? Is it possible to still champion the values of the global over the national? How do the values of internationalism stay relevant? And, more important for this volume, how does education ensure continued equitable access and opportunity for all students? What does it mean to advocate for social justice and education in the shadow of these powerful forces?

This chapter seeks to provide a deeper understanding of how nationalist ideologies are affecting higher education, illuminate some emerging challenges in schools where nationalist ideologies are prevalent, and offer some thoughts on how we as international educators can create a culture of dissonance to combat the fear of pushing back against the larger forces of nationalism to support internationalism.

The chapter comes against the backdrop of other negative global forces that have the potential to reverse trends and move toward greater inequity on a relatively global scale. The intersection between neoliberal policies that cede to the power of markets and capital, emboldened nativist and nationalist rhetoric, and the more pronounced experience of misogyny in schools have constrained teachers, created apprehensive parents, and buffeted students who are influenced by systems that seek to measure success, prove accountability, and, oftentimes, create an unhealthy competitive environment around which learning is supposed to occur. While these issues are not the focus of this chapter, it is impossible to separate the ways in which social justice and equity are under pressure from this triple threat. The mission of those organizations and entities that value and champion internationalism and international mindedness cannot ignore these concerns, which further influence shifts in policy and practice around the world. It is within these systems that educators who advocate for social justice issues are struggling to argue relevancy, ensure transparency, and speak to the larger idea of an unmeasurable good.

Nationalism Through Education

While the focus of this chapter is on the growing nationalist movements and their impact on education, the larger economic argument of how neoliberal agendas percolate through these conversations—due in part to the continued dominance of the powerful over the powerless—cannot be ignored. Within the sphere of education, the continued marginalization of people often depends upon their collective naiveté regarding the continued inequity and unequal delivery of educational systems worldwide.

Ensuring a more just and equitable education, especially as we look at international higher education, depends on making these entanglements visible and accountable. Toward that effort, this section examines how nationalism is theorized, the rhetoric of internationalism in education, and the ways in which nationalism and education are increasingly intersecting.

Dimensions of Nationalism

Numerous scholars have explored the roots, spread, and impact of nationalism in multiple spheres, including education (Au 2017; Moskal 2016). Ashcroft, Griffiths, and Tiffin (2013, 168) argue that nationalism remains one of, if not the, "most implacably powerful force in 20th-century politics." They theorize that nationalistic "identifiers are employed to create exclusive and homogenous conceptions of national traditions" (Ashcroft, Griffiths, and Tiffin 2013, 167). Such identifiers become unifying factors to reject the varied nature of diversity in communities that seek to exemplify nationalism. This becomes a critical facet of power: to represent and to "consolidate the interests of the dominant power groups within any national formation" (Ashcroft, Griffiths, and Tiffin 2013, 167). Holding tight to the badge of nationalism creates the ability for those in power to determine what is legitimate patriotism and what might be illegitimate patriotism (McDonough and Cormier 2013). This is illustrated in the current U.S. political dialogue where hugging the flag is seen as legitimate patriotism, while kneeling during the national anthem is portrayed as illegitimate. The decision to value one over the other allows nationalists to question the patriotism of the individual they seek to marginalize and silence.

Another key facet of nationalism is the notion of self-determination, where the argument for a nationalist platform for action is built on a fragile rationale that the self-determination of a particular group is at risk. While there are often cases of groups of people who argue that their rights are being suppressed by the state apparatus, the use of self-determination in nationalist ideologies by certain movements speaks to the transfer of these ideas to political purposes, where the ideas are designed to "capitalize on the dramatic political weight… as a means of advancing very different sorts of political goals" (McDonough and Cormier 2013, 138). For instance, this is evident in the west, with the rising incel (involuntary celibate) movement or other misogynistic groups that argue that men are the ones who are being suppressed and marginalized. The suppression of self-determination, which hinders the successful functioning of democracy, blurs the lines between the nation-state, patriotism, and citizenship, ultimately making it more challenging to counter the narrative of nationalism as it takes deeper root in society. According to Ashcroft, Griffiths, and Tiffin (2013, 167):

> The confusion of the idea of the nation with the practice and power of the nation-state makes nationalism one of the most powerful forces in contemporary society. It also makes it an extremely contentious site, on which ideas of self-determination and freedom, of identity and unity collide with ideas of suppression and force, of domination and exclusion.

Leading philosopher and ethicist Kwame Anthony Appiah (2018, 90) more recently finds that:

> the ideal of national sovereignty remains a profound source of legitimacy, however obscure and unstable our definition of the people….Yes, "we" have the right to self-determination, but this idea can guide us only once we've decided who "we" are. That question…almost never has a single possible answer.

Unfortunately, with the spread of a more populist rhetoric, the definitions of who "we" are seems to have shrunk, resulting in a more specific answer. This answer is becoming increasingly singular as politicians and heads of state impose a more uniform and faux utopian ideal of the nation. I use the term "faux utopian" to signal the discourse that is used in political rhetoric to return citizens to a more perfect time—one that never existed but can be summoned to create a sense of nostalgia for a more perfect past. It is this return to an unrealistic past that allows people to demonize the "other," to amplify fears, and to foster divisiveness, which spreads from the home to the community and the school. Schools, in part, and education, more broadly, have always been seen as vehicles to both support and expand an awareness of national unity and national identity on to future generations; whether this is through indoctrination or critical thinking depends oftentimes on both who is viewing the education and who is being educated.

Internationalism in Education

While early education was often considered an instrument through which people could learn the tenets of religion, in the United States, there was an evolution in the middle of the nineteenth century where education expanded to include the notion of "making good citizens" (Pierce 1934, 117). While Pierce (1934, 121) recounts the delicate balance that is at play between the school and the state, she also recognizes that the promotion of international "amity" was a critical need for the world at that time.

In the development of prejudice, there is a "human tendency to divide the social world into two categories—us and them" (Woolfolk 2008, 187). However, for much of the post-World War II era, there has been a cogent expectation that education should aspire to provide people with more unifying tendencies than dividing (Sevier 2009). For instance, UNESCO (2019) argues:

> Education should be a means to empower children and adults alike to become active participants in the transformation of their societies. Learning should also focus on the values, attitudes and behaviors, which enable individuals to learn to live together in a world characterized by diversity and pluralism.

The goals of education, perhaps most particularly higher education, are designed to support the development of people, to engage in the development of their societies, but also to enhance their ability to get along as members of a global community. In the United States, the mission of the U.S. Department of Education (n.d.) is to promote the economic heft of a country, with a focus on "student achievement and preparation for global competitiveness by fostering educational excellence and ensuring equal access."

The Global Rhetoric

The rhetoric of internationalism in education takes many forms. For instance, Gunesch (2004, 2007) defines cosmopolitanism as "feeling at home in the world...as interest in or engagement with cultural diversity by straddling the global and the local spheres in terms of personal identity" (Gunesch 2004, 256). While certain international educators might still speak to the influence of cosmopolitanism, others have critiqued the notion as more elitist, masculine, and highly individualistic (Matthews and Sidhu 2005). Yet, the characteristics of international education oftentimes include the development of certain traits and dispositions, including social justice perspectives, inclusion, respect, empathy, global issues responsibility, and the ability to take multiple perspectives.

Curricular models that include ways to inculcate such dispositions include service-learning, outreach, and global issues programs that foster the development of social justice, equity, and responsibility. For example, the Global Issues Network (GIN)'s mission is "to help students realize they can make a difference by empowering them to work with their peers internationally to develop solutions for global issues" (East Asia Regional Council of Overseas Schools 2018, 2). Educators take on the responsibility to promote the development of personal identity for those students, fostered by independent action to solve global issues. Curricular frameworks that prepare teachers to think from both the inside-out and from the outside-in allow for the nuances of nation-state issues to remain present and to create a level of sensitivity to historical and cultural underpinnings (Levy and Fox 2007).

Education is a critical stage on which the tensions of society play out. Issues of class, race, caste, color, ability, gender, sexuality, and other identity markers are buttressed and confronted. Norms of society are reinforced, and privilege can be deeply entrenched. The use of language shapes the experience of students and, as Grimshaw (2007, 365) notes, "language can be manipulated to shape ideology and maintain power relations within a society." For instance, there is already a tendency to see English as the language of power, especially for the middle and upper classes around the world that are quickly adopting the ways of the west (Stromquist and Monkman 2000). This adoption of

English is seen as a fundamental threat to the nationalist movements that strike back by creating factions of people to battle against, including the global elite, the local elite, the minority populations, and the dangerous "other." These strawmen make convenient foils for populist movements that seek to consolidate power.

The global rhetoric around international education and its role in providing access, engaging the world, and supporting social justice initiatives is one side of the fight for education as a powerful transformative tool to influence minds to engage in larger power struggles. Friedman (2018, 248) speaks to the tension between the role that higher education plays in both fostering the goodwill of an international ideology and the neoliberalism and growing anger of nationalist agendas toward such efforts:

> [H]igher education's globalization has been narrated over the past decade, particularly concerning the world's elite universities. For, with their doors open to international students and scholars, their public commitments to multicultural diversity, and their professed desire to help solve humanity's most pressing challenges, these universities have commonly been imagined as engines of cosmopolitanism and harbingers of peace. Their broad embrace of internationalization—across various academic programs and numerous operational domains—has been viewed as a natural reflection of their core globalist values. If today's wave of nationalism is seen as a populist "mutiny" against globalization and "cosmopolitan elites" (Calhoun 2016), then elite universities have been firmly positioned in the latter camp.

As more and more families move around the globe for various reasons, and "individuals, commercial organizations, educational organizations and national systems grow increasingly reliant on interaction with those in other parts of the globe, an understanding of what it means to be 'international' becomes ever-more relevant to increasing numbers of individuals worldwide" (Hayden, Rancic, and Thompson 2000, 120). Yet, as the rhetoric expanded and grew more inclusive, education, as a space to engage in global ideals, now battles the growing nationalist movements.

International Education: Strengths and Weaknesses

Across the global, national, and local domains, schools are viewed as spaces to ensure the agency of students, promote equity, and speak to global engagement and the ability to seek out meaningful and economically productive lives (The World Bank 2019). At the turn of the twentieth century in the United States, historian Frederick Jackson Turner wondered how the country would sustain itself amidst all the social upheaval of the time (VanOverbeke 2009). In VanOverbeke's (2009, 18) exploration of Turner's influence on social justice in education, he argues that Turner believed "historical knowledge and appreciation...would build a strong nation comprised of democratic citizens working to further strengthen the nation." This engagement with democracy was an effort to create independent-minded thinkers, but as VanOverbeke (2009, 20) concludes, "Turner also never questioned that the masses [might not want to]... transform their thoughts and feelings into actions for the good of the nation." In fact, one can argue that Turner was fighting a larger machinery: education's centrality to the "preservation of the nation-state machinery by helping it shape a national consciousness and ideology" (Bekerman 2009, 139).

International education can be seen as one domain that threatens the nationalists. Research shows that "people with higher education are less prejudiced toward ethnic outgroups than are those with lower education" (Coenders and Scheepers 2003, 313), but it is the type of education that matters. Education that is rooted in progressive, liberal, and international ideals can promote a more socially just mindset. Oftentimes, it can be argued that international schools (pre-K to grade 12, usually) or those schools designed for the purposes of working with "culturally diverse, internationally mobile students" (Hill 2015, 66), are spaces that promote such curricula. On the other hand, international schools are also often seen as spaces of opportunity and privilege, limited to wealthy populations and operating without concern for the well-being of those beyond their social circle. Research conducted in Australia, for example, found that international school students' "everyday experiences were marked by separation and disconnection from local students" (Matthews and Sidhu 2005, 59). While this observation is not uncommon in the international school environment, it reiterates the discourse of divisiveness and disunity. Although it was established that international education may promote a more unified world, Matthews and Sidhu (2005, 50) argue that depending on the context, curricula, and mission of any school, an international education is just as likely to "give rise to profoundly conservative ethnocultural affiliations and largely instrumental notions of global citizenship as to generate a collective and compassionate global subject."

When the lines of demarcation between people are based on socioeconomics, race, class, caste, ethnicity, gender, sexuality, and ability, it becomes easy to create divisions to ensure that those at the top—most often cis, wealthy male members of the dominant race—maintain power. Struggles over the preparation of teachers, curriculum, textbooks, school culture, and rituals have long been spaces of disagreement and disavowal of politics in education. It is in this current climate of jockeying for power and for a particular brand of nationalism that we need to explore the challenges that continue to decay democratic principles and hinder social justice and equity through international education.

Social Justice in Education

The rise of nationalism, the vulnerability of internationalism, and the recognition that education can be pivotal in the fight to find allies often leads to the focus on the ways in which social injustice is renewing its hold on schools and students. The current global political climate shows the rise of education as a place to renew or reinforce marginalization, as well as a lack of commitment from authorities and political leaders in rectifying these new attacks on education (Bondy and Braunstein 2019). Two particular concerns to track include a growing pressure for (a) greater conformity among students, schools, and educators, resulting in less risk-taking and questioning; and (b) greater compliance, making it easier to break down norms and barriers to promote acceptance of small changes, leading to the loss of individuality. In the following sections, I draw connections between the growth of nationalism and the dangers of conformity and compliance, both of which can weaken internationalization as a mode of thinking and further constrain efforts around social justice and equity in international education.

Conformity in Education

At an international education conference I attended a few years ago, a former leader from a number of different international schools spoke to me about how international schools created leaders and other schools created followers. This statement indicates recognition that a student's socioeconomic status can determine his or her educational opportunities, and schools are structured to provide enough education based on the outcomes or goals society anticipates that a particular student needs to access. This would be why schools in poorer neighborhoods often focus on vocational training programs and work-study or skills-based classes, as these might be the boundaries a society expects of a particular student's aspirations. This educational divide exists around the world (GPE Secretariat 2019). While we consistently hear of increasing access, opening doors, and ensuring equity, as long as education is seen as a pathway to maintain hegemonic control over resources and opportunities, competition will remain the driving factor to ensuring that we maintain the status quo.

It is this competitive edge in education that promotes conforming attitudes and actions in pursuit of institutionally recognized academic standards. Taking risks and exploring nondominant ideas and identities lose primacy when faced with obligations to meet neoliberal determinations of excellence. No matter what strata of society a person comes from, the risks of nonconformity can be high both personally and professionally. It can lead to loss of income and livelihoods, limited access in certain fields of study, or closed doors to places of worship. There might even be a real fear of losing one's place in a social hierarchy. Such structural forms of oppression and violence are grounded in the type of education one has access to; thus, schools are further supporting both implicit and complicit forms of conformity.

Conformity in education can take on multiple forms. There is conformity in policy, in practice, and in perception. Conformity in policy can be implemented through national oversight of textbooks or ensuring certain gaps or lapses in content to project a more positive view of the nation. For example, Fukurai and Alston (1992) found that the history of minorities in Japan was eliminated or shown in a far more positive light in textbooks to encourage national unity. Conformity in practice is highlighted in the types of schools and educational opportunities students have access to as an extension of their socioeconomic status. It is not uncommon for teachers working in poor or low-resourced schools to recognize the structural barriers that prevent their students from aspiring to be doctors or engineers because they live in communities where they do not see themselves represented in these professions in their day-to-day lives. People conform to the expectations of social worth based on the context in which they live. Such conformity of ambition results in those in power ensuring there is no additional competition that comes from outside their own income brackets. This was in some ways the foundation of the caste system, an economic system in India that co-opted certain jobs and roles in society to certain groups in an effort to make sure there were enough people to serve in those roles. This stratification led to the oppression of large groups of people over the centuries, in part adding layers of demarcation between "us" and "them" to uphold the separation and consolidation of power and resources. Finally, there is conformity of perception. This is not about changing oneself to fit in, it is more about the perception that some people conform in certain situations better than others by sheer dint of who they are—be they men, women, people of color, or able-bodied.

Opposing conformity in policy, practice, and perception can be challenging, but as nationalist governments consolidate power, a conforming society makes resistance more dangerous. It also makes the identification of outliers simpler. Speaking up against injustice becomes harder and, as such, conformity allows for rules to be made to ensure that those who are considered to be dangerous are corralled. Education is a key space through which conformity can be inculcated, and in creating a more conforming society, the work of international education is further diluted, if not completely eliminated.

Compliance

Compliance, in its simplest form, is agreement without critical thinking. As schools push for greater conformity of ideas, compliance works in tandem to build concurrence without disagreement. At the policy level, compliance oftentimes relates to the maintenance of quality across varied delivery, but in schools, compliance weakens dissent and creates a culture where fear of being seen as out of step with the majority can be dangerous. Compliance in education can affect governance, is oftentimes the bedrock of standardization practices, and undermines the expansion and championship of creativity.

Over the past 20 years, there has been a shift in how people around the world view school. The *idea* of school is growing in popularity, but the *practice* of school is one of compliance and completion (Goodman and Uzun 2013). Policymakers find that it is easy to identify education as a common interest, with a clear sense among voters around the world that making education more accessible is a popular stance to take. What most people around the world have realized is that to move forward economically, which would then enhance their standards of living, requires some form of certification proving that they have a particular expertise in a specific topic, which has primarily been distributed through formal schooling. This narrative is clear and has a deep sense of buy-in, especially in countries that have large populations of middle-class families who are placing their hopes of economic security on the success of their children in school.

This compliance ensures that those people who have a voice and resources are able to make the loudest noise and, as such, their children are privileged over the other students (Lareau, Weininger, and Cox 2018). These actions are neither isolated nor unpopular, thus it is easy for us to ignore the trends around equity and marginalization in schools, especially when there are limited resources. A clear example of this is found in the history of the state of Virginia. In her dissertation, Mann (2015) finds that in the 1960s, after the schools were bound by law to desegregate, Prince Edward County decided that rather than desegregate the schools, the county would close all public schools. Under the guise of closing schools, White schools created a parallel process where they could admit the White students who were removed from the public schools to make sure that their education was not interrupted (Mann 2015). For nearly 5 years, non-White students in Prince Edward County either did not have access to schools, were removed from their families to move to areas where they could attend school, or transitioned into the labor force earlier than expected as a result of not being able to attend school (Mann 2015).

Many years later, the state of Virginia sought to right this wrong by providing reparations to those who suffered from the closures, but these reparations came with so many conditions that they did little to ease the pain and suffering experienced by the African American community (Mann 2015). Mann (2015) found that scholarships were provided to only those individuals directly affected, but many of those affected were in their sixties, seventies, and eighties. They were not permitted to use the scholarships for their children or grandchildren (Mann 2015). The lack of access to education limited the opportunities people could have, reduced their ability to build their net worth, and affected their capability to provide greater opportunities for subsequent generations.

International education, at its best, speaks to building opportunities and access for students on the fringes of society. Oftentimes, policies that are implemented at the national level speak to the rhetoric of international education, but the practice is far removed, as illustrated in the case of Prince Edward County. Compliance with the law often means that the school is trying to meet the letter of the law, not the spirit of the law. Compliance tends to make us fearful. Compliance tends to make us want to fit in and be agreeable. Compliance tends to make us good followers, but not good leaders.

The Unmeasurable Good in International Education

In the previous sections, I presented the argument that with the rise of nationalism, schools are weighed down by increasing conforming and complying behaviors, and those behaviors extend to the individual, the school, and the local community. This, in turn, allows for nationalist ideologies to become easier to accept and follow, as people are more afraid and unsure of what it might mean to resist. Nationalism depends on the marginalization of others, creating an unjust system lacking in values of social justice and equity for all people. Across schools, the choice of textbooks and curricula, the decisions on the language of instruction, the inclusion of greater patriotic practices, and the overall social and political messaging of nationalist movements is challenging the more internationalist world order that has been fostered over the past 50 years. This shift requires both an urgent response and a collective understanding of what international education offers in terms of ensuring social justice and equity.

How can international education stand firmer in this environment? How can we as international educators learn from research and practice around the world to ensure that the values of internationalism and the experiences that come from international education are not lost? How can we counter the messages of nationalism as a unifying facet to engage people to think about internationalism as a vehicle for positive social change, especially as global competition and insecurity remain dominant messages to promote nationalism?

International education is dependent on individuals at multiple levels promoting policies and practices that can both address the rise of nationalism and speak to the continued need for social justice in education. To do so, it is important for international educators to take a comprehensive look at global economics, politics, and law. The changes that are happening in one part of the world are replicated in other parts of the world. Boylan and Woolsey (2015, 63) contend that: "Given that social justice…is enacted in and through embodied relationships, attention must be given…to the social…issues—such as school organisation and societal outcomes—but also to the personal and the micro and the interplay between them." Addressing the lack of awareness of these global ideologies must be the first thing we do to ensure the collective movement within international education on these matters.

Second, teachers and teacher educators must have more support and preparation to hold firmer ground on these issues as they arise in their classrooms. Hamilton (2018, 19) studied the reasons for Roma youth disengagement in school and found that policymakers and practitioners are often unaware of the "emotional and social pressure…experienced by individuals whom choose to deviate from cultural norms." The key word is "deviate," which aligns with the earlier sections on conformity and compliance. The fear of not fitting in is universal and is especially potent among adolescents. Furthermore, Baily and Katradis (2016, 224) found that:

> Teachers think and are often willing to talk about inequity….They remember incidents in their classrooms where they are unprepared and

hesitant to take on problematic social issues. While the forces of justice and injustice exist in the context of schools, teachers reflect on their experiences and in our data, often found themselves lacking an awareness of how to handle themselves and provide knowledge, support and guidance to their students.

Educators, teachers, and teacher educators must learn to be comfortable speaking up about these issues and must learn to educate themselves on local ideologies that might challenge a more international focus in education. Educating themselves, feeling comfortable with talking about these issues, and finding support in having these conversations can provide a foundation so that teachers do not choose to avoid and ignore issues of social justice and equity in education. Furthermore, the more that dominant ideologies are accepted without uncritical reflection, the more they are able to take control of larger audiences. Applebaum (2014, 2) argues that dominant ideologies are "difficult to dislodge" and "hijack the discussion and re-center dominant interests," and by giving dominant voices equal time allows for those ideas to be given credence that their "perspective is equally valid," supporting the systematic ignorance of all.

Third, understanding how to truly foster critical thinking should be the responsibility of teacher educators and teachers around the world. Hjerm, Sevä, and Werner (2018, 56) advocate for greater critical thinking to help students "move beyond stereotypes and prejudice when confronted with out-group members." Working with teachers is critical to challenging the narratives that emerge from textbooks, nationalist dialogue, and politically motivated speeches. The power of teachers to teach about marginalization is more effective when there are particular models of citizenship that do not depend purely on one homogenous lived experience and when teachers can address "citizenship in ways that acknowledge the multiple affiliations that people hold. These affiliations need not be framed as problematic and could be viewed as opportunities for extending the ongoing struggle for justice beyond the boundaries of any one nation-state" (El-Haj 2010, 270).

But beyond these recommendations, who are other nontraditional allies we might seek out? How do we create a culture of dissonance to make nationalist rhetoric be seen as the dog whistle it is meant to be? How can we combat attacks on patriotism when people stand against nationalism? Those involved in international education have a special place to be able to make those connections and advocate more fiercely for the principles and actions of social justice around the world. Writing in newspapers, speaking in forums that might not be friendly to these messages, and engaging actively with those people who feel marginalized must be the work we do as international educators. The fear that has allowed the flames of nationalism to be fanned requires those of us involved in international education to be willing to run inside the burning building.

Conclusion

Bassie Louise Pierce (1934, 121) wrote that "the school can have no more dangerous foe than nationalism." With World War II still to come, Pierce entreated people to support teachers' groups through international agencies to stem the tide of nationalist ideologies. She argued, "[P]olitical and economic movements today [are] apparently directed toward setting higher national walls" (Pierce 1934, 121). As conformity and compliance increase, we might be forced to endure what Pierce saw happen to the world merely 4 years after the publication of her essay.

This volume looks at how international education intersects with social justice. The definition of international education has been one of breadth and width. Social justice intersects in every domain across the fields of comparative and international education, development education, international education through exchange and study abroad, intercultural competence, and international education policy. Spring (2018, 61) states that "[t]he divisiveness of nationalism and patriotism outweighs any feelings of fellowship, particularly when they reflect racism, anti-immigrant and religious intolerance….[They] may distort rational thinking and hinder the ability to envision a better world." The power of international education has been to help craft a vision of a better world. The spread of nationalism, and the corresponding factors that are affecting education directly, risk affecting how we envision that better world.

References

Appiah, Kwame Anthony. 2018. *The Lies That Bind: Rethinking Identity*. New York, NY: Liveright Publishing Corporation.

Applebaum, Barbara. 2014. "Hold That Thought." *Democracy and Education* 22, 2:1–4.

Ashcroft, Bill, Gareth Griffiths, and Helen Tiffin. 2013. *Postcolonial Studies: The Key Concepts, Third Edition*. United Kingdom: Routledge.

Au, Wayne. 2017. "When Multicultural Education Is Not Enough." *Multicultural Perspectives* 19, 3:147–150.

Baily, Supriya, and Maria Katradis. 2016. "'Pretty Much Fear!!' Rationalizing Teacher (Dis)Engagement in Social Justice Education." *Equity & Excellence in Education* 49, 2:215–227.

Bekerman, Zvi. 2009. "Social Justice, Identity Politics, and Integration in Conflict-Ridden Societies: Challenges and Opportunities in Integrated Palestinian-Jewish Education in Israel." In *Handbook of Social Justice in Education*, eds. William Ayers, Therese Quinn, and David Stovall. New York, NY: Routledge.

Bondy, Jennifer M., and Lauren B. Braunstein. 2019. "Racial Politics, Latin@ Youth, and Teacher Education." *Journal of Latinos and Education* 18, 2:93–106.

Boylan, Mark, and Ian Woolsey. 2015. "Teacher Education for Social Justice: Mapping Identity Spaces." *Teaching and Teacher Education* 46:62–71.

Coenders, Marcel, and Peer Scheepers. 2003. "The Effect of Education on Nationalism and Ethnic Exclusionism: An International Comparison." *Political Psychology* 24, 2:313–343.

East Asia Regional Council of Overseas Schools. 2018. *Global Issues Network Conference Handbook*. East Asia Regional Council of Overseas Schools. https://www.earcos.org/forms/GIN%20Handbook%20Rev2018.pdf.

El-Haj, Thea Renda Abu. 2010. "'The Beauty of America': Nationalism, Education, and the War on Terror." *Harvard Educational Review* 80, 2:242–275.

Friedman, Jonathan Z. 2018. "Everyday Nationalism and Elite Research Universities in the USA and England." *Higher Education* 76, 2:247–261.

Fukurai, Hiroshi, and Jon P. Alston. 1992. "Sources of Neo-nationalism and Resistance in Japan." *Journal of Contemporary Asia* 22, 2:207–223.

Goodman, Joan F., and Emily Klim Uzun. 2013. "The Quest for Compliance in Schools: Unforeseen Consequences." *Ethics and Education* 8, 1:3–17.

GPE Secretariat. 2019. "A Stubborn Education Crisis as Global Progress Flatlines." Global Partnership for Education. November 20, 2019. https://www.globalpartnership.org/blog/stubborn-education-crisis-global-progress-flatlines.

Grimshaw, Trevor. 2007. "Critical Perspectives on Language in International Education." In *The SAGE Handbook of Research in International Education, First Edition*, eds. Mary Hayden, Jack Levy, and Jeff Thompson. London, United Kingdom: SAGE Publications.

Gunesch, Konrad. 2004. "Education for Cosmopolitanism: Cosmopolitanism as a Personal Cultural Identity Model for and Within International Education." *Journal of Research in International Education* 3, 3:251–275.

Gunesch, Konrad. 2007. "International Education's Internationalism: Inspirations from Cosmopolitanism." In *The SAGE Handbook of Research in International Education, First Edition*, eds. Mary Hayden, Jack Levy, and Jeff Thompson. London, United Kingdom: SAGE Publications.

Hamilton, Paula. 2018. "Engaging Gypsy and Traveller Pupils in Secondary Education in Wales: Tensions and Dilemmas of Addressing Difference." *International Studies in Sociology of Education* 27, 1:4–22.

Hayden, Mary C., Bora A. Rancic, and Jeff J. Thompson. 2000. "Being International: Student and Teacher Perceptions from International Schools." *Oxford Review of Education* 26, 1:107–123.

Hill, Ian. 2015. "What Is an 'International School'?" *International Schools Journal* 35, 1:60–70.

Hjerm, Mikael, Ingemar Johansson Sevä, and Lena Werner. 2018. "How Critical Thinking, Multicultural Education and Teacher Qualification Affect Anti-immigrant Attitudes." *International Studies in Sociology of Education* 27, 1:42–59.

Lareau, Annette, Elliot Weininger, and Amanda Barrett Cox. 2018. "When Wealthy Parents Hold Sway in Public Schools." *The Hechinger Report*. https://hechingerreport.org/opinion-when-wealthy-parents-hold-sway-in-public-schools.

Levy, Jack, and Rebecca Fox. 2007. "Pre-service Teacher Preparation for International Settings." In *The SAGE Handbook of Research in International Education, First Edition*, eds. Mary Hayden, Jack Levy, and Jeff Thompson. London, United Kingdom: SAGE Publications.

Mann, Linda Jean. 2015. "Restorative Justice Unfulfilled: A Case Study of African Americans from Prince Edward County, Virginia." Doctoral dissertation, George Mason University. http://mars.gmu.edu/handle/1920/9669.

Matthews, Julie, and Ravinder Sidhu. 2005. "Desperately Seeking the Global Subject: International Education, Citizenship and Cosmopolitanism." *Globalisation, Societies and Education* 3, 1:49–66.

McDonough, Kevin, and Andrée-Anne Cormier. 2013. "Beyond Patriotic Education: Locating the Place of Nationalism in the Public School Curriculum." *Education, Citizenship and Social Justice* 8, 2:135–150.

Moskal, Marta. 2016. "Spaces of Not Belonging: Inclusive Nationalism and Education in Scotland." *Scottish Geographical Journal* 132, 1:85–102.

Pierce, Bessie Louise. 1934. "The School and the Spirit of Nationalism." *The ANNALS of the American Academy of Political and Social Science* 175, 1:117–122.

Sevier, Brian R. 2009. "Between Mutuality and Diversity: The Project in Intergroup Education and the Discourse of National Unity in Post World War II America." *Educational Foundations* 23, 1–2:21–46.

Snyder, Jack. 2019. "The Broken Bargain: How Nationalism Came Back." *Foreign Affairs*. https://www.foreignaffairs.com/articles/world/2019-02-12/broken-bargain.

Spring, Joel. 2018. "The Well-Schooled World: An Introduction." In *Global Impacts of the Western School Model: Corporatization, Alienation, Consumerism* by Joel Spring. New York, NY: Routledge.

Stromquist, Nelly P., and Karen Monkman, eds. 2000. *Globalization and Education: Integration and Contestation Across Cultures*. Lanham, MD: Rowman & Littlefield.

UNESCO. 2019. *Role of Education*. UNESCO. http://www.unesco.org/new/en/social-and-human-sciences/themes/fight-against-discrimination/role-of-education.

U.S. Department of Education. n.d. "About ED: Overview and Mission Statement." Washington, DC: U.S. Department of Education. https://www2.ed.gov/about/landing.jhtml.

VanOverbeke, Marc A. 2009. "Educating the Democratic Citizen: Frederick Jackson Turner, History Education, and the University Extension Movement." In *Handbook of Social Justice in Education*, eds. William Ayers, Therese Quinn, and David Stovall. New York, NY: Routledge.

Woolfolk, Anita. 2008. *Educational Psychology, Tenth Edition*. Boston, MA: Allyn & Bacon.

The World Bank. 2019. "Overview." The World Bank Group. https://www.worldbank.org/en/topic/education/overview.

3
The Evolution of Social Justice in International Higher Education

AARON CLEVENGER, EdD

Any study of social justice must begin with the question: Who has the right to govern others? Said another way: Do you have the right to wield power over me? Is there some form of superior strength, trait, or intelligence that would make one person more of a leader than others? Do these perceived strengths manifest through race, age, sexual orientation, gender, or other characteristics? Or is there a feature in all human life and in the abilities and differences in each of us that make anyone capable of leading others, or at least determining our own fate?

Working to answer these deeply complex issues gives rise to many other questions: How does one lead fairly? Whose sense of fairness should people follow? Are there such things as universal ethics that we each should, or even could, agree on? Over the years, there have been lived experiments in governance, like democracy and socialism, which have been accepted by the governed; while other forms of oppression, like chattel slavery and totalitarianism, have been brutally forced upon generations of individuals. History is full of examples of the powerful imposing themselves on those perceived to be less powerful, less educated, less wealthy, less pious, or less capable.

It is this history and debate over who has the right to rule over others from which social justice was originally born (Burke 2011). While many people today believe that social justice was formed out of religious teachings, it can be argued that it actually has its beginnings in the modern-day concept of political security (Jackson 2005; Brodie 2007). This chapter provides an overview of the history of social justice, its relationship with higher education, key terminology surrounding the discourse, and the impact of educational activities and experiential learning.

History of Social Justice

In 1843, Jesuit philosopher Luigi Taparelli d'Azeglio coined the concept of social justice as part of what Burke (2011) describes as his desire to convince the people of Italy that there was no such thing as equality in terms of governance. Burke (2011) argues that Taparelli believed that there was a divine and natural need for an aristocratic class. Taparelli penned his opus, *Saggio teoretico di dritto naturale,* during the debate over the future political standing of Italy in the mid-1800s, just after the Napoleonic War. The chief question of the debates became whether Italy would remain as multiple separate kingdoms or would form one unified government. Taparelli, a devout Catholic, worked to develop a philosophy of politics that kept the Pope and Catholicism at the center of power, while his rival philosophers of the day, John Locke and Adam Smith, advocated for governances built on liberalism and free market capitalism, respectively.

According to Behr (2003), in espousing this Catholic-centered authority, Taparelli found himself at deep odds with Locke's concept of the governed being in a contract with those who govern them. Taparelli believed that there was a divine province and a divinely chosen ruling class. He thought that, whether by wealth, education, or strength, this class of people should naturally be able to rule over others. He was convinced of the idea of a "social justice" where those who had the power to bring about stability should rule over those who were unable to bring about stability. Taparelli believed in a concept of "natural authority," which posits that all men were naturally equal but that the application of a person's choices provides him or her with a different and unequal path. He philosophized that choices made some people wealthy and powerful and made others subject to those with that power. Burke (2011), an ardent critic of social justice, draws attention to the paradox of Taparelli being the founder of social justice, pointing out that Taparelli's form of social justice was a defense of inequality and extreme conservatism.

Instead of rejecting this concept, the Catholic church, under the influence of Pope Leo XIII, Cardinal Tommaso Maria Zigliara, and others, eventually transformed the concept into a more centralist approach. During Pope Leo XIII's papacy, Cardinal Zigliara composed the *Rerum novarum*, and the teachings of social justice moved away from pure politics into a more modern philosophy, stating that the role of the state is to protect and promote the rights of its citizens. Through the *Rerum novarum*, the Catholic church adopted the idea that God is on the side of the poor and the working man rather than the rich and the greedy. This philosophy went as far as to condemn many of the practices of capitalism and advocated for the need for trade unions and collective bargaining. Concurrently, the Catholic church pivoted to a more biblical message of helping the less fortunate, the infirm, the less educated, and the poor. Guided by the belief that humans are divinely judged by their acts of charity and faith, the Catholic church transformed the concept of social justice into a responsibility that asked those who had been blessed with more to provide for those with less. The church pointed to the concept of Jesus and his acts in caring for those that society had abandoned as God's example of how society should act toward one another.

Social Movements of the Twentieth and Twenty-First Centuries

As the world emerged from World War I, social justice became more secular in its aims against injustice. During this time, a number of social movements developed, including the fight for the needs and concerns of the working class (Waites 1976), protections against child labor (Cox 1999), the initial adoption of women's suffrage (Hume 2016), and the earliest beginnings of the fight for equality for lesbian, gay, bisexual, and transgender (LGBT) individuals (Bullough 2002).

As World War II came to an end, the civil rights movement in the United States rose in national prominence. During this time, the concepts of racial hierarchy, social Darwinism, and Aryanism—previously held as mainstream beliefs throughout Europe and the United States—fell out of favor thanks, in part, to their association with nazism. However, despite scientifically disproving White supremacy and the idea of any superior race, violence, segregation, and hatred continued, especially in the United States and South Africa.

To battle these racially motivated injustices, numerous leaders in the African American community during the 1950s and 1960s led marches, boycotts, and peaceful protests in an attempt to make real progress and change in the lives of African Americans and the politics of the United States. Beginning then and progressing into the 1980s, leadership from Nelson Mandela and the African National Congress, among others, fought to end the evils of the ferocious violence, segregation, and discrimination against "non-Whites" under the apartheid laws of the South African Afrikaners. While much progress has been made in the areas of civil rights and racial equality, many radical racist theories and behaviors have transformed over the years from overt mainstream beliefs and laws to a more covert form of systematic and institutional racism.

In conjunction with the fight for social and political equality, civil rights leaders such as Martin Luther King Jr. and Ralph Abernathy began to demand economic and human rights for the poor, regardless of race. As these civil rights leaders made direct connections between poverty and inequality, they enabled others to take action. Another champion of the day was Michael Harrington, a political theorist and member of Dr. King's National Advisory Committee. Harrington, author of *The Other America: Poverty in the United States* (1962), made the argument that poverty was no longer temporary for people; it had become a permanent state of being that was inherited from one generation to the next, becoming systematically engrained into the lives of many within the United States and the other global north countries of the world. Harrington's text became so influential that it is often credited as a major influence on U.S. Presidents Kennedy and Johnson. Harrington's text and the civil rights movement are both cited as leading to Johnson's 1964 War on Poverty (Heise 1989; Isserman 2009; Matthews 2014).

Building on the principles of those major events, John Rawls's (1971) *A Theory of Justice* criticizes the widening gap between the rich and the poor and calls for a Locke-like contract between the government and the people, guaranteeing all individuals their basic human rights. Rawls (1971) espoused the idea that the poor must be given the opportunity to work, and the notion that the government owes its people the ability to afford and/or receive free healthcare and education. Critics and proponents alike began to see social justice as an economic philosophy that calls for the rich to pay a representative percentage of taxes, that income and wealth should be distributed, and that all citizens should benefit from one another's labor.

Social Justice Today

Too often, the first lesson in teaching social justice requires that it be demystified, redefined, and explained, absent from the political jargon it has been assigned. As an administrator in international education and an adjunct professor in both ethics and global studies, I find that my students often misunderstand what social justice is and why it is important to society. I have seen students become defensive, skeptical, and even angry on occasion. These emotions seem to emerge from the perception that social justice is somehow a desire that seeks to forcibly redistribute the wealth, opportunities, and privilege of the rich. In reframing social justice, it is important to define it as a concept of human rights and equality that requires the removal of systematic barriers that prevent individuals from succeeding and meeting their full potential. It is this concept of equality of opportunity that social justice stands for today.

TERMINOLOGY

While it is essential that students understand that social justice is not simply moving wealth from one person or class of people to another, it is also vital that they recognize and accept that there is a universal need for equality and opportunity for all people. In order to teach the concepts of social justice, equality, and opportunity, either in a traditional classroom setting or in a more hands-on experiential environment, we must define and understand a number of terms. I have narrowed the terms to 10. While my list is by no means comprehensive, I have found these terms to be essential for student comprehension if they are to truly grasp the concept of social justice.

- Prejudice: an assumed belief or judgment about a culture or a group of people.

- Discrimination: an intentional or unintentional action against a person or a group of people based upon one's prejudiced beliefs about that person or group.

- Power: the ability to control, influence, or direct the action of others with or without their permission or despite their resistance to one's control or influence.

- Oppression: exercising unjust or cruel power over another person or group of people.

- Equity: a state of being where all people or a group of people are afforded access to, and the correct amount of, necessary resources to achieve equal results as the dominant group.

- Privilege: social, legal, and institutional rights and power afforded to someone merely because of the person's membership in one or more social identity groups; in the U.S context, these would include White people, able-bodied people, heterosexuals, males, Christians, cisgender persons, and those people who speak English as their first language.

- Systematic Barriers: written or unwritten, spoken or unspoken policies, practices, and procedures that create unequal challenges or limit access to opportunity.

- Culture: the norms, values, customs, terminology, laws, religion, institutions, and social groups of a people.

- Socialization: the lessons and behaviors one learns in order to conform to and understand a particular culture; family, friends, cultural influences, and personal experiences often influence one's socialization.

- Peacebuilding: nonviolent activities undertaken to resolve injustices caused by violence, deadly conflict, or destructive behaviors.

While the definitions above are a compilation that I have developed over the years, they have been inspired by Sensoy and DiAngelo's (2017) *Is Everyone Really Equal?* Sensoy and DiAngelo (2017) informed not only my thinking around the essential terminology and definitions applied but also the examples, stories, and analogies I use in class and in the field. As one begins to teach or facilitate social justice curriculum, one will likely find it essential to become familiar with other terminology, like the lexicon surrounding gender, sexuality, and disability scholarship and research.

Social Justice and Higher Education

Higher education, like social justice, has changed and transformed over time, becoming what Karaca (2018) labeled the "Third Generation University," comprising institutions of academics, research, and innovation. In considering U.S. higher education, Thelin (2011) points to a number of historical moments that have led to the transformation of the academy from a curriculum reflecting colonial vocations and values to a more holistic and modern pedagogy. The passage of the Morrill Land-Grant Colleges Acts of 1862 and 1890 and the founding of schools for women, historically Black colleges and universities for the descendants of former enslaved African Americans, and other institutions that serve minority students are two examples of this shift. The transformation is further demonstrated by Columbia College's 1919 introduction of the Core Curriculum and the G.I. Bill. These examples represent only some of the laws and social movements that have helped transform U.S. higher education from its purpose of educating young, White men to the current ambitious vision for U.S. higher education.

Today, the public expects higher education to produce useful research that benefits society in a tangible way, improve the economic future of its graduates, and, in turn, enhance the communities in which the graduates live and work. In the United States, higher education is an important vehicle for class and social mobility. It is this aspect that has led some higher education institutions to prioritize social justice as an important aspect of the curriculum. These institutions advocate for the idea that, in order to produce educated individuals and future responsible leaders, their students must be able to understand their place within the world while also acknowledging what systematic barriers prevent individuals from succeeding and meeting their full potential; this has not always been the belief, even among academics.

Theories and Concepts

Bennett (2010) points out in his consequential chapter "A Short Conceptual History of Intercultural Learning in Study Abroad" that before the world wars, society, including academia, was mired in the history of European colonialism and still advocated and endorsed the theory of social Darwinism. Many educated individuals still believed in concepts such as eugenics (Dikötter 1998) and a hierarchy of cultures ranging from what was labeled "the savage to the civilized" (Kenny 2015, 176). With these ethnocentric beliefs came the imperialistic concept that the "global north" needed to either control or save the people of the uneducated and barbarous communities of the "global south."

Not wanting to continue the normalization of these racist concepts, anthropologists like Frank Boas and his students began debunking these erroneous and specious beliefs and instead espoused the concept of cultural relativism (Tilley 2007). Cultural relativism is the belief that a culture should not be judged through the lens of another person's culture, but that it must be experienced and understood through direct exposure to the culture and understood on its own terms (Bennett 2010). In this way, cultural relativism can be seen as the original goal of international education and one of the first consequential intersections of social justice and international education.

International Exchanges

In conjunction with the rise of cultural relativism and the end of World War II, the global community began to realize that relationships were needed between nations to develop a sense of mutual understanding and respect around the differences of cultures, peoples, and their governments. Individuals saw the need to explore other places and understand other people's lived experiences, not through the judgment of their own lives but through direct exposure to other countries. To this end, a number of international education efforts were born, such as the long-standing Experiment in International Living (Bennett 2010) and the foundation of the Peace Corps (Wetzel 1966), both of which served to provide international exposure and experience for Americans and still exist today.

While these and other programs of the time sent U.S. citizens to other countries, it was the 1946 legislation that created the Fulbright Program that created a full bilateral exchange. The Fulbright Program sent Americans abroad to represent the United States, and, simultaneously, people from around the world would come to study in the United States. Often considered by some experts to be the greatest international exchange program ever conceived (Gearhart 2014), the Fulbright Program was envisioned to encourage students to learn, research, and communicate across borders—both physical and intellectual. With the help of funds from war reparations, the Fulbright Program set up an exchange for all aspects of academics, ranging from science and technology to culture and politics to the arts and public service.

The Fulbright Program has been proven over the years to "increase mutual understanding between the people of the United States and the people of other countries" (SRI International Center for Science, Technology and Economic Development 2005, 51). World leaders agreed that international collaboration was a means of using research to produce knowledge that would benefit society collectively. To perpetuate these collaborations, U.S. and other institutions of higher education throughout the world further adopted the current concept of exchanges, study abroad, and other forms of academic mobility.

Social Justice Learning

In considering the intersections of social justice and international education, I offer a number of examples from my own experience as a faculty member and administrator, both in the classroom and through experiential learning opportunities that I have helped to facilitate. At my current institution, Embry-Riddle Aeronautical University, we have the unique mission of teaching the science, practice, and business of aviation and aerospace, preparing students for productive careers and leadership roles in service around the world. It is my belief that to prepare students to be global leaders, they must have an understanding of the importance of social responsibility and social justice.

In terms of demographics, the majority of my students are White, middle-class males with academic interests in science, technology, engineering, or mathematics. This student demographic is underrepresented in study abroad, but they benefit from the opportunity to broaden their perspectives and challenge their worldviews. As both the senior international officer and a professor, I find it essential to introduce my students to social justice education because it is every student's responsibility to lead the world to a more equitable place. The pursuit of social justice is about removing the barriers of success for all people. Social justice is not some form of power shift designed to lessen men or punish one group of people; it is a movement to provide opportunity and resources for all, regardless of their status or ability.

Additionally, I believe it is essential to expose my classes to social justice learning outcomes because, despite the students' homogeneous appearance, the students represent diverse backgrounds and experiences. Among them, there are international students, gay men, differently abled students with visible or invisible disabilities, veterans, liberals, and conservatives, to name a few. Moreover, there are non-majority groups represented within the classroom, including non-White men and women of all races. Despite any perceived similarities among my students, each of them has a different voice and perspective and each deserves the opportunity to be exposed to the lessons of social justice. The inherent diversity of these classes, though sometimes not immediately apparent, provide a strong argument for the use of a social justice curriculum. Once exposed to social justice, students are often interested in understanding how to leverage the concepts to champion themselves, or perhaps to advocate for their friends, family, or society as a whole.

Position of Privilege

In teaching my students, I have found it nearly impossible to move forward if they cannot agree that some of us are more privileged than others. In coming to this agreement, I believe it is necessary for the students to understand that this privilege is not due to their hard work and determination but because they face far fewer, or no, structural or social barriers working against their success and because of the arbitrary circumstances into which they were born. Making the point that we should perhaps feel a sense of responsibility to provide others the same opportunities that we have received is controversial, often leading to contentious discussions about the amount of work and determination that they and their family have put forth for years.

Regularly in these discussions, my students have felt that they and their families' hard work is being dismissed and disrespected. Some of these students believe that on the topic of inequality, individuals who are oppressed by systematic barriers are really just less enterprising people, some individuals are unlucky, and others are too lazy to fight and sacrifice for the same opportunities as others who have "pulled themselves up by the bootstraps." It is a rewarding but challenging task for me to convince someone that systematic barriers exist or that oppression based on race, age, religion, or sexual orientation does have a profound impact on someone's self-worth, opportunity to succeed in a career, or even the ability to see a future where the individual is considered equal. In the next section, I will discuss the ways in which I use educational activities and exercises to help students confront their own biases and understand their privilege.

Educational Activities

While I have heard the advice and always attempt to ensure that my lessons are more about the students discovering their own opinions and coming to their own conclusions than adopting my way of thinking, it is essential to attempt to educate individuals on the difference between equality of opportunity and equality of outcome. I use activities like Global Beads® to attempt to create a visual representation of socialization and privilege; I show documentaries like *The Eye of the Storm* (Peters 1970) to drive home the concept of discrimination and its effects on individuals; I have even used movies like *Crash* (Haggis 2004) and *Remember the Titans* (Yakin 2000). These Hollywood films give my students a window into the various cultures and life experiences to which they would usually not be exposed, including lessons on bias, prejudice, and racism.

Often, these activities, personal stories during the classroom reflection, and other forms of experiential learning have the desired impact on the students, and they come away with a better understanding of discrimination, privilege, and the purpose of social justice.

Experiential Learning

While there are strengths and weakness that can be attributed to lecture-based social justice education, there is research that has shown that experiential pedagogy, such as international service-learning, exchange programs, and international volunteerism, is actually a more effective way to learn about oppression, privilege, and peacebuilding. Social justice education leaders Adams and Bell (2016) advocate for social justice education to be conducted through experiential learning, suggesting that the participants benefit from experiences that confront previous assumptions and biases while disrupting the students' incorrect social presumptions. Since international education's purpose, in addition to academic study, is to expose learners to new cultural experiences, increase student empathy and awareness of social injustices, and promote understanding of the world and its people, the intersection of social justice and international education could not be more appropriate.

International Service-Learning

In my experience, teaching social justice in a lecture rarely resonates in the same way as exposing a student to a real-life experience, which is why I find it so fulfilling when I have the opportunity to lead an international service-learning program. My first foray into utilizing experiential learning as a modality for teaching social justice education was in the late 1990s, when I co-led an alternative spring break program to Atlanta, Georgia, around the theme of homelessness and hunger. The program was my graduate practicum, and I had a number of faculty and staff members helping to guide me in the concepts of cocurricular facilitation, reflection exercises, and social justice curriculum design.

ALTERNATIVE SPRING BREAK IN ATLANTA

Each day of the weeklong experience provided me, my cofacilitator, and our 25 undergraduate students with a window into the lives and experiences of citizens in the Atlanta metro area. Among the 25 student participants, about 60 percent were women and 40 percent were men and about 75 percent were White and 25 percent were people of color. Together, we aimed to serve the Atlanta community while learning about poverty and the food insecurity of the region. Specifically, the educational experiences included volunteering at a soup kitchen, the Second Harvest food bank, a halfway home for men reentering society after incarceration, a community food garden, and a homeless shelter's children's day care center. Each night included several hours of reflection exercises and discussions regarding food security, poverty, and the systematic barriers that are the root causes of homelessness.

GLOBAL SERVICE INITIATIVE

Several years later, I combined this alternative spring break experience with my role as a fraternity and sorority adviser, which led me to my work with the Global Service Initiative (GSI) and Project Jamaica. The award-winning GSI is a social justice and civic engagement program designed to teach fraternity members from the United States and Canada about the importance of global engagement, social justice, and human insecurity. According to GSI, the typical participant is a White, college-aged male attending his sophomore or junior year of college or university in the United States or Canada. There is not an observable pattern of economic class, as there have been students of upper-, middle-, and lower-class means attending the program. Of the participants I have worked with, approximately 90 percent have been White and 10 percent have been students of color.

In terms of the experience, GSI is a seven-day, international service-learning program that runs three times annually, with a service component taking place on four of the seven days. The service portion of the program runs between 7 and 8 hours daily; the typical service experience is manual labor and often involves mixing and laying concrete, framing walls, roofing buildings, arranging plumbing, setting tile, building fences, painting, and, occasionally, demolishing or clearing ground for projects. Each year, the participant cohorts accomplish at least three projects that span the week of the program; these projects have occurred each January, May, and June for the last 9 years of the program. Members of the group can choose to stay with one project throughout the week or rotate through all three projects. The host community itself becomes a part of the format of learning. As Lewin (1946) suggests, the educational environment is part of the experience.

Cultural experiences occur over two of the seven days. The first cultural day includes a Sunday church service, an island boat tour, and lunch at an authentic Jamaican restaurant. The second day is spent experiencing music at the Zimbali Retreats. Here, the participants experience drum lessons and see where their lunch is grown and harvested. In addition, a hike from the Zimbali Retreats to a Rastafarian commune occurs; participants follow a Rastafarian guide up the Canaan Mountains. The tour serves as an introduction to how the Rastas live, farm, and survive.

Logistically, Jamaica was chosen because of a long-term, existing relationship between the local government and the founder and main facilitator of GSI. These ties with the local government enable GSI to better connect with local schools and engage in the local culture; it also ensures that the local community is both invested and involved in any decisions involving site selection and projects. The GSI experience has spawned an off-shoot program, titled Project Jamaica, that brings this same social justice program to other collegiate and non-collegiate groups, such as the Girl Scouts of Central Indiana, multiple university honors programs, and numerous university leadership programs.

During the four times that I have facilitated one of the GSI programs, I have seen how international service can open the eyes and hearts of young men who otherwise have not been exposed to poverty, homelessness, childhood hunger, and limited access to work and school. An empirical review of the GSI, in the form of pre- and post-tests, has shown that this exposure has led to a statistical improvement in the following areas: (a) the participants' ability to identify privileges that they have in their lives; (b) their understanding of how to have an impact on global and social justice issues through their actions; and (c) their commitment to address issues they see in their community. In addition, from a qualitative perspective, participants have shared direct feedback that demonstrates their growth in social justice learning outcomes. A sampling from the 2019 cohort follows:

- "When I return home, I want to have an impact globally.... Eventually, I'd also love to do Doctors Without Borders and do dental work in third-world countries."

- "I want to become further educated on the issues through immersing myself in various cultures."

- "I myself can make a huge impact into the lives of others. I also learned the importance of helping vs. service as well as acknowledging my privilege."

- "During this week, I learned that other cultures have really interesting and differing viewpoints to be appreciated."

Undergraduate Research Abroad

When I transitioned from student affairs to an academic position as executive director of undergraduate research, I brought my interest in social justice education with me. In this role, Embry-Riddle gave me the opportunity to create an annual research abroad program (George and Clevenger 2019). In my 4 years in the role, my cofacilitator and I shared in the responsibilities of serving as research supervisors to the dozens of students who traveled to one or more of the nine international locations, including Brazil, China, Hong Kong, Hungary, Indonesia, Japan, Malaysia, Romania, and Singapore.

My cofacilitator, a professor of economics, supervised students' research in areas such as finance labor, industry, and innovation; I supervised research in culture, social justice, education, and human security. The undergraduate researchers who conducted social justice or cultural-based research programs met with me biweekly for 6 months before traveling with me and a cofacilitator to the country in which they were doing research. During these predeparture meetings, the students developed baseline knowledge of social justice terminology, human security concerns, and cultural norms for each of the countries that were visited. In addition, the students were taught qualitative research methods such as life story interviews (Atkinson 1998), Rapid Qualitative Inquiry (Beebe 2014), and Quick Ethnography (Handwerker 2011) that could be used as methodologies for their studies.

While each year and country provided a unique set of excursions, in-person interviews, opportunities for observations, and individual discussions, each of the experiences exposed students to the different cultures, human security challenges, and social justice concerns in the various countries they were studying. Upon the students' return, they each produced a scholarly work about their experience that was presented either in a scholarly journal or via poster at one of numerous undergraduate research conferences. Examples of relevant topics included how the ethnic fragmentation and class division of cities contributes to human trafficking and complex criminal activity in Southeast Asia, cultural attitude shifts among multiple generations in Singapore, and women's access to higher education in a global context.

Hybrid Courses

My professional and personal interests in international education and social justice became even more closely aligned in 2014 when I moved into the university's senior international officer role and began teaching courses on ethics and social responsibility, international studies, and world politics and globalization. It was through this lens, and nearly 20 years of teaching social justice education, that I have designed hybrid courses with short-term social justice experiences as culminating course experiences.

My next two scheduled course experiences are eco-agriculture experiences where my students and I will be working on a macadamia nut farm that was designed to assist with economic development and sustainable agriculture in Guatemala. During our time on the eco-agricultural project, we will be discussing the connections between poverty, social justice, and environmental injustice. We will see firsthand how the communities we visit are developing self-sustaining agriculture. We will assist in educating the general public about the environment, while they teach us about their customs and lifestyle. The following year, students in my international studies course are scheduled to become a participant cohort in Project Jamaica.

Reflection

Whether we are talking about lectures in class or these programs in Jamaica, China, or Atlanta, each day of these varied learning opportunities have ended with a reflective exercise designed to assist participants in considering how they have been influenced by and have grown through their exposure and experience, as well as how their work relates to social justice and their values. Reflection questions and daily activities include discussions regarding the culture, poverty, and its effect on the people we met and the world; the difference between direct service and indirect philanthropy; ways to be active and engaged global citizens; and how to serve as an advocate for human development and social justice causes. Other discussions throughout the different programs include dialogues about privilege and equality, social injustice, and both equality of opportunity and equality of outcome.

Once my students or participants are exposed to the reality of poverty in many parts of the world, including in the United States, conversations about privilege take place more honestly and with the students better understanding the nuances of why someone might not have the same opportunity to learn, earn, or thrive. As individuals see the barriers to equality of opportunity, some feel helpless, while others are inspired to serve in their own communities, international communities, or even in some global or industrial leadership role.

Sustainable Development Goals

To provide the students who are inspired during or after their international experience with a framework for making a difference in the service to others, many international educators have adopted the United Nations's (UN) 17 Sustainable Development Goals (SDGs). The SDGs were created in 2012 during the United Nations Conference on Sustainable Development in Rio de Janeiro, Brazil. The attendees and subsequent leaders in human security and social justice created what the United Nations considers to be a blueprint for overcoming the global challenges that all humankind face. Through international education experiences that include social justice education and the SDGs, our students are able to contribute to the eradication of poverty, inequality, and environmental degradation.

My experiences with the SDGs as a framework for actionable items have provided me with a dual-sided paradigm. On one side, I see the need for a structure that gives both a plan and tangible goals; on the other side, I have found that the SDGs can sometimes cause well-meaning people to feel that they understand the situations on the ground more than those actually living them. It is imperative when we are working alongside individuals in their own community that we listen, learn, and take direction on the projects that we work and the support that we give. The SDGs have the potential to put blinders on our students and to provide us with goals that are not supported by the community we are serving. In terms of how the SDGs can intersect with social justice and international education, it is essential that we only consider these as goals if and when they fit within the expressed objectives of the community leaders.

Conclusion

As more international educators choose to adopt a role in social justice education, it is important to realize that, even though higher education is a generally welcoming environment for the ideas espoused by social justice, there has been little formal agreement on what social justice education should look like or what learning outcomes social justice educators should teach. The future of social justice through international education needs more scholarship and a wider set of agreed upon definitions.

We need more international education leaders to be able to articulate why social justice is a worthy goal for college graduates, as well as experiential reflective programs designed with those students and social justice in mind. International education has the power to impact social justice education today and long into the future, not only as a field of scholarship but also as pedagogy of hope. The concepts of social justice and international education are inextricably linked, as are the goals that each espouse. I am eager to see us all write the next chapter of social justice and its intersections with international education.

References

Adams, Maurianne, and Lee Anne Bell, eds. 2016. *Teaching for Diversity and Social Justice*. New York, NY: Routledge.

Atkinson, Robert. 1998. *The Life Story Interview*. Thousand Oaks, CA: SAGE Publications.

Beebe, James. 2014. *Rapid Qualitative Inquiry: A Field Guide to Team-Based Assessment*. Lanham, MD: Rowman & Littlefield Publishers.

Behr, Thomas. 2003. "Luigi Taparelli D'azeglio, SJ (1793-1862) and the Development of Scholastic Natural-Law Thought as a Science of Society and Politics." *Journal of Markets & Morality* 6, 1:99–115.

Bennett, Milton J. 2010. "A Short Conceptual History of Intercultural Learning in Study Abroad." In *A History of U.S. Study Abroad: 1965-Present*, eds. William W. Hoffa and Stephen C. DePaul. Carlisle, PA: Frontiers: The Interdisciplinary Journal of Study Abroad and The Forum on Education Abroad.

Brodie, Janine M. 2007. "Reforming Social Justice in Neoliberal Times." *Studies in Social Justice* 1, 2:93–107.

Bullough, Vern L. 2002. *Before Stonewall: Activists for Gay and Lesbian Rights in Historical Context*. London, United Kingdom: Routledge.

Burke, Thomas Patrick. 2011. *The Concept of Justice: Is Social Justice Just?* London, United Kingdom: Continuum International Publishing Group.

Cox, Katherine. 1999. "The Inevitability of Nimble Fingers—Law, Development, and Child Labor." *Vanderbilt Journal of Transnational Law* 32, 1:115–150.

Dikötter, Frank. 1998. "Race Culture: Recent Perspectives on the History of Eugenics." *The American Historical Review* 103, 2:467–478.

Gearhart, G. David. 2014. "The Fulbright Program: Too Remarkable to Be Cut." *Chronicle of Higher Education*. May 5, 2014. https://www.chronicle.com/blogs/conversation/2014/05/05/the-fulbright-program-too-important-to-be-cut.

George, Kelly W., and Aaron D. Clevenger. 2019. "Preventing a Boondoggle: Assuring a Short Term Research Abroad Activity is an Educative Experience." *Journal of Research in Innovative Teaching & Learning*. Published electronically December 9, 2019.

Haggis, Paul. 2004. *Crash*. Santa Monica, CA: Lions Gate.

Handwerker, Penn W. 2011 *Quick Ethnography: A Guide to Rapid Multi-Method Research*. Plymouth, United Kingdom: AltaMira Press.

Harrington, Michael. 1962. *The Other America: Poverty in the United States*. New York, NY: Macmillan.

Heise, Kenan. 1989. "Michael Harrington, 61, Socialist Who Wrote 'The Other America.'" *Chicago Tribune*. August 2, 1989. https://www.chicagotribune.com/news/ct-xpm-1989-08-02-8901010409-story.html.

Hume, Leslie. 2016. *The National Union of Women's Suffrage Societies 1897–1914*. Routledge Revivals. London: Routledge. Citations based on Routledge edition.

Isserman, Maurice. 2009. "Michael Harrington: Warrior on Poverty." *New York Times*. June 19, 2009. https://www.nytimes.com/2009/06/21/books/review/Isserman-t.html.

Jackson, Ben. 2005. "The Conceptual History of Social Justice." *Political Studies Review* 3, 3:356–373.

Karaca, Mehmet. 2018. "Universities at 21st Century: Conversion of Istanbul Technical University to New Generation University." *Balkan Universities Association* 62.

Kenny, Robert. 2015. "Freud, Jung, Boas: The Psychoanalytic Engagement with Anthropology Revisited." *Notes and Records: The Royal Society Journal of the History of Science* 69, 2:173–190.

Lewin, Kurt. 1946. "Active Research and Minority Problems." *Journal of Social Issues* 2, 4:34–46.

Matthews, Dylan. 2014. "Everything You Need to Know About the War on Poverty." *Washington Post*. January 8, 2014. https://www.washingtonpost.com/news/wonk/wp/2014/01/08/everything-you-need-to-know-about-the-war-on-poverty.

Peters, William. 1970. *The Eye of the Storm*. San Francisco, CA: California Newsreel.

Rawls, John. 1971. *A Theory of Justice*. Cambridge, MA: Harvard University Press.

Sensoy, Özlem, and Robin DiAngelo. 2017. *Is Everyone Really Equal? An Introduction to Key Concepts in Social Justice Education*. New York, NY: Teachers College Press.

SRI International Center for Science, Technology and Economic Development. 2005. *Outcome Assessment of the Visiting Fulbright Scholar Program*. Arlington, VA: SRI International. Retrieved from https://files.eric.ed.gov/fulltext/ED495810.pdf.

Thelin, John R. 2011. *A History of American Higher Education*. Baltimore, MD: Johns Hopkins University Press.

Tilley, John J. 2007. "Cultural Relativism." In *The Blackwell Encyclopedia of Sociology*, ed. George Ritzer. Malden, MA: Blackwell Publishing.

Waites, Brian A. 1976. "The Effect of the First World War on Class and Status in England, 1910–20." *Journal of Contemporary History* 11, 1:27–48.

Wetzel, Charles, J. 1966. "The Peace Corps in Our Past." *The Annals of the American Academy of Political and Social Science* 365, 1:1–11.

Yakin, Boaz. 2000. *Remember the Titans*. Burbank, CA: Walt Disney Studios Motion Pictures.

4

Being "Black" in a U.S. Context
Racialized Experiences of African and Caribbean International Students

SHONTAY DELALUE, PhD

In the United States, there is a distinct and ongoing difficult dialogue surrounding race. Charged by social, political, and historical factors, some critical race theorists argue that race is the basis for how we do business in the United States. In their seminal book *Racial Formation in the United States: From the 1960s to the 1990s,* Omi and Winant (1994, 55–56) argue that "racial categories are created, inhabited, transformed and destroyed and race is a matter of both social structure and cultural representation."

Given how embedded race is in the discourse, experience, and society of the United States, it is essential for international educators to examine the ways in which systems and policies adversely impact certain groups—particularly the connections between social justice and the international student experience. Operating from a social justice lens entails acknowledging inequities in society and working to address them.

As many higher education institutions in the United States and around the world have been tasked with developing comprehensive internationalization strategies, we as international educators must also examine how race impacts international students' experiences. Gary Althen, former president of NAFSA: Association of International Educators, wrote in his *International Educator* article "Educating International Students About 'Race'" that "Many international student offices address the general issue of intercultural relations, without a particular focus on race relations," but "most advisers agree that learning about race is an important part of understanding culture in the United States" (Althen 2009, 88, 93).

In this chapter, I explore the impact of U.S. racialization—the process of ascribing a racial identity to a person or group—for African and Caribbean students by sharing excerpts from my doctoral research (Delalue 2014) on how the concept of race was conceived and maintained over time in the United States. I also consider the experience of "Black" international students who are often ascribed a racial status with which they do not personally identify.

The Origins of Race

The origins of race and racial classifications have long been disputed. Scholars in the eighteenth and nineteenth centuries purported that race had a biological element, but that theory has been refuted. Many people now agree that race is a socially constructed, yet well-maintained, system of classification. One of the many organizations that formerly backed the biological race theory was the American Anthropological Association (AAA). Having since changed its position, AAA (2019) now offers the following definition of race:

> Race is a recent idea created by western Europeans following exploration across the world to account for differences among people and justify colonization, conquest, enslavement, and social hierarchy among humans. The term is used to refer to groupings of people according to common origin or background and associated with perceived biological markers… Ideas about race are culturally and socially transmitted and form the basis of racism, racial classification and often complex racial identities.

Race as a concept was embedded in the early founding of the United States. Omi and Winant (1994, 79) posit that "[s]ince the earliest days of colonialism in North America, an identifiable racial order has linked the system of political rule to the racial classification of individuals and groups. The major institutions and social relationships of U.S. society—law, political organizations, economic relationships, religion, cultural life, residential patterns, etc.—have been structured from the beginning by the racial order." While race has come to have a distinct meaning in the United States, the practice of classifying humans in a hierarchical manner based on physical characteristics originated in Europe.

The notion of race as a loose concept can be traced back to the seventeenth century. According to the AAA (n.d.), one of the first documented efforts of work on human variation by a European was done by French physician Francois Bernier. In 1684, Bernier published *A New Division of the Earth, According to the Different Species or Races of Men Who Inhabit It*. Bernier relied on categories based on outward physical characteristics, such as skin color, to distinguish between humans. Half a century later, Swedish botanist Carolus Linnaeus published a system of biological classifications in *Systemae Naturae* (1735), and Johann Friedrich Blumenbach followed suit.

> [Linnaeus] formalized the distinction among the continental populations of the world and his work helped characterize the concept of race. In the tenth edition of *Systemae Naturae,* published in 1758, Linnaeus proposed four subcategories of Homo sapiens: Americanus; Asiaticus; Africanus; and Europeanus. Expanding on the work of Carolus Linnaeus, German professor of medicine Johann Friedrich Blumenbach introduced one of the race-based classifications in *On the Natural Variety of Mankind*. In the second edition, Blumenbach changed his original geographically based four-race arrangement to a five-group one that emphasized physical morphology (the study of the form of an organism). Blumenbach's five categories were: Caucasian, the white race; Mongolian, the yellow race; Malayan, the brown race; Ethiopian, the black race; and American, the red race. Although he retained geographical names for his categories, the change marked a shift from geography to physical appearance. (AAA n.d.)

These ideas, which were professed to be rooted in science, were propagated in the United States in the 1700s by those who wished to justify slavery. Among them were some of the nation's founding fathers, such as Thomas Jefferson who, during his tenure as governor of the state of Virginia, said in *Notes on the State of Virginia 1781–1785*: "I advance it therefore as a suspicion only, that the blacks, whether originally a distinct race, or made distinct by time and circumstances, are inferior to whites in the endowments of both body and mind." Prior to European scientists developing pseudoscientific theories of race, origins of racist ideas were being planted by Puritans who "used them in the 1630s to legalize and codify New England slavery—and Virginians had done the same in the 1620s" (Kendi 2016, 22).

The Introduction of Slavery

Many historians contend that August 1619 marked the first arrival of Africans to what would eventually become the United States of America. Some scholars argue that due to the complexity of slavery being a transnational endeavor, this date should be seen as one historical point in a complicated series of abominable events. Michael Guasco (2017) notes, "Telling the story of 1619 as an 'English' story also ignores the entirely transnational nature of the early modern Atlantic world and the way competing European powers collectively facilitated racial slavery even as they disagreed about and fought over almost everything else."

The slave trade "was not a distinct enterprise but rather an institution that permeated every aspect of social and economic life in Rhode Island, the Americas, and indeed the Atlantic World" (Brown University Steering Committee on Slavery and Justice 2006, 13). The vast majority of enslaved Africans were brought to the Caribbean and South America, namely Brazil. While, in the U.S. context, the focus is often on the southern states, for decades the business of slavery was one of the most lucrative endeavors in the northern part of the United States, including Rhode Island, the smallest state in the country.

The dispersion of Africans across the Americas and the Atlantic with no acknowledgment of shared linkages furthers the assumption of distinct Black experiences with no common thread: one in the United States, the Caribbean, Brazil, and various countries in Africa. The complexity of discussing the Black race is made all the more complicated by the way the word "race" is defined and used—specifically "Blackness," as it takes on a different meaning depending on location.

U.S. Racial Categorization

In the United States since 1790, by law, data are collected on race and ethnicity (among other data) every 10 years, which illustrates just how embedded the notion of race is in the country. Article I, Section 2 of the U.S. Constitution states that "Representatives and direct Taxes shall be apportioned among the several States which may be included within this Union, according to their respective Numbers, which shall be determined by adding to the whole Number of free Persons, including those bound to Service for a Term of Years, and excluding Indians not taxed, three fifths of all other Persons." In this instance, "all other Persons" referred to Black people (namely, enslaved Africans at that time).

The Constitution goes on to say, "The actual Enumeration shall be made within three years after the first meeting of the Congress of the United States, and within every subsequent term of ten years, in such manner as they shall by law direct." In essence, it means that every household in the United States must answer a survey in the form of the census every 10 years.

In attempting to understand the concept of "three fifths of all other Persons," Annenberg Classroom's (2019) *Annenberg Guide to the United States Constitution* states:

> Article I, Section 2, creates the way in which congressional districts are to be divided among the states. A difficult and critical sticking point at the Constitutional Convention was how to count a state's population. Particularly controversial was how to count slaves for the purposes of representation and taxation. If slaves were considered property, they would not be counted at all. If they were considered people, they would be counted fully just as women, children and other non-voters were counted. Southern slave-owners viewed slaves as property, but they wanted them to be fully counted in order to increase their political power in Congress. After extended debate, the framers agreed to the three-fifths compromise— each slave would equal three-fifths of a person in a state's population count. (Note: The framers did not use the word slave in the document.) After the Civil War, the formula was changed with the passage of the 13th Amendment, which abolished slavery, and Section 2 of the 14th Amendment, which repealed the three-fifths rule.

Some people have asked why the question of race is not removed from the census given that race has been proven to be socially constructed. As race is woven into the fabric of the country through its laws and practices, so too is it tied to funding: "Congress must determine how many representatives (at least one required) are to come from each state and how federal resources are to be distributed among the states. The Constitution set the number of House members from each of the original 13 states that was used until the first census was completed" (Annenberg Classroom 2019).

In the 2010 U.S. Census, the racial designation of "Black" encompasses "A person having origins in any of the Black racial groups of Africa. It includes people who indicated their race(s) as 'Black, African American, or Negro' or reported entries such as African American, Kenyan, Nigerian, or Haitian" (Humes, Jones, and Ramirez 2011, 3). The U.S. Office of Management and Budget, the federal government department responsible for maintaining racial categories, states, "The racial categories included in the census questionnaire generally reflect a social definition of race recognized in this country and not an attempt to define race biologically, anthropologically, or genetically" (United States Census Bureau 2018).

If racial categories in the United States reflect a social definition that is understood here, how are international students who are new to the country supposed to understand the meanings?

International Student Mobility

The Institute of International Education (IIE) has been collecting data on international student mobility to the United States since its founding in 1919. Additionally, colleges and universities in the United States that receive federal funding must submit a Common Data Set, which requires providing data on racial, ethnic, and international student numbers through the Integrated Postsecondary Education Data System. The data are searchable on the National Center for Education Statistics's (NCES) website (nces.ed.gov). The NCES is the primary federal entity in the United States responsible for collecting and analyzing data related to education. Although most international educators would argue that the term is outdated, the U.S. Code of

Federal Regulations still categorizes international students on non-immigrant visas as "non-resident alien."

According to IIE's (2019b) *Open Doors* report, the United States welcomed 872,214 international students in the 2018–2019 academic year, with another 223,085 on Optional Practical Training. The majority of the 1,095,299 students in the country for the purpose of study or work come from two Asian countries, with a little more than 52 percent representing China and India alone (IIE 2019b).

Students from sub-Saharan Africa and the Caribbean represent a small percentage of the total number (see table 1). The top sending countries in sub-Saharan Africa are Nigeria, Ghana, and Kenya (IIE 2019a). The top sending countries in the Caribbean are Jamaica, the Bahamas, and the Dominican Republic (IIE 2019a).

Table 1. Sub-Saharan African and Caribbean Students in the United States in 2018–2019

	Sub-Saharan Africa	Caribbean
Undergraduate	21,194	7,242
Graduate	12,525	2,318
Optional Practical Training	5,344	1,264
Nondegree	1,227	241
Total	40,290	11,065

Source: Institute of International Education (2019a).

For African and Caribbean students studying in the United States, what does it mean to be categorized as non-resident aliens *and* be treated as "Black" in a U.S. context, yet lack the knowledge and lived experience of the complexity of race in the United States?

International Students and Race

The vast majority of international students who come to the United States travel on an F-1 student visa, which allows them to study and work (with restrictions) in the United States for a specified amount of time. However, in recent years, the number of international students enrolling in U.S. colleges and universities has slowed down, or even declined at some institutions (IIE 2019b).

In higher education spaces in the United States today, campus communities are engaged in heightened conversations around race. Still, at times, international students may not be fully cognizant of the political, economic, or historical factors at play. Some international students are not aware of the in-depth history of race relations in their own country, let alone its complex role in the history of the United States.

Anthropologist Carolyn Fluehr-Lobban (2006, 1) states, "Race is now viewed as a social construction that is primarily recognized by physical appearance, or phenotype. In the United States this means that Americans are socialized first to identify a person's race by skin color, and second by hair form, along with other physical features." For some international students, this can mean being viewed as something other than Black in their home country but being labeled "Black" in the United States based on skin tone (even if light), hair, and/or facial features, such as nose and lips.

Through my doctoral research study, "Assumed to Be 'Black': A Critical Examination of Being Ascribed a Racial Status on a Predominately White Campus," in 2013–14, I conducted extensive qualitative interviews with seven Black students from various African and Caribbean countries who were studying in the United States. The objective was to learn more about their experiences of being racialized as "Black," which was most often based on their physical appearance. This distinction regarding appearance is important because non-Black African students and Black African students do not have the same experiences in the United States (Constantine et al. 2005). Additionally, as students coming from nations where they represent a racial majority, it can be startling to be thrust into the racial dynamics of the United States, where they are now a racial minority.

Student Identity Markers and Acculturative Stress

Students come into university settings with an ultimate goal: to obtain a degree and find a good job upon graduating. Embedded in that quest for knowledge, Lee Hawkes (2014) explains, is students' secondary goal of having an academic identity and a sociocultural identity. According to Hawkes (2014, 4), "Academic identity is what students do, how they feel, how they fit in, how they see themselves as students and their relationships with their peers and teachers." Much of the research on international students' experiences looks at acculturative stress in relation to their academic identity. "Acculturative stress" can be described as greater levels of conflict that are experienced in relation to cultural changes due to group encounters, such as psychological, socio-cultural, and economic adjustments. While these can be daunting for international students to confront, they are "controllable and surmountable" (Boafo-Arthur 2013, 117).

On the other hand, not as much research has been done to examine the role of international students' sociocultural identity. "Sociocultural identity is where they see themselves in the world, what their position is in relation to adults, what societal and cultural expectations are in terms of being 'good' and 'successful,' fundamental epistemological and ontological notions and understandings of identity, belief, truth, and validity" (Hawkes 2014, 4). For many international students, their academic identity and sociocultural identity are greatly affected by the racial dialogue found across the United States.

Experiences of Black African Students

Since the early 2000s, more studies have begun to look specifically at the experiences of Black African students in the United States. Through a qualitative study, Constantine et al. (2005) examined the cultural adjustment experiences of students from the top three sending African countries: Nigeria, Kenya, and Ghana. Almost a decade later, Boafo-Arthur looked further at the acculturative experiences of Black African international students. Her findings highlighted three main problems these students often face once in the United States: prejudicial or discriminatory treatment, social isolation, and, for some, financial difficulty (Boafo-Arthur 2013, 118). These challenges were experienced in addition to issues such as culture shock, which is faced by the vast majority of international students.

In Boafo-Arthur's (2013, 118) study, Black African international students reported being labeled as minorities once in the United States, "regardless of their personal affinity towards other groups, and whether or not they believe they have something in common with the minorities raised in the United

States...while Black-African students as well as African-Americans may be discriminated against based on race, Black-African students face discrimination from multiple sources (e.g., cultural differences, accents, and negative stereotypes about their countries of origin). These experiences collectively put these students at risk for acculturative stress."

This imposed racial identity adds another layer of transition for some students: "Upon moving to the U.S., [Black-African students] often find that they are evaluated with the same stereotypes that are ascribed to African-Americans by the dominant culture" (Boafo-Arthur 2013, 119). Some students, particularly those assumed to be "Black" in a U.S. context, may need an even deeper level of support regarding what they may experience relative to race because "most Black-African students prior to moving to the United States have no experience of [overt] racial discrimination" (Boafo-Arthur 2013).

Experiences of Black Caribbean Students

There is a notable gap in the research pertaining to Black Caribbean students. In 2018–19, they represented roughly 1 percent of all international students in the United States (see table 1). Despite this small number, it is important to understand how they are experiencing their time in the country and navigating issues of race and identity.

The topic of race becomes even more complex for students from countries such as the Dominican Republic because intertwined in a conversation on Blackness is the ethnic Hispanic/Latinx identity. The Pew Research Center published a study in 2016 that tackled the complexity of race among Latinx communities in the United States. The findings showed that "in the U.S., Latinos with Caribbean roots are more likely to identify as Afro-Latino or Afro-Caribbean than those with roots elsewhere" (López and Gonzalez-Barrera 2016).

A misguided correlation is often made that those Caribbean individuals who identify as Afro-Latino would racially identify as Black or of mixed race, with Black being one of the races. However, the Pew Research Center study found that:

> Afro-Latinos' views of race are also unique. When asked directly about their race, only 18% of Afro-Latinos identified their race or one of their

races as black. In fact, higher shares of Afro-Latinos identified as white alone or white in combination with another race (39%) or volunteered that their race or one of their races was Hispanic (24%). Only 9% identified as a mixed race. These findings reflect the complexity of identity and race among Latinos. For example, two-thirds of Latinos (67%) say their Hispanic background is a part of their racial background. This is in contrast to the U.S. Census Bureau's own classification of Hispanic identity–census survey forms have described "Hispanic" as an ethnic origin, not a race. (López and Gonzalez-Barrera 2016)

Following the release of the 2010 U.S. Census, when the question on race was updated, social media was abuzz with Latinx people who were raised in the United States asking questions regarding how they should identify their race. The changes were such that the "Hispanic or Latino" category was no longer a racial category but a question of ethnic origin where a person of Hispanic or Latino background could be of any racial category (American Indian/Alaska Native, Asian, Black or African American, Native Hawaiian or Other Pacific Islander, White). If the issue of race is this complex and confusing for those raised in the United States, imagine the experience of Black Caribbean international students.

Like their Black African international counterparts, Black Caribbean students' experiences surrounding race affects their student journey in more ways than they anticipate before arriving in the United States. Based on my own lived experiences as a Black African American born and raised in the United States, I recognize how important it is to help others grapple with the complexities of race.

My Experience with Race and the African Atlantic Diaspora

I self-identify as Black/African American. Though my father's side of the family has roots in the Caribbean, I did not grow up with him, so my entire cultural frame of reference is connected to my maternal lineage. In tracing the lineage of my mother's parents, my family knows the names of relatives in the United States going back eight generations on my grandfather's side and seven generations on my grandmother's side (both inclusive of living generations). While we have not found slave records, we have made the assumption that we are the descendants of enslaved Africans in the United States given the dates of birth and death of our relatives and their locales in Virginia and South Carolina.

I grew up in New Jersey in a racially diverse, albeit segregated, neighborhood. I went to college in Maine, where, for the first time in my life, my Blackness was a topic of discussion on a regular basis. I was intrigued by the fact that my peers from Ghana, Haiti, Nigeria, and Swaziland and I were all lumped into the broad category of "Black." Growing up 30 minutes from New York City, I was used to a cultural salad bowl where each unique ethnic group was able to retain its cultural identity even when blended together into a beautiful and often chaotic mosaic. (I personally refrain from the "melting pot" reference as it engenders feelings of forced assimilation and loss when, instead, unique cultural attributes should be celebrated and maintained.)

My friends from Nigeria, for example, had very specific ethnic and cultural traditions that shaped their worldview—as did I. This was my first taste of the Black monolith myth: the notion that all Black people, regardless of their country of origin, shared a similar cultural experience. Unfortunately, the centrality of our shared experience was often connected to instances of racial discrimination. Nigerian author Chimamanda Ngozi Adichie touched on this in her 2009 TEDGlobal talk, "The Danger of a Single Story." During her talk, Adichie (2009) wove together an honest account of the dangers of assuming things about individuals and entire groups of people: "So that is how to create a single story, show a people as one thing, as only one thing, over and over again, and that is what they become."

Her words made me recall an experience I had in college. Sitting in a large lecture hall next to some Black peers, the professor pointed to us and said, "Can I get a response from the scholarship section?" The professor's words perpetuated the assumption that all Black students were in college on a scholarship, when in fact there were both U.S. students and international students in the group who were not on scholarship. This story, which is just one of many, reiterates the need to reject the Black monolith myth that has allowed racism and vestiges of slavery to exist for so long.

The Chains of Slavery

In March 2009, I had the opportunity to travel to Ghana and shadow a group of students from Rutgers University in New Jersey who were participating in an intense cultural immersion experience. This international trip, coupled with my activism and passion for impacting race relations in the United States, helped solidify the focus of my doctoral study. One of the most transformative moments on the trip were the visits to the Elmina and Cape Coast slave castles. As a Black/African American traveling to West Africa, it was one of the most anticipated and anxiety-producing events to look forward to: stepping foot inside of a slave castle.

In her book *Lose Your Mother: A Journey Along The Atlantic Slave Route*, Saidiya Hartman (2007, 112) masterfully describes the experience of being inside one of the castle dungeons:

> The interior of the dungeon exposed an open wound of the earth, and the roughly hewn walls perspired, making the chamber dank....The arched ceiling of the vault and the tubular shape of the connecting cells resembled a large intestine. Walking from one end of the dungeon to the other, I did feel as though the castle were ingesting me, as though I were inching my way along the entrails of power.

In Ghana, I recall standing in the female dungeon of the Cape Coast Castle and walking up to what is now referred to as the "Door of No Return." As I attempted to walk through it, I realized I did not fit through the narrow door. I began to weep. The tour guide came to console me by resting his hand on my shoulder and said, "yes, my sister...this is what our ancestors would have experienced. A woman of your stature would have been returned to the dungeon to waste away a little more as they wanted them strong enough to survive the journey but too weak to fight back." It is not known how many Africans lost their lives in the dungeons or on the ships, some choosing to jump overboard rather than face some unknown fate. As Ashun (2004, 81) notes:

> It needs to be emphasized also that the captives did not move freely since they were in chains and chained to each other. In these chains, they went through a very short door from whence they were made to exit through a door (now known as the "Door Of No Return"), descend a ladder to canoes and finally enter the ships to begin another dreadful and despicable journey to unknown places in the world.

Ashun's words rang through me as I stood in that doorway. It will forever be etched in my mind: the sound of the waves crashing against the shore and the glimmer of light that shone through the narrow passage that would lead Africans to the Americas and feed the false notions of Black inferiority.

In my third trip to Ghana in 2019—this time as the professor of a course on race, identity, memory, and belonging in the African Atlantic diaspora—I was further moved by the passage. A full decade had passed since my last trip there with a group of students, and yet the castles remained the same: hollowed spaces that held the blood, tears, and stench of fear of my ancestors, but no bold answers to the complexity of race. It was through the dialogue with the students, all of whom happen to be Black (African international, African first-generation immigrant in the U.S., and African American descendants of slaves), that pushed me to continue to grapple with the questions of: Who is Black? In what context? And who gets to decide? Throughout our dialogue, themes of anti-Blackness, miseducation, and belonging prevailed. This course, and future research in this space, strives to bridge the artificial divide that has left us in these invisible chains.

Research Study

While I worked on my doctoral research study, it was increasingly evident that there is a significant lack of research that examines the sociocultural identity experiences of students from the African Atlantic diaspora relative to the racial ascription they are given in the United States. One of the challenges in the field of international education centers on how educators work with students to understand the lingering effects of colonialism, subsequent hierarchy of racial classification, and its continued impact on Africa and the Americas.

How, then, do we as international education professionals engage students from Africa and the Caribbean who are faced with the twenty-first-century racial dynamics of the United States? How are we preparing African American and Latinx students (some heritage seekers) in the United States for sociocultural experiences they may encounter when traveling to places like Cuba, Brazil, and Ghana? Many students are not prepared to participate in racial dialogue in the host country because of a limited scope of knowledge on race. Oftentimes, cultural values, family dynamics, the media, education, and peers influence what students learn about race before embarking on an experience abroad.

Racial Identity Development

In the United States, there is an ideological framing around racial identity and racial identity development. In discussing the work of Janet Helm, Thompson and Carter (2012, 2) state that racial identity refers to "a sense of group or collective identity based on one's *perception* that he or she shares a common heritage with a particular racial group....Racial identity development entails changes or shifts in worldviews, the byproduct of a series of experiences, self-reflections, and more decision making." The definition of race and the method of racial categorization can vary across the African Atlantic diaspora. Therefore, a collective identity is not present. This can lead to a misguided reliance on stereotypes, as Beverly Daniel Tatum (1997, 62) notes: "What is problematic is that the young people are operating with very limited definitions of what it means to be Black, based largely on cultural stereotypes."

Contradictions arise from this classification because, for a number of people, "Black" has a varied meaning depending on one's cultural frame of reference (Davis 1991; Román and Flores 2010). In the United States, for example, "Black" becomes complicated and often one-dimensional (Omi and Winant 1994, 22)–complicated because there is a history associated with the term and one-dimensional because Blackness gets reduced to a single, often negative, story (Adichie 2009). In addition, "Black" is commonly interchanged with "African American," and thus becomes a label with which some people who are perceived to be "Black/African American" do not associate. To analyze this topic further in my doctoral research study, a utilization of Critical Race Theory (CRT) and cultural values widely held in Africa and the Caribbean were employed.

CRT was born in the field of law and has since made its way into social science fields such as education. Delgado and Stefancic (2012, 8–10) outlined the following main tenets to frame and unpack race in a U.S. context:

- Race is ordinary: Approaching situations from a racial perspective is the ordinary way that society does business (in the United States).

- Interests converge on the topic of race: Large segments of U.S. society have little incentive to eradicate race because racism advances the interests of both White elites (materially) and working-class Whites (physically).

- Race is a social construct: "Races" are categories that society invents, manipulates, and retires when convenient.

- Differential racialization exists: Groups are racialized at different times in history.

- Race is complex due to the intersectionality of identities: People have multiple overlapping identities.

- Representation is viewed through the unique voice of color: Minority status brings with it a presumed competence to speak about race and racism.

Critical Race Theory served as the necessary theoretical foundation to ground my essential question of wanting to better understand the experience of international students being racialized as Black in a U.S. context.

Study Methodology

A goal of my doctoral research study was to bring awareness to the unique experiences of Black African and Caribbean international students. By understanding the insidious nature of race in the United States, it established the need to explore how students who are racialized upon arriving make meaning out of their experiences. To accomplish this effectively, I collected narratives of international students who were ascribed the racial label and subsequent stereotypes of being "Black" in the United States.

The criteria for a student participating in my study included the following:

- Based on skin color, is recognized as Black by others in the United States;
- Identify as Black but not U.S. Black/African American;
- Comes from Africa or the Caribbean or has family origins from a country in the African Atlantic diaspora and identifies mainly with that ethnic background/ heritage; and
- Attends or has attended a college or university that is predominately White (more than 50 percent of the population is White).

I held extensive interviews with seven participants using a phenomenological methodology. Phenomenology is the essence of the lived experience of a group of people who share in a phenomenon. The participant size is typical of a qualitative research project using these methods (Smith 2008; Constantine et al. 2005). I used Irving Seidman's (2006) individual interviewing technique, as well as open focus groups using similar criteria as outlined above. The focus groups were helpful as they yielded Caribbean students from Jamaica, one of the largest Caribbean constituent groups in the United States.

Of my participants, I asked the following questions in order to better frame their sociocultural experiences:

- What is the essence of the experience for students from Africa and the Caribbean who are assumed to be "Black" in a U.S. context?
- How do the participants racially/ethnically self-identify? How does this differ from how others identify them based on observable physical characteristics, such as skin color and hair type?
- What contradictions exist between the participants' racial self-identification and the racial ascription of "Black/African American"?

- Prior to college, what informed the participants' racial/ethnic self-identity?
- How is the participants' racial identity impacted when they are in predominantly White campus settings?

In asking these in-depth questions using a qualitative methodological framework, my doctoral research study attempted to address the dearth of literature specifically focused on the racialization of Black African and Caribbean international students in the United States and move beyond the confines of acculturative stress to further unpack their experience.

Participants' Voices

The study revealed some of the stereotypes that students of African and Caribbean descent hold regarding Blackness in the United States, and how those stereotypes are developed and maintained. I am most certain that had the study focused on African American students' perceptions of African students, it, too, would have been steeped in false generalizations based on how the concept of racial hierarchy was originally formed and is currently manifested. It should be understood that because race is socially constructed and fueled by misconceptions and negative falsehoods masked as truths, it is no wonder that individuals and groups internalize and perpetuate stereotypes based on a centuries-old, carefully crafted web of lies.

I employed Jonathan Smith's (2008) interpretive phenomenological analysis when synthesizing my results. This method is known as a "double hermeneutic," whereby participants are trying to make sense of their experience, and the researcher is trying to make sense of the participants trying to make sense of their world. In the essence of interpretive phenomenology, below are some direct quotes from the participants that aided in substantiating my findings. The participant quotes are coupled with scholarly quotes from leading researchers who have studied race relations in the United States for the past 100 years.

Participants' quotes from the focus group discussions (Jamaica and Ghana):

> *In the media...they try to portray a different culture and they don't even use people from that culture. The media itself doesn't give way for Black people*

being different...they have to fit into that stereotype of how a Black person is supposed to act.

It is hard to imagine a more famous fictional character during the twentieth century than Tarzan—and it is hard to imagine a more racist plot than what Burroughs wrote up in the Tarzan adventure series books.... The defining message of the Tarzan series was clear: White people will do it better than the African apelike children, so much better that Whites will always, the world over, become teachers of African people. (Kendi 2016, 300)

Participant 1 (Ghana):

In school, ethnicity was basically the different tribes in Ghana. And race, I don't recall even talking about race because it wasn't an issue to us....It's like it never really came up. [Once on campus] *I would immediately disassociate myself and say I'm African because I was proud of my culture....I would kind of look down on them [African-Americans]. You know, which is not right. Because I feel like, even though people in Africa have a much lower standard of living than the Black people here, we see ourselves as...still living an amazing life. Over here, it's like you hear crime, you automatically think of a Black person. It's like automatically you don't want to be associated with that group because the way they act.*

[O]ur very ways of walking, talking, eating, and dreaming become racially coded simply because we live in a society where racial awareness is so pervasive. (Omi and Winant 1994, 60)

Participant 2 (Ghana):

Well, back home I never really thought about race that much. I think about it more now than I ever had in my lifetime because like it's constantly brought up here. On campus, I think people just assume that I am Black.

[D]efinitions of who is black vary quite sharply from country to country and for this reason people in other countries often express consternation about our [U.S.] definition. (Davis 1991, 13)

Participant 5 (Dominican Republic):

Just trying to understand what are all these perceptions that people already have before they even know me. It's almost like—creating double the work because you've been robbed of your first impression in that sense.

It is a peculiar sensation, this double-consciousness, this sense of always looking at one's self through the eyes of others, of measuring one's soul by the tape of a world that looks on in amused contempt and pity. (Du Bois [1903] 2009, 7)

Participant 6 (Dominican Republic):

There's this idea—it was like 'mejorar la raza,' you have to 'better the race.' It's basically saying that you can't date a Black man—you can't even date darker than your skin color even in the Dominican Republic. When I think of the word 'Black' I simply think of African-American.

I am a Latinegra, born to a world that denies my humanity as a Black person, a woman, and a Latina...a child of a White Puerto Rican mother, whose family counted their drops of pure Spanish blood and resented our dark presence, and a very prieto (dark Black) Puerto Rican father. Teachers and other adults in the community openly commented to me and my siblings that my mother had disgraced her family by marrying a Black man...my father was retinto (double-dyed Black) and moyeto, meaning Black and ugly. At best I was mejorando la raza [improving the race]. (Cruz-Janzen 2010, 282)

Participant 7 (Puerto Rico):

As to your skin color...you don't want to be white; you don't want to be a gringo because you're going to forget who you are but you also don't want to be Black because you don't want to be ghetto. So either way, it's like, who am I?

We utilize race to provide clues about who a person is. This fact is made painfully obvious when we encounter someone whom we cannot conveniently racially categorize. (Omi and Winant 1994, 59)

Study Findings

What I surmised through my study is that the notion of "Blackness" as an identity has different meanings in various cultural contexts. As Omi and Winant (1994, 59) state: "A racialized social structure shapes racial experience and conditions meaning" and "we utilize race to provide clues about *who* a person is." Some of the themes culled from my analysis include the following:

- The participants valued their own cultural/ethnic/national backgrounds and would have preferred to be associated with that heritage alone.

- There are widely held assumptions about what it means to be Black/African American throughout the African Atlantic diaspora.

- "Black" in the United States is often interchanged with "African American," and "African American" is coded negatively as dangerous, ghetto, loud, poor, uneducated, and lazy (as described by the participants throughout the study in regard to what they learned at home, in school, and in the media prior to coming to campus).

- The participants were ascribed a racial identity that they had no lived experience and/or cultural frame of reference for, and thus they disassociated from that racialization.

Gary Younge, London-based author, broadcaster, and editor-at-large for the *Guardian*, gave the keynote address at the NAFSA 2017 Annual Conference Symposium on Leadership, which had a focus on internationalization and diversity and inclusion. Of his talk, Charlotte West (2017, 4) writes: "Younge argued that identity has been central to some of the most inspirational and lurid moments in human history….He argued that no one is fully in control of their own identity, which is not only a product of self-definition but also must make sense to others. Identities are furthermore dependent upon context, which is rooted in power."

At the core of the creation and institutionalization of racial hierarchy is power, privilege, and oppression. Social justice is about acknowledging this truth and using one's platform to dismantle a system designed to perpetuate inequity: "Social justice is both a goal and a process...a reconstructing of society in accordance with principles of equity, recognition, and inclusion" (Bell 2018, 34). As an administrator committed to equity, I have learned to use my voice to advocate for positive change and recognize that I am not responsible for single-handedly eradicating systems of oppression such as racism. My accountability lies within my sphere of influence.

Actions to Break the Chains

A natural reaction to the quotes from the participants in my study may be feelings of hurt, sadness, disbelief, empathy, and/or guilt (based on one's lived experience). But once we move past that visceral reaction, we must engage in an ongoing process of critical self-reflection (Sisneros et al. 2008) to understand how we are personally impacted by and contributing to socialized systems that disproportionately affect members of the global majority who are marginalized.

As international education practitioners, we can partner with other colleagues on campus (e.g., domestic cultural affairs practitioners, faculty, etc.) to create mechanisms to help keep international students informed and engaged in the dialogue (Althen 2009; Boafo-Arthur 2013). For example, I have been invited by students to participate in structured dialogue nights where leaders from student organizations (i.e., Black student union, African student association, and Caribbean student association) facilitate a dialogue focused on the tensions (particularly intergroup anti-Blackness) and the possibilities for racial healing and unity among the group using research, data, and students' narratives.

Additionally, when I oversaw the intercultural center at a small institution, we held a joint new student orientation, in addition to transition workshops, for international students and domestic students of color where we focused on topics of social justice, namely, race in the United States. The evaluations from the workshops were very positive, and the students remarked on how important it was to learn about power, privilege, and oppression and begin to break down preconceived notions they had of one another—especially since both groups were underrepresented on that particular campus.

Providing opportunities for ourselves and our students to engage in a process of unlearning stereotypes and gaining tools to practice equity and justice is a type of freedom that cannot be quantified. Social justice work does not happen overnight. It requires a commitment to lifelong learning and the daily exercising of cultural humility.

Conclusion

Colleges and universities continue to add diversity and internationalization as major components of their strategic planning efforts. Students from various racial, ethnic, and national backgrounds are expected to expand their intellectual curiosity through international experiences, while bringing with them various views on race that are maintained through myths and misconceptions. We must challenge ourselves to ask: What new ways of thinking about culture and society are students expected to gain? We must also encourage students to engage in dialogue about race from personal, historical, and critical lenses. The only way to do that effectively is to provide the space, tools, and expertise to ensure that all voices and perspectives are heard and valued.

Through the development and implementation of comprehensive internationalization plans, colleges and universities have an obligation to help acclimate international students to the social realities of living in the United States. This can be achieved through a number of ways, such as orientation, ongoing dialogue programs, courses designed specifically with international students in mind, and so on. Assigning readings such as Chimamanda Adichie's 2014 novel *Americanah* can highlight the experience of race, nationality, and class in the United States and the social implications of being classified as "Black" to spark a dialogue. Students can journey with Yaa Gyasi's characters in the novel *Homegoing* (2017) to begin to unpack the complex and enduring interconnected legacies of the middle passage. Together, students and educators can watch Henry Louis Gates Jr.'s documentary *Black in Latin America* (2011) to hear the historical and present-day accounts of what meanings race takes on in places like Cuba and Haiti.

In order to do this work, we must be willing to grapple with and simultaneously dismantle the Black monolith myth. As a first step, international education practitioners can further their knowledge and understanding of social justice issues by examining the history of race in the United States. This foundational knowledge can be applied to other facets of international education as well as deeper understandings of other social identities (e.g., gender, class, etc.). Engaging in this work promises to be intense yet rewarding.

References

Adichie, Chimamanda Ngozi. 2009. "Transcript of 'The Danger of a Single Story.'" Filmed July 2009 in Oxford, England. TED video, 18:34. https://www.ted.com/talks/chimamanda_adichie_the_danger_of_a_single_story/transcript.

Adichie, Chimamanda Ngozi. 2014. *Americanah*. New York, NY: Anchor Books.

Althen, Gary. 2009. "Educating International Students About 'Race.'" *International Educator* 18, 3:88–93.

American Anthropological Association (AAA). n.d. "Early Classification of Nature." *Understanding Race*. Arlington, VA: American Anthropological Association. http://www.understandingrace.org.

American Anthropological Association (AAA). 2019. "AAA Statement on Race." https://www.americananthro.org/ConnectWithAAA/Content.aspx?ItemNumber=2583.

Annenberg Classroom. 2019. "Article I, Section 2." *The Annenberg Guide to the United States Constitution.* Philadelphia: PA: Annenberg Classroom, The Annenberg Public Policy Center. https://www.annenbergclassroom.org/article-i-section-2.

Ashun, Ato. 2004. *Elmina, The Castles and The Slave Trade*. Cape Coast, Ghana: Nyakod Printing & Publishing.

Bell, Lee Anne. 2018. "Theoretical Foundations for Social Justice Education." In *Readings for Diversity and Social Justice*, eds. Maurianne Adams, Warren J. Blumenfeld, D. Chase J. Catalano, Keri "Safire" DeJong, Heather W. Hackman, Larissa E. Hopkins, Barbara J. Love, Madeline L. Peters, Davey Shlasko, and Ximena Zúñiga. New York, NY: Routledge Taylor & Francis Group.

Boafo-Arthur, Susan. 2013. "Acculturative Experiences of Black-African International Students." *International Journal for the Advancement of Counselling* 36, 2:115–124. Published electronically August 9, 2013. https://link.springer.com/article/10.1007%2Fs10447-013-9194-8.

Brown University Steering Committee on Slavery and Justice. 2006. *Slavery and Justice Report of the Brown University Steering Committee on Slavery and Justice.* Providence, RI: Brown University. https://www.brown.edu/Research/Slavery_Justice/documents/SlaveryAndJustice.pdf.

Constantine, Madonna G., Gregory M. Anderson, Laverne A. Berkel, Leon D. Caldwell, and Shawn O. Utsey. 2005. "Examining the Cultural Adjustment Experiences of African International College Students: A Qualitative Analysis." *Journal of Counseling Psychology* 52, 1:57–66.

Cruz-Janzen, Marta I. 2010. "Latinegras: Desired Women: Undesirable Mothers, Daughters, Sisters, and Wives." In *The Afro-Latin@ Reader: History and Culture in the United States*, eds. Miriam Jiménez Román and Juan Flores. Durham, NC: Duke University Press.

Davis, F. James. 1991. *Who Is Black?: One Nation's Definition.* University Park, PA: Penn State University Press.

Delalue, Shontay. 2014. "Assumed to Be 'Black': A Critical Examination of Being Ascribed a Racial Status on a Predominately White Campus." Doctoral dissertation, University of Rhode Island.

Delgado, Richard, and Jean Stefancic. 2012. *Critical Race Theory: An Introduction, Second Edition.* New York, NY: New York University Press.

Du Bois, W.E.B. [1903] 2009. *The Souls of Black Folk.* New York, NY: Simon and Schuster Paperbacks.

Fluehr-Lobban, Carolyn. 2006. *Race and Racism: An Introduction.* Lanham, MD: AltaMira Press.

Gates, Henry Louis, Jr. 2011. "Black in Latin America." PBS. http://www.pbs.org/wnet/black-in-latin-america.

Guasco, Michael. 2017. "The Fallacy of 1619: Rethinking the History of Africans in Early America." *Black Perspectives* (blog). September 4, 2017. https://www.aaihs.org/the-fallacy-of-1619-rethinking-the-history-of-africans-in-early-america.

Gyasi, Yaa. 2017. *Homegoing: A Novel.* New York, NY: Vintage Books.

Hartman, Saidiya V. 2007. *Lose Your Mother: A Journey Along the Atlantic Slave Route.* New York, NY: Farrar, Straus and Giroux.

Hawkes, Lee. 2014. *The Development of the Social and Academic Identities of International Students in English-speaking Higher Education Institutions.* London, England: BPP University.

Humes, Karen R., Nicholas A. Jones, and Roberto R. Ramirez. 2011. "Overview of Race and Hispanic Origin: 2010." *2010 Census Briefs*. March 2011. https://www.census.gov/prod/cen2010/briefs/c2010br-02.pdf.

Institute of International Education (IIE). 2019a. "Data by Region Fact Sheets." *Open Doors Report on International Educational Exchange*. Institute of International Education. https://www.iie.org/Research-and-Insights/Open-Doors/Fact-Sheets-and-Infographics/Data-by-Region-Fact-Sheets.

Institute of International Education (IIE). 2019b. "International Students." *Open Doors Report on International Educational Exchange*. Institute of International Education. https://www.iie.org/Research-and-Insights/Open-Doors/Data/International-Students.

Kendi, Ibram X. 2016. *Stamped from the Beginning: The Definitive History of Racist Ideas in America*. New York, NY: Nation Books.

López, Gustavo, and Ana Gonzalez-Barrera. 2016. "Afro-Latino: A Deeply Rooted Identity Among U.S. Hispanics." *Pew Research Center*. https://www.pewresearch.org/fact-tank/2016/03/01/afro-latino-a-deeply-rooted-identity-among-u-s-hispanics.

Omi, Michael, and Howard Winant. 1994. *Racial Formation in the United States: From the 1960s to the 1990s, Second Edition*. New York, NY: Routledge.

Román, Miriam Jiménez, and Juan Flores, eds. 2010. *The Afro-Latin@ Reader: History and Culture in the United States*. Durham, NC: Duke University Press.

Seidman, Irving. 2006. *Interviewing as Qualitative Research: A Guide for Researchers in Education and the Social Sciences, Third Edition*. New York, NY: Teachers College Press.

Sisneros, Jose, Catherine Stakeman, Mildred C. Joyner, and Cathryne L. Schmitz. 2008. *Critical Multicultural Social Work*. New York, NY: Oxford University Press.

Smith, Jonathan A., ed. 2008. *Qualitative Psychology: A Practical Guide to Research Methods*. London, United Kingdom: SAGE Publications.

Tatum, Beverly Daniel. 1997. *"Why Are All the Black Kids Sitting Together in the Cafeteria?": And Other Conversations About Race*. New York, NY: Basic Books.

Thompson, Chalmer E., and Robert T. Carter. 2012. "Race, Socialization, and Contemporary Racism Manifestations." In *Racial Identity Theory: Applications to Individual, Group, and Organizational Interventions*, eds. Chalmer E. Thompson and Robert T. Carter. New York, NY: Routledge.

United States Census Bureau. 2018. "Race." United States Census Bureau. https://www.census.gov/topics/population/race/about.html.

West, Charlotte. 2017. *Internationalization & Diversity and Inclusion*. NAFSA 2017 Symposium on Leadership. Washington, DC: NAFSA: Association of International Educators.

5

"Rebeldes en Acción"
A Case Study in English Teaching in a Marginalized Colombian High School

YECID ORTEGA, MA

Colombia has experienced more than 50 years of political violence perpetrated by leftist guerrillas, right-wing paramilitary organizations, organized crime, the armed forces, and the police (González González 2014; Sherman 2015; Vargas and Caruso 2014). This conflict has filtered down into school violence that teenage students experience daily (López de Mesa-Melo et al. 2013; Rodríguez 2014). However, a peace agreement signed in November 2016 has offered hope to Colombian citizens that the country can move forward toward reconciliation. The Colombian government is working to develop effective ways to promote citizenship education for national unity and prosperity. The education sector, in particular, has been identified as crucial for promoting social cohesion. Consequently, there is a concerted effort to include peace and social justice education in the national curriculum (Barrera, Chaux, and Trujillo 2015; Chaux et al. 2017).

Typically, conflict and peace in Colombian classrooms are addressed in history or social studies classes (Bickmore, Kaderi, and Guerra-Sua 2017). English classes in Colombia have mainly focused on teaching linguistic content in an uncritical manner that is unrelated to the cultural and social realities of students in both urban and rural areas (Usma 2015; Usma and Pelaez 2017). Furthermore, the English curricular content proposed by the Ministry of Education (Colombia Bilingüe 2014–2018) states that English language teaching should provide students with the professional and academic skills needed to succeed in the global market. The larger goal of the policy is to advance Colombia's economic competitiveness to place the country as the economic leader of Latin America (Ministerio de Educación 2016).

Although learning the English language is important for many reasons beyond purely economic ones (particularly in "postconflict" societies), there has been little discussion in Colombia on the role that English as a foreign language (EFL) curriculum and instruction can have in promoting peace and social justice. Generally, English teachers in Colombia teach conversation skills and strategies to use the language in a possible future reality that is not necessarily related to the sociopolitical context in Colombia. For example, teachers have used songs to promote English proficiency (Palacios and Chapetón 2014); used writing strategies to address issues beyond the classroom (Chapetón and Chala 2013); and employed cooperative learning principles to foster student interaction, dialogue, and reflection in the English language classroom (Contreras León and Chapetón Castro 2016).

However, these attempts are not enough to address the social core issues that Colombia and the rest of the world currently face—nor do they give students the social skills needed to solve problems in their communities. Critiques to EFL pedagogies and contradicting policies have emerged in the last few years (Miranda 2016; Miranda and Valencia Giraldo 2019; Miranda Nieves 2018; Usma 2015; Usma and Pelaez 2017), thus creating the need for more research to explore the possibilities of social justice and peacebuilding curriculum in EFL classrooms.

This chapter discusses pedagogies that attempt to address social justice issues in Colombia, as they connect to other global social problems. I present some findings of a critical ethnographic case study of how high school students from a marginalized neighborhood gained social justice awareness while engaging in English tasks that helped them to understand the intricacies of social problems and build the necessary social and linguistic skills to accomplish their personal and professional goals.

Conceptual Considerations

This section examines these main conceptual underpinnings that framed this research: social justice, peace, and violence. I argue that both social justice and peace approaches to education, particularly in EFL instruction, are powerful means of critically questioning the status quo. Social justice challenges the notions of inequality in an unstable society, while peace and violence are two opposing concepts that help us understand the roots and intricacies of the struggle in which contemporary Latin American societies live, especially in a conflict/postconflict context.

In education, pedagogies that borrow concepts from social justice, peace, and violence mainly look at including and privileging students' voices in teaching and learning, and by connecting learning to students' lived experiences and larger problems confronting the community (Macrine 2009). These interconnected concepts support each other and find their convergence in praxis (see figure 1). For Freire (1970), "praxis" refers to the actions and reflections directed toward the transformation of social structures that oppress the marginalized. Praxis empowers the oppressed to acquire a critical awareness of the social topography of power and to question their marginal position in society.

Figure 1. A Framework for Social Justice and Peace in Language Teaching

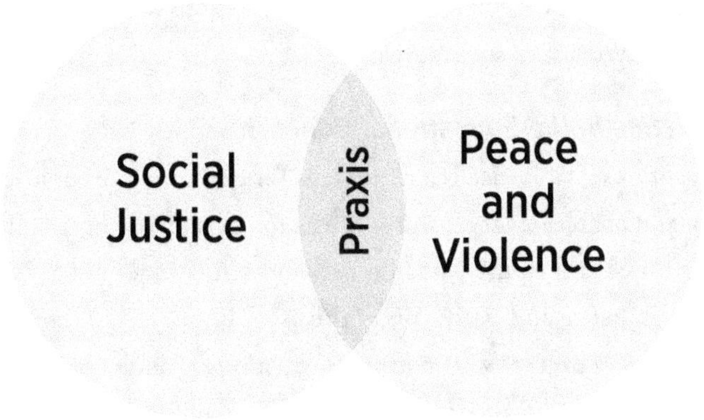

Social Justice

Social justice is understood in different ways by different people. Some define social justice as a philosophical approach that seeks to treat all people with fairness, respect, dignity, and generosity (Nieto and Bode 2012). Miller (1999) argues that our understanding of social justice must be practical and real, rather than imprecise, conceptualizing social justice as the just distribution of benefits and burdens within society. He poses questions regarding how ordinary people understand justice and address social justice in their real-life contexts. Miller (1999) proposes three principles by which people should evaluate the fairness of society: (a) outcomes of distribution according to need; (b) distribution according to "desert" (claiming rewards based on performance); and (c) distribution on the basis of equality.

Like Miller, Zajda (2010) views justice as a set of principles. Her concept of social justice includes economic, legal, and political dimensions that are guided by a sense of responsibility to work with others. Capeheart and Milovanovic (2007) encourage us to examine the conceptions of dominant and nondominant justice and how these are applied to people and groups. They explain that social justice is not a narrow system that looks for the justice of an individual alone, but a complex and challenging task for all of society (Capeheart and Milovanovic 2007). As humans, we must aspire to a vision of changing and transforming society (Johannessen and Unterreiner 2008). In short, social justice is about fairness, and it should be practical. Social justice should be rooted in people's experiences and realities (i.e., not some abstract ideas), with economic, legal, and sociocultural-political dimensions that must be addressed at different personal and social levels.

Social Justice in the Educational Context

The concept of social justice is a useful lens for examining social inequities in schooling and enables teachers and students to envision teaching and learning for social justice and equity (Johannessen and Unterreiner 2008; Ukpokodu 2010). Social justice and peace concepts cannot be conceived separated from a critical stance. Giroux (1994) notes that questions of audience, voice, power, and evaluation actively work to construct particular relations between teachers and students, classrooms and communities, and institutions and society. Ukpokodu (2010) contends that social justice is an action-oriented process that pursues social reconstruction; therefore, a social justice approach to education inherently challenges hegemonic ideologies and tries to confront and dismantle unequal structures in society and the educational system. Moreover, education must commit to empowering the powerless to transform their conditions that perpetuate injustice and inequity (McLaren 1988). Critical pedagogy ultimately looks at questioning power relations and the structures that reproduce the injustice, exploitation, and oppression of the status quo while hindering students' liberation (Freire 1970).

Peace and Violence

Although theorizing around peace—what it is and how it is constructed in our societies—hails from a very different academic tradition than the scholarship surrounding social justice, the two concepts have important similarities that are worth exploring. Peace is often best understood by defining and delineating its opposites: violence and conflict. Galtung (1990) describes three types of violence:

- Direct violence: any form of physical or verbal abuse (e.g., killing or torture, rape and sexual assault, and beatings)

- Cultural violence: beliefs and attitudes that have been inculcated since childhood and prevail with us in our daily lives

- Structural violence: groups, classes, genders, and nationalities that tend to have more access to goods, resources, and opportunities than others

The three forms of violence are interrelated as they become part of structural and unequal advantages that are built into the very social, political, and economic systems that govern societies. Galtung's (1990) conceptualization of peace is linked to this triangle of violence; notably, he differentiates between "negative peace," which he defines as the absence of direct physical violence, and "positive peace," which he theorizes more broadly as the absence of structural and cultural violence.

As points of entry, Galtung's (1969) negative peace refers to the absence of ceasefire and passive coexistence (*Convivencia*) (Silva and Chaux 2005), while positive peace actively represents love and the union of body, mind, and spirit in the presence of cooperation, equity, equality, and dialogue. For the purposes of this chapter, I use a simplified version of Galtung's (1969) quadrant model (see figure 2) in which to the right, we find positive peace, and to the left, we find negative peace. That is, suffering increases the more we move to the left, suffering decreases the more we move to the right, and zero (0) is a state in between.

Figure 2. Positive and Negative Peace (Galtung's Adaptation)

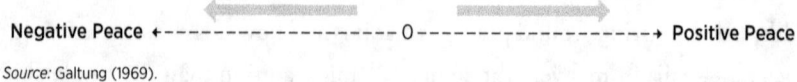

Negative Peace ←------------------- 0 -------------------→ Positive Peace

Source: Galtung (1969).

While on the one hand we have a type of peace that refers to the absence of violence, war, and conflict, on the other hand we have the idea of the integration of human society within a structural model of social justice. Although for Galtung (1969) these concepts mainly refer to contexts of war and conflict, in this chapter, I borrow the ideas to refer to negative peace as the violence and struggles faced by the students and teachers in the community, and positive peace as the classroom projects that address issues of social justice and attempt to challenge the precarious situations in which they live.

Nixon (2011) adds further nuance to the concept of violence by appending a temporal dimension. He argues that many types of violence are so "slow" and temporally distant from the causes of this violence, that what he labels "slow violence" is largely imperceptible except to the poor and marginalized who suffer disproportionately from its effects (Nixon 2011). Although Nixon uses the concept mostly to examine the impact of environmental pollution on the disempowered, conflict-affected situations like Colombia also suffer from multiple consequences of violence that take place incrementally, hidden from view.

Culture of Peace

Valenzuela (2005) states that peace can be manifested in each person, the person's family, and the sociopolitical and economic community. He believes that the individual can create a culture of peace by challenging and dismantling hidden manifestations of structural and cultural violence. Valenzuela (2005) guides individuals on how to positively affect the sociopolitical, economic, and religious dimensions of life that foster a culture of peace and eradicate war.

Furthermore, UNESCO and the United Nations (1997) state that a transdisciplinary approach must be pursued in which Valenzuela's principles, school initiatives, and other social ideas can be enacted to foster respect for fundamental rights and freedoms, understanding, tolerance, and solidarity with the marginalized. For nation-states that have lived through conflict, such as Colombia, education has a pivotal role in pursuing a culture of peace and the social transformation that the world needs in times of crisis (Lin and Oxford 2011).

Social transformation can be accomplished once structural and cultural forms of violence are made visible. This creates space for a human journey to respond to real-life problems, which Lederach (2006) calls "conflict transformation." This journey recognizes the dialectic nature of relationships: Because conflict is socially created by humans, it can also be transformed by humans. The world and its cultures are socially constructed, not fixed; therefore, as social beings, we do not need to take the world "as is," but we can change it.

For Lederach (2006), this transformation must occur at two levels. First, at a personal level, conflict transformation is characterized by the pursuit of awareness, growth, and commitment to change (Lederach 2006). Second, at the system level, conflict transformation includes the elimination of oppression, the sharing of resources, and the promotion of nonviolent conflict resolution between disputing groups (Lederach 2006). Education is seen by many scholars and educational professionals as a means of transforming both interpersonal and societal conflict.

I posit that social justice and peace can work concomitantly to address issues of inequality, discrimination, and race across the curriculum. Teachers and researchers must connect theory and practice toward social change, leading to praxis. Chapman and Hobbel (2010) specifically suggest that social justice in education should invigorate students to know the world through a critical understanding of themselves, the communities in which they live, and their larger society, from multiple curricular perspectives and sides in order to transform the world. Nieto and Bode (2012) propose that social justice should challenge, confront, and disrupt misconceptions and stereotypes that lead to structural inequality and discrimination based on race, social class, gender, and other social and human differences.

Ethnographic Case Study

Building off of the work of Chapman and Hobbel (2010), I completed a critical ethnographic case study in 2018 with English teachers and their high school students from a marginalized neighborhood in Colombia to examine how social justice awareness affected their skill development and attainment of goals. I was interested in exploring and understanding the participants' stories, as well as exposing the inequalities they face and how they counter them. Like Creswell (2009, 16), through this study, I "sought to establish the meaning of a phenomenon from the views of the participants [and] one of the key elements of collecting data in this way is to observe participants' behaviors by engaging in their activities." To accomplish this, I employed critical ethnographic and case study approaches, situating them in the critical research paradigm.

This research study employed critical ethnographic (Madison 2011) and case study (Merriam 2009) approaches to examine the characteristics, strengths, and weaknesses of a social justice and peacebuilding approach to teaching English. Specifically, I looked at the following questions: How do participants envision and enact an English curriculum based on social justice and peacebuilding? And how does this curriculum influence their perceptions and experiences of social inequalities in their lived experiences?

Study Methodology

The participants in the study are three middle-aged English teachers who have been teaching English for more than 20 years in different public and private schools in Colombia. They self-identified as either Christian or Catholic, and they claim that this part of their identities is well reflected in their pedagogy because their work is in line with shaping a new generation of social agents of change for a better humanity. Many of the teachers' students (grades 6 to 11), who come from diverse ethnic backgrounds (Afro-Colombians, *campesinos*, and Indigenous descent), have voiced that they experience daily violence, gang recruiting, drug dealing, and class discrimination. Both the teachers and the students are aware of the Colombian sociopolitical situation and collaboratively create lessons to address some of the issues they face on a daily basis (see Appendix A for ideas on social justice and peacebuilding activities that are oriented to teach English).

The research study employed different data collection instruments, including (a) school and classroom observations; (b) individual and group interviews in the form of focus groups; (c) documents such as policy documents, lesson plans, and students' and teachers' journals; and (d) artifacts such as students' cultural productions (e.g., paintings, posters, videos, music, etc.). The collected data were transcribed and a grounded theory analytical approach was used with Nvivo 11 software to code for the subsequent content and theme analysis (Creswell 2015) for emerging patterns across the different data sets (Hsieh and Shannon 2005).

I collaborated with the students and teachers to conduct the interviews in a more dialogical manner in what I call *Charlas*. *Charla* is my own research approach that is similar to an interview but is also a form of conversational engagement about a specific topic in which the participants explore an issue, problematize it, and offer possible solutions. I use the term *Charla*, which in Spanish means conversation or talk but is more relevant to the research context, as the discussions are richer and culturally embedded. The questions in this dialogue mode of collecting data emerged based on the conversations we were having.

The students, teachers, and I engaged in numerous classroom conversations on how to solve problems in their communities and how to be critical of the current global and local social issues. By the end of the fieldwork, I attest to my own personal and professional transformation as I became part of the class/school. I became part of their day-to-day activities, and they expected me to actively participate alongside them. Taking this critical ethnographic lens, I believe, is the first step in moving forward to not only better understanding the communities we work with but also challenging the status quo.

Preliminary Findings

Based on the classroom observations and interviews, there were two main findings. First, the study revealed that there are four forms of resistance: (a) native speakerism resistance; (b) language policy resistance; (c) administration resistance; and (d) capitalism resistance. Second, the findings showed that these four resistances were grounded on the teachers' beliefs that other pedagogies are possible to potentialize students' futurities and teachers' pedagogies as anticolonial practice.

Forms of Resistance

In one of the *Charlas,* a teacher mentioned that the reason why they were able to approach English teaching in an alternative manner was that they see themselves as "rebels with a cause." The teachers promoted agency and gave students the skills to create projects that foster social cohesion while ignoring mandated administrative or government guidelines to train the students for the local standardized tests. After analysis of the data, the following four types of resistance were revealed.

RESISTANCE TO NATIVE SPEAKERISM

The teachers allowed the students to use their home language (Spanish) in class. During one of my class observations, the students were giving presentations about their social justice projects when one of the students struggled to present his topic in English. The teacher immediately jumped in and told him to use his Spanish, if necessary. This type of resistance is already in line with concepts of translanguaging (Garcia and Wei 2014) and trans[cultura]linguación (Ortega 2019), in which the cultural and linguistic backgrounds of the students are at the front of the day-to-day practice.

RESISTANCE TO LANGUAGE POLICY

The teachers argued that the government curricular guidelines are insufficient to address students' social needs and instead called for a cocreated, participatory English curriculum design. Toward the end of my fieldwork, I noticed how the teachers created a "hidden" curriculum that is not evident to their eyes but is embedded in their classroom practices. I have called this emerging curriculum "social justice and peacebuilding curriculum (SJPBC)." Unlike curricula that are based on agendas of educational systems that use schooling to prepare students for a capitalistic world (Zajda 2010), a social justice and peacebuilding curriculum promotes English teaching for students to navigate a world in which they learn the larger purposes of economic social mobility and social cohesion. This social justice-oriented mindset is emphasized by the school environment, classroom environment, teachers' expectations, and lesson planning. In a sense, a social justice and peacebuilding curriculum counters Colombia's educational policies (such as *Colombia Bilingüe*) that promote English education for economic development and leadership in Latin America (Ministerio de Educación 2016).

RESISTANCE TO ADMINISTRATION

The teachers fronted their social justice projects and foregrounded the standardized English testing training. From my observations, it was evident that the teachers had to train their students for the local standardized test at least once a week, as mandated by the academic coordinators, thus restricting the possibilities for socially oriented tasks. Sol, one of the teachers interviewed, argues that regardless of these constraints, the students still manage to learn some English:

> *Nos toca entrenarlos para las pruebas del estado y no nos queda tiempo para hacer el trabajo real, pero con lo poco que hacemos, ellos aprenden.* (We have to train them [the students] for the standardized tests and we do not have time to do the real work, but with the little that we do, they do learn.) (Sol in discussion with the author, August 12, 2018)

RESISTANCE TO CAPITALISM

The teachers promoted pedagogical approaches that look at students as human beings who care about others and resist their violent context. Rather than treating the students as factory products of knowledge that feed a capitalistic neoliberal system, the teachers portrayed them as potential agents of social change.

Data analysis evidenced the connection between teachers' practices and their actions to counter global and neoliberal discourses of learning English. For example, parents and the administration tend to believe that learning English is important for securing well-paid jobs in the future. However, the teachers strongly believe that caring about students' well-being is imperative because what happens in their students' lives affect teachers' lives as well. For example, Hadasa, another one of the teachers interviewed, believes that she is touched by what happens to her students.

> *uno se enfrenta con seres humanos que manejan vidas complejas…a mí me afecta lo que le pase a ellos.* (We face human beings who manage complex loves…I am affected by what happens to them.) (Hadasa in discussion with the author, August 1, 2018)

Finally, on the one hand, although many of the students in this research study face everyday violence, gang recruitment, drug dealing, and family abuse, they believe they have found hope in education because learning English becomes a conduit to pursuing their dreams and hopes of moving up socially. On the other hand, the teachers' pedagogies crack a dent on neoliberal discourses of English language teaching. The teachers explicitly do not want their students to acquire English skills to feed the capitalistic system, but rather to visualize community problems and solve them. The teachers believe this "*rebeldia*" (rebellion) to fight the system must be done with concrete actions that counter dehumanization and connect the students with the world. According to Sol:

> *un profesor que sea humano y que sienta la humanidad de su grupo ya es un excelente profesor, porque ya esta conectado, cuando usted se conecta con la humanidad del otro ahí tiene ganado el 90% del aprendizaje de los estudiantes.* (A teacher who is human and that feels humanity is already an excellent teacher because he/she is already connected, and when you connect with humanity you win 90 percent of learning.) (Sol in discussion with the author, August 12, 2018)

Futurities: Hopes and Dreams

The interviews and data collected on classroom observations showed evidence that school and classroom policies to language teaching are geared toward teaching to the test. The school's academic coordinators push the teachers to focus their classes on practicing for the Colombian standardized test. However, the teachers push back by supporting the students in accomplishing their personal goals. In an interview with one of the teachers, she expresses this sentiment by offering students an invitation to pursue their dreams:

> *entonces yo siempre los invito a soñar que hay más posibilidades.* (I always invite them to dream, that there are more possibilities.) (Hadasa in discussion with the author, August 13, 2018)

The pedagogical tasks used in the classroom foster students' sense of belonging to their culture and help them to dream and hope for a better future. Most of the activities are focused on providing the strategies and techniques for the students to learn English meaningfully, as the students hope to secure jobs that allow them to move socially and support their families and communities. According to one of the students interviewed:

> *quisiera ser periodista cuando sea mayor y esto me sirve para darme cuenta de cosas que la sociedad normalmente olvida de estas zonas marginales.* (I would like to be a journalist when I grow up. That helps me to be aware of the things that happen out there in society and that people do not normally pay attention to.) (Horacio in discussion with the author, September 24, 2018)

As a critical ethnographer who engaged in classroom activities, I witnessed how the teachers and students work in collaboration to forge a better future. In a sense, the teachers have become *guerreros* (warriors) and *rebeldes* (rebels) of the system by fighting back on the school administration's standardized testing mentalities and by prioritizing the students' hopes and dreams instead.

Anticolonial Praxis: Social Agents of Change

Another key finding of the research study is that the teachers do not necessarily follow the suggested curriculum provided by the government. The teachers argue that although the current curriculum tries to incorporate some tasks that are culturally relevant, the students need more than just content, especially when they live in a very violent setting. The teachers decided to use the overarching English curriculum themes and adapt them to the students' own context. For example, instead of teaching the American or British culture, a teacher developed a project to highlight human rights and responsibilities and how understanding these would help students to respect others. According to one of the students interviewed:

> *Por ejemplo ella con el tema de derechos y deberes, ella nos mostro muchas formas de tratar a las personas y sus deberes y como puede uno ser con ellos tratarlos bien y ser respetuosos.* (For example, she [the teacher] with the theme of rights and responsibilities showed us different ways of dealing with others, their rights and how we should be with them, treat them well and be respectful.) (Daniel in discussion with the author, September 27, 2019)

Through classroom observations, it was also noted how the teachers tend to highlight the importance of involving the students in the decisionmaking process when it comes to lesson design. The teachers strive to cocreate projects related to social justice and peace, while using activities that help students resolve problems such as unemployment, bullying, and drug addiction. One student commented on how motivating the classes are when they do activities related to their interests and how these somehow help the students to challenge inequalities that their communities face:

> *[aprendimos] lo de comercio justo, adicciones, problemáticas sociales y ella [la profesora] aterriza eso en problemas más cotidianos, y que identifique esos problemas en entorno y nos hace identificar el problema y buscar alternativas de solución.* ([We learned] about fair trade, drug addiction, social problems and she [the teacher] makes connections with our daily lives and helps us to identify the problem and find alternative solutions.) (Cesar in discussion with the author, September 24, 2018)

Finally, the teachers in this study posit that altering the curriculum and adapting it to tailor the students' needs and preferences are important to take them away from the gangs, drugs, and other violent street experiences that disrupt their education and their lives, so that they can become active social agents of change. In general, the teachers believe that "the interactions of education with the other spheres of social life" have allowed them to connect with their students on a personal level (Bondarenko and Kozulin 1991, 74).

The teachers in Colombia acting as *rebeldes* (rebels) fight the system with concrete actions that counter government capitalist and neoliberal discourses. For Dei (2019, viii), decolonial praxis is seen as a concrete, action-oriented task or a purposeful and intentional act of doing decolonization: "for us to be more effective, our decolonial praxis must be about resistance to all forms of oppression given that colonialism and colonization are fundamentally about exploitation and oppression of peoples." In other words, teachers pushing back against the administration and government curricular guidelines help them to challenge, problematize, and counter oppressive narratives that are part of a decolonial project in action that is "deeply implanted in the ways we transform our political, economic, cultural and school systems" (Dei and Lordan 2016, vii).

After spending 8 months in the field working with teachers, students, and others in the schools, I noticed how classroom pedagogies are not only connected with larger-scale national problems, as the teachers and students seek to create some kind of social awareness, but also how education is connected to globalization and the internationalization of education.

Internationalization of Education

Knight (1994) proposes that the purpose of internationalization varies depending on the institution, but it fundamentally speaks to the integration of international and intercultural lenses into teaching and research activities, policies, and services at any given institution. This was evident during my study when the teachers and students expressed an ongoing belief that learning English will help them to move socially, even given the uncertain future. In a broader sense, internationalization refers to the processes by which an institution encourages faculty and students to develop global connections beyond their own realms (de Wit 1999). However, that is also why so many teachers are required to train students for standardized testing in English based on the Common European Framework of Reference (Council of Europe 2001), thereby hindering the possibilities for social justice-oriented pedagogies.

Globalization as a multifaceted and complex phenomenon has become a symbol that leads nation-states to a postmodernity state in which new dimensions of socioeconomic stratification have emerged with equity and equality implications of educational opportunities (Zajda 2010). "Internationalization" and "globalization" are merely two terms that have become a reflection of the current sociopolitical times of neoliberalism that have permeated into the many levels of society, one of which is language education. Specifically, English language teaching has become a language teaching industry around the world by commodifying languages and identities (Heller 2003). English has been used as a tool for modernization. The teaching and learning of the English language have turned into a device for global communication as it is used to stay in contact with speakers around the world (Gnutzmann and Intemann 2005).

Conclusion

Although teachers in Colombia must pursue the government's agenda to help students gain the English language skills that will position the country for Latin American economic leadership, they still try to resist it and believe that there is much more to education than just teaching for managerial skills that will help students get into the labor market. Students need to develop a critical consciousness (Freire 1970) for humanization.

The social justice and peacebuilding work that these Colombian teachers do to fight neoliberal discourses may be difficult, especially given the challenges to get school support. Notwithstanding, the students have found that the approaches used by the teachers have helped to raise local and global social awareness. Classroom projects have prompted students to take actions outside of school and have promoted solutions to social problems that are connected to global issues. The very dialogical nature of this research project, between me as a researcher and the participants, may encourage other researchers to work collaboratively with teachers and other stakeholders in research projects that attend to the social needs of the community.

This research study may advance scholarship on social justice and peacebuilding in postconflict contexts in the field of educational research. This study may also prompt further research on culturally informed pedagogy and curriculum by contextualizing the importance of students' backgrounds and experiences in the creation of social justice and peacebuilding curriculum in a manner that is sustaining and relevant to their context (Ladson-Billings 1992; Paris and Alim 2017). Specifically, this study may translate experiential knowledge and critical research into innovative discussions on curriculum design that may enhance students' social engagement in English language learning, and thereby equip them with the necessary skills for critically evaluating global and local issues that better serve the needs of our educational systems. Finally, this project has demonstrated the need for humanizing pedagogies that are more in tune with the balance and harmony among human beings and directly challenge exogenous and systemic structures of neoliberalism, capitalism, and globalization through a decolonial praxis.

References

Barrera, Madeleine, Enrique Chaux, and Daniela Trujillo. 2015. "¿Los Mejores Perfumes Vienen en Envases Pequeños?: Potencial de las Intervenciones Breves en el Contexto Educativo." *Revista Colombiana de Psicología* 24, 2:285–300.

Bickmore, Kathy, Ahmed Salehin Kaderi, and Ángela Guerra-Sua. 2017. "Creating Capacities for Peacebuilding Citizenship: History and Social Studies Curricula in Bangladesh, Canada, Colombia, and México." *Journal of Peace Education* 14, 3:282–309.

Bondarenko, Ye. G., and A. V. Kozulin. 1991. "The Democratization of Education: Basic Principles." *Higher Education in Europe* 16, 1:74–78.

Capeheart, Loretta, and Dragan Milovanovic. 2007. *Social Justice: Theories, Issues, and Movements*. New Brunswick, NJ: Rutgers University Press.

Chapetón, Claudia, and Pedro Chala. 2013. "Undertaking the Act of Writing as a Situated Social Practice: Going Beyond the Linguistic and the Textual." *Colombian Applied Linguistics Journal* 15, 1:25–42.

Chapman, Thandeka K., and Nikola Hobbel. 2010. *Social Justice Pedagogy Across the Curriculum: The Practice of Freedom*. New York, NY: Routledge.

Chaux, Enrique, Madeleine Barrera, Andres Molano, Ana Velásquez, Melisa Castellanos, Maria Paula Chaparro, and Andrea Bustamante. 2017. "Classrooms in Peace Within Violent Contexts: Field Evaluation of Aulas en Paz in Colombia." *Prevention Science* 18, 7:828–838.

Contreras León, Janeth Juliana, and Claudia Marcela Chapetón Castro. 2016. "Cooperative Learning with a Focus on the Social: A Pedagogical Proposal for the EFL Classroom." *HOW Journal* 23, 2:125–147.

Council of Europe. 2001. *Common European Framework of Reference for Languages: Learning, Teaching, Assessment*. Cambridge, United Kingdom: Press Syndicate of the University of Cambridge.

Creswell, John W. 2009. *Research Design: Qualitative, Quantitative, and Mixed Methods Approaches, Third Edition*. Los Angeles, CA: SAGE Publications.

Creswell, John W. 2015. *Educational Research: Planning, Conducting, and Evaluating Quantitative and Qualitative Research, Fifth Edition*. Boston, MA: Pearson.

Dei, George J. Sefa. 2019. "Foreword." In *Decolonization and Anti-colonial Praxis. Shared Lineages*, ed. Anila Zainub. Leiden, The Netherlands: Brill Sense.

Dei, George J. Sefa, and Meredith Lordan. 2016. "Introduction: Envisioning New Meanings, Memories, and Actions for Anti-colonial Theory and Decolonial Praxis." In *Anti-colonial Theory and Decolonial Praxis*, eds. George J. Sefa Dei and Meredith Lordan. New York, NY: Peter Lang Publishing, Inc.

de Wit, Hans. 1999. "Changing Rationales for the Internationalization of Higher Education." *International Higher Education* 15, 1: 2–3.

Freire, Paulo. 1970. *Pedagogy of the Oppressed*. New York, NY: Seabury Press.

Galtung, Johan.1969. "Violence, Peace, and Peace Research." *Journal of Peace Research* 6, 3:167–191.

Galtung, Johan. 1990. "Cultural Violence." *Journal of Peace Research* 27, 3:291–305.

Garcia, Ofelia, and Li Wei. 2014. *Translanguaging: Language, Bilingualism and Education*. New York, NY: Palgrave Macmillan.

Giroux, Henry. 1994. *Disturbing Pleasures: Learning Popular Culture*. New York, NY: Routledge.

Gnutzmann, Claus, and Frauke Intemann. 2005. *The Globalization of English and the English Language Classroom, First Edition*. Tübingen, Germany: Narr.

González González, Fernán E. 2014. *Poder y Violencia En Colombia. Colección Territorio, Poder y Conflicto*. Bogotá, Colombia: Odecofi, Cinep.

Heller, Monica. 2003. "Globalization, the New Economy, and the Commodification of Language and Identity." *Journal of Sociolinguistics* 7, 4:473–492.

Hsieh, Hsiu-Fang, and Sarah E. Shannon. 2005. "Three Approaches to Qualitative Content Analysis." *Qualitative Health Research* 15, 9:1277–1288.

Johannessen, B. Gloria Guzman, and Ann Unterreiner. 2008. "Pedagogical Ethics for Teaching Social Justice in Teacher Education." *Educational Practice and Theory* 30, 1:27–39.

Knight, Jane. 1994. *Internationalization: Elements and Checkpoints. CBIE Research No. 7*. Canadian Bureau for International Education (CBIE) / Bureau canadien de l'éducation internationale (BCEI).

Ladson-Billings, Gloria. 1992. "Reading Between the Lines and Beyond the Pages: A Culturally Relevant Approach to Literacy Teaching." *Theory into Practice* 31, 4:312–320.

Lederach, John Paul. 2006. "Defining Conflict Transformation." *Peacework* 33, 368:26–27.

Lin, Jing, and Rebecca L. Oxford. 2011. *Transformative EcoEducation for Human and Planetary Survival*. Charlotte, NC: IAP.

López de Mesa-Melo, Clara, César Andrés Carvajal-Castillo, María Fernanda Soto-Godoy, and Pedro Nel Urrea-Roa. 2013. "Factores Asociados a La Convivencia Escolar En Adolescentes." *Educación y Educadores* 16, 3:383–410.

Macrine, Sheila L. 2009. *Critical Pedagogy in Uncertain Times: Hope and Possibilities*. New York, NY: Palgrave Macmillan.

Madison, D. Soyini. 2011. *Critical Ethnography: Method, Ethics, and Performance*. Los Angeles, CA: SAGE Publications.

McLaren, Peter L. 1988. "On Ideology and Education: Critical Pedagogy and the Politics of Empowerment." *Social Text* 19, 20:153–185.

Merriam, Sharan B. 2009. *Qualitative Research: A Guide to Design and Implementation*. San Francisco, CA: Jossey-Bass.

Miller, David. 1999. *Principles of Social Justice*. Cambridge, MA: Harvard University Press.

Ministerio de Educación. 2016. *Colombia Bilingüe*. http://aprende.colombiaaprende.edu.co/es/colombiabilingue/86689.

Miranda, Norbella. 2016. "Bilingual Colombia Program: Curriculum as Product, Only?" *Working Papers in Educational Linguistics (WPEL)* 31, 2:19–38.

Miranda Nieves, Norbella. 2018. "Política Educativa Para El Bilingüismo Español-Inglés En Colombia: Rastreo de Su Trayectoria Desde Las Aulas." Doctoral dissertation, Universidad del Quindio.

Miranda, Norbella, and Silvia Valencia Giraldo. 2019. "Unsettling the 'Challenge': ELT Policy Ideology and the New Breach Amongst State-Funded Schools in Colombia." *Changing English* 26, 3:282–294.

Nieto, Sonia, and Patty Bode. 2012. *Affirming Diversity: The Sociopolitical Context of Multicultural Education*. Boston, MA: Pearson.

Nixon, Rob. 2011. "Slow Violence." *Chronicle of Higher Education*. June 26, 2011. http://www.chronicle.com/article/Slow-Violence/127968.

Ortega, Yecid. 2019. "'Teacher, ¿Puedo hablar en Español?' A Reflection on Plurilingualism and Translanguaging Practices in EFL." *Profile: Issues in Teachers' Professional Development* 21, 2:155–170.

Palacios, Nilsen, and Claudia Marcela Chapetón. 2014. "Students' Responses to the Use of Songs in the EFL Classroom at a Public School in Bogotá: A Critical Approach." *GIST Education and Learning Research Journal* 9:9–30.

Paris, Django, and Samy Alim, eds. 2017. *Culturally Sustaining Pedagogies: Teaching and Learning for Justice in a Changing World*. New York, NY: Teachers College Press.

Rodríguez, Edwin Cruz. 2014. "Hipótesis Sobre El Matoneo Escolar o Bullying: A Propósito Del Caso Colombiano." *Intersticios. Revista Sociológica de Pensamiento Crítico* 8, 1:149–156.

Sherman, John W. 2015. "Political Violence in Colombia: Dirty Wars Since 1977." *History Compass* 13, 9:454–465.

Silva, Alexander, and Enrique Chaux. 2005. *La Formación de Competencias Ciudadanas*. Asociación Colombiana de Facultades de Educación, ASCOFADE. http://www.academia.edu/download/31807215/La_formacion_de_competencias_ciudadanas.pdf.

Ukpokodu, Omiunota Nelly. 2010. "Engagement and Social Justice and Institutional Change: Promises and Paradoxes." *The International Journal of Critical Pedagogy* 3, 2:104–126.

UNESCO and United Nations. 1997. *UNESCO and a Culture of Peace: Promoting a Global Movement, Second Edition*. Paris, France: UNESCO.

Usma, Jaime. 2015. *From Transnational Language Policy Transfer to Local Appropriation: The Case of the National Bilingual Program in Medellin, Colombia*. Blue Mounds, WI: Deep University Press.

Usma, Jaime, and Oscar Pelaez. 2017. "Teacher Autonomy: From the Conventional Promotion of Independent Learning to the Critical Appropriation of Language Policies." In *Innovations and Challenges in Applied Linguistics and Learner Autonomy*, eds. Christine Nicolaides and Walkyria Magno. Campinas, São Paulo: Pontes Editores.

Valenzuela, Edmundo. 2005. *Cultura de La Paz*. Biblioteca de Estudios Paraguayos, v. 65. Asunción, Paraguay: Universidad Católica Nuestra Señora de la Asunción.

Vargas, Juan, and Raul Caruso. 2014. "Conflict, Crime, and Violence in Colombia." *Peace Economics, Peace Science and Public Policy* 20, 1:1–4.

Zajda, Joseph, ed. 2010. *Globalization, Education and Social Justice*. Dordrecht, The Netherlands: Springer Netherlands.

Notes: Thanks to the English teachers (Hadasa, Sol, Camello) who keep working on social justice and peacebuilding strategies to address issues of violence. Some of the research and pedagogical work related to social justice in language teaching can be found at www.andjustice4all.ca/.

Funding: Part of this research project was funded by The Social Sciences and Humanities Research Council of Canada (SSHRC) and The International Research Foundation for English Language Education (TIRF).

Appendix A: Classroom Activities

During the time I spent with the teachers, I observed three kinds of activities that look at humanizing the pedagogical practice, as these are related to the students' and teachers' lived experiences. The following is a summary of these types of activities.

Social Justice-Oriented Projects

One of the many concerns related to teaching has to do with how to connect the English lessons to problems that the community faces on a regular basis. In order to address this, the teachers discussed with the students some of the problems they experienced every day. The teachers asked the students to organize themselves into groups and map out as many problems as they could and how these problems could be solved. Upon sharing and reflecting on the problems, these were the salient ones:

- Bullying
- Homelessness
- Teenage pregnancy
- Family violence
- Drug addiction
- Unemployment
- Stray dogs and cats

The next step was to figure out how to connect the problems and the possible solutions. The English textbook suggested that the students create companies because their main goal is to talk about business and entrepreneurship. However, instead of creating companies for business and profit, the students and teachers agreed to create nonprofit organizations to solve some of the problems they previously discussed. Subsequently, students drafted mission and vision statements, goals, and timelines in Spanish to later be translated into English. The teachers then reviewed and revised the drafts, corrected the grammar, and gave the students feedback. The students did fieldwork in which they went around their neighborhood and took photos, interviewed people, and proposed solutions to the problems they identified. Finally, the students presented the outcomes of their projects in front of the class and to the larger school community. Examples of project topics were sports for health, which encouraged students to stay away from gangs and drug addiction; food for dogs, which raised funds to buy and make food for stray dogs; and unemployment support, whereby the students conducted interviews and surveys in order to get a sense of the unemployment rate in the neighborhood and then provide the necessary resources for people to find jobs. The lessons learned in this experience were not only to sensitize students to the local problems and connect with global issues, but to find a concrete solution to a problem so that students could see the immediate impact of their learning. In other words, students used the English language as a means to discuss their local problems, promote social awareness, and provide solutions.

Dreams and Hopes Project

Students from grades 9, 10, and 11 usually learn certain skills to prepare themselves for their future in the job market post-high school. All high school teachers need to tailor their activities to help the students acquire these skills. In the English class, one of the teachers created a project related to the students' dreams and hopes called the "project of life." The teacher started the project by posing some exploratory questions about what the students want to do in the future, about their strengths, weaknesses, their favorite person or role model, and how they see themselves and the communities in which they live. She then asked the students to write down their reflections based on the answers to these questions. The teacher checked the students' grammar, coherence, and cohesion, and the students then shared their ideas with the class. After that, the students created artistic booklets and presented them during a cultural activity with other grades during the English week at school. The main lesson learned in this experience was to set out a larger purpose for students' lives and to encourage students to have a vision of what they want to do in their profession or personal life after they graduate from high school.

Cultural Awareness Projects

For one of the teachers, it was important to encourage students to acknowledge their own culture before learning about another one. A project about Colombian culture was designed and assigned to engage students in learning more about their own country. The students formed groups to research a topic related to Colombian culture, prepared presentations, and then shared them with peers in the school. For example, some students presented on Colombian food, delivered the presentations in English, and prepared some questions to ask the audience. When other students answered the questions correctly, they would get a sample of the food. This project helped the students gain a sense of community and respect for their own culture, and it set the groundwork for learning about other cultures in a respective and engaging way.

Part II
Social Justice in Practice

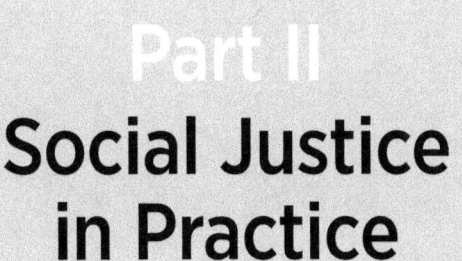

6

View, Voice, and Visibility
A Liberating Framework for Social Justice in Education Abroad

EDUARDO CONTRERAS JR., EdD

On one spring afternoon in San Antonio, Texas, an eager group of educators took their seats to listen to a Distinguished Lecture given by Sara Lawrence-Lightfoot at the American Educational Research Association (AERA) 2017 annual meeting. As the nearly standing-room-only audience settled to a willing hush, AERA President Vivian Gadsden introduced the speaker as a MacArthur Fellow, pioneering sociologist, and endowed professor with a long list of notable publications. Most of the people in the room knew the author or were familiar with her prodigious work; the remaining folks were interested in learning more about principles of equity in education.

As Lawrence-Lightfoot (2017) brought her lecture to a close, she shared a story from her own history, which was an internal reflection on *injustice* in education. Her fifth-grade teacher had sought to honor her, the only African American student in his class, during "Negro History Week" by introducing the class to the poetry of Harlem Renaissance poet Jean Toomer. Years later, Lawrence-Lightfoot vividly recalled the quiet stares of her classmates when she was singled out. She lamented the unintended consequence of her teacher's earnest effort to acknowledge her presence. Yet she also recalled a powerful metaphor from Toomer's epic poem, "The Blue Meridian," which she read to the attentive audience at AERA. The poem by Toomer ended with the line, "Whoever lifts the Mississippi/ Lifts himself and all America;/ Whoever lifts himself/ Makes that great brown river smile" (Jones and Latimer 1988, 50). This memory and powerful metaphor was an exclamation point to Lawrence-Lightfoot's talk, and it demonstrated the potential of achieving social justice in education.

In this chapter, I argue that the liberating framework she introduced on that sunny day in Texas can be directly applied to supporting social justice in education abroad. I offer a working definition for *critical social justice* education, then I introduce Lawrence-Lightfoot's liberating framework, followed by a discussion of the specific ways in which the three core elements of the framework intersect with education abroad. Finally, I present core questions that we as international educators should consider in the context of education abroad:

- In what ways can we reframe the view of critical social justice in education abroad?
- How can we amplify the widest array of voices in education abroad to dismantle hierarchies and support educational equity and equal access?
- How can we advocate for students to ensure that all students are visible?
- How can we interrogate our own biographies and advocate for ourselves so that we, too, are visible?

Ultimately, these questions will provide the basis for achieving social justice in education abroad and supporting greater access and equity in the field.

Social Justice: A Critical Perspective

In its most simplistic terms, "social justice" can be defined as any endeavor that maintains and enhances equitable treatment of all individuals in ways that advance inclusive learning opportunities. As Sensoy and DiAngelo (2012) note, when addressing social justice, it is important to acknowledge the role that power, privilege, and stratification play in the world. Since there is ample evidence that there are inequalities in the world along the lines of race, class, gender, sexuality, ability, age, and other intersectional identifying factors, a critical perspective is essential. Sensoy and DiAngelo (2012, 145) explain that anyone engaged in critical social justice must be able to:

> recognize that relations of unequal social power are constantly being negotiated at both the micro (individual) and macro (structural) levels. We must understand our own positions within these relations of unequal power. We must be able to think critically about knowledge. And most

importantly, we must be able to act from this understanding in service of a more just society.

This general definition can be applied in multiple contexts, and it corresponds well with the liberating framework offered by Lawrence-Lightfoot.

Liberating Framework: View, Voice, and Visibility

Lawrence-Lightfoot's (2017) AERA Distinguished Lecture, "'Let the Great Brown River Smile.' Liberating Frames and Educational Discourses: On View, Voice, and Visibility," establishes a firm foundation for engaging in critical social justice in education abroad. First and foremost, her idea is grounded in equity at the structural (macro) and individual (micro) levels, so it aligns with the first principle of Sensoy and DiAngelo's (2012) definition. As Lawrence-Lightfoot said, "I want to address my comments to researchers and practitioners, scholars, and activists…and *to all of us who are focused on achieving the promise of equal education opportunity*" (Lawrence-Lightfoot 2017; emphasis added). In the lecture, Lawrence-Lightfoot encouraged the audience members to reframe their view by asking everyone to lift up their voices. Then, she expressed the imperative that everyone be visible. Again, this harkens back to Sensoy and DiAngelo (2012) who encourage those who do social justice work to understand their own positions and be mindful of serving a just society.

The Three Vs Framework in an Education Abroad Context

The three *Vs* framework of View, Voice, and Visibility offered by Lawrence-Lightfoot (2017) provides educators with unique perspectives that challenge existing paradigms around educational equity and support for social justice. In asking the AERA audience to reframe their view, Lawrence-Lightfoot challenged the room to shift away from the darkness of focusing on obstacles and problems and move toward the light of finding success and solutions. According to Lawrence-Lightfoot (2017), the tendency to seek problems and pathology often leads to victim blaming, so, in her mind, it is necessary to reframe one's view. For many of us working in education abroad, the story of obstacles and roadblocks to access is a familiar tune, which speaks to the collective focus on pathology in this field and the need to reframe this view.

Next, by urging those in the room to lift their voices, Lawrence-Lightfoot encouraged everyone to speak up for the powerless and voiceless in schools and universities. Voice also applies to the field of education as a whole. Lawrence-Lightfoot advocated for diversity in education by asking for everyone to be heard, thus dismantling academic hierarchies and encouraging a multiplicity of perspectives and voices in teaching, scholarship, practice, and policymaking. Within the study abroad context, it is evident that diversity in students outpaces diversity in staff and faculty, so the need for amplifying voices is particularly poignant. This amplification of voices in education abroad will serve both the students and the profession.

Finally, when Lawrence-Lightfoot (2017) implored the audience to "cut through the layers of hard distorted glass and see the full humanity of our research subjects, participants, protagonists," her message of visibility had a dual meaning. Not only did she ask educators to make sure that all students are visible, but she also asked that scholars and practitioners, who themselves are on the margins, make themselves *be* visible. As she noted, "To be visible, we must live lives of vigilant observation, criticism, and action. To be seen, we must see" (Lawrence-Lightfoot 2017). In this way, View, Voice, and Visibility offer those who work in education abroad a critical framework to support social justice.

View

In the first frame, Lawrence-Lightfoot asks researchers, practitioners, and policymakers to reject the established narrow definition of achievement and reframe their "view." According to Sue Swaffield's (2017, 493) summary of this lecture, Lawrence-Lightfoot argued "that the relentless scrutiny of failure is distorting, and the documentation of pathology often bleeds into blaming the victim." Rather than blame the students and institutions that are the victims of systemic oppression, Lawrence-Lightfoot encouraged educators to focus on "goodness."

Lawrence-Lightfoot has a long history of finding goodness. Her seminal work, *The Good High School: Portraits of Character and Culture* (1983), chronicles six successful high schools: two from poor, urban districts; two from suburban regions; and two elite preparatory institutions. Her observations are not naïve, romanticized, fluff pieces, but rigorous, nuanced, and scholarly observations grounded in established research methodology and informed real-world social and historical context. This reframing view of goodness in those high schools served as a counterpoint to the prevailing discourse of the early 1980s around minimum requirements for academic success and poor academic achievement, as epitomized by U.S. President Ronald Regan's National Commission on Excellence in Education's (1983) publication *A Nation at Risk: The Imperative for Educational Reform.* The commission's report chronicled many failures of the U.S. educational system and set the negative tone around education discourse for years to come. As Lawrence-Lightfoot (2017) argued in her AERA Distinguished Lecture, "Social scientists have a long legacy of focusing their investigations on pathology and disease rather than health and resilience....they often confuse difference with deviance, or difference with dysfunction, conflating illness and identity."

To reframe views, Lawrence-Lightfoot encouraged educators to shift the focus away from the problems, while still acknowledging the grand challenges, and instead ask these questions: What is good here? What is working well? What is strong? What is worthy? In this way, she suggested, "We will discover a different reality. We may even uncover a lever of change, a spark of promise, that had been formally obscured by our well-worn negative prophecies" (Lawrence-Lightfoot 2017).

A Reframed View in Education Abroad

Shifting from a look at pathology in education broadly to study abroad specifically, there are some important questions to ask: What are the general views of social justice in education abroad? What are our "well-worn negative prophecies"? And how might the field of education abroad move away from these negative prophecies to find avenues of hope and success? When it comes to access and equity, the dominant view has long been preoccupied with barriers and bottom lines. By barriers, I refer to the work in the field that has focused on defining the roadblocks for students from underrepresented groups. For example, consider the "Four *F*s" framework introduced by Spelman College President Johnnetta Betsch Cole at the Council on International Educational Exchange (CIEE)'s 1991 annual conference. In her keynote address, Cole (1991) argued that the barriers to study abroad for African Americans could be boiled down to four *F*s: Faculty and staff, Finances, Family and community, and Fear. Cole also stated in her address that the barriers to studying abroad that she described pertaining to her Spelman College students could apply to all underrepresented minority students. Cole (1991) listed the barriers in her speech:

- Faculty members can be a barrier because of their predilection to recruit only a selective body of students for overseas study, and their tendency to neglect students who are not part of dominant groups.

- Finances pose another challenge because underrepresented students are more likely to be on financial aid than students in majority groups.

- Families, particularly parents, can also undermine underrepresented students' abilities to study abroad because of parental worries about health, safety, and the impact of racism on their children abroad.

- Fears of the students are the final major obstacle to overcome for minoritized students because they, too, fear the impact of racism while abroad.

Cole's Four *F*s framework has been foundational and still shapes many of today's discussions around access. Although many in the field know the Four *F*s framework—and some know that Cole is its original author—very few remember the context from which it emerged. The framework was presented at a CIEE conference focused on advancing strategies for increased access, describing rationales for sending more students abroad, and addressing barriers to overseas study. But nearly 30 years later, what most people remember, and continue to write about, are the barriers.

Indeed, as a personal example, as I completed the first draft of this chapter, the latest issue of *International Educator* magazine arrived in my mailbox. The issue included an article titled "Breaking *Barriers* to Study Abroad" (West

2019; emphasis added). Although the article's intent is to illuminate the avenues to access, the rhetoric in the author's title foregrounds the barriers. This preoccupation with barriers has plagued the field since Cole's seminal speech in 1991. I do not chastise other colleagues for using this paradigm because I have also been guilty of perpetuating these views of barriers in national presentations. I engaged in the same rhetoric with two colleagues (Trixie Cordova and Sara Spiegler) at the Forum on Education Abroad's 2017 annual conference with a panel presentation called "The New *F* Words: Rethinking Access in the 21st Century" (Contreras, Cordova, and Spiegler 2017). As we noted in our presentation, barriers are a part of the dialogue on access. Our presentation discussed the old barriers and noted two new roadblocks: Future (long-term career objectives) and Fit (curricular alignment). Like Cole, our impetus for reintroducing old barriers (and, indeed adding a few new impediments) to the discussion was access and social justice. As Cole mentioned in 1991, "we have the awesome and doable responsibility of making enriching experiences possible for larger numbers of African American students—*indeed all students*" (emphasis added). Of course, the field's preoccupation with barriers does not undermine or disrespect Cole's influential work, but it is important to keep in mind that the dominant view often focuses on what is wrong (Four *F*s framework) rather than on what is good or right.

As international educators, our preoccupation with barriers has focused our gaze on the *impossibilities*, so it is important to reframe our view around what is *possible* in education abroad. Although the studies that address such possibilities are minimal, there are scholars who have considered these potentials. For example, the eye-opening work of Tasha Willis (2015) in "'And Still We Rise…': Microaggressions and Intersectionality in the Study Abroad Experiences of Black Women" powerfully demonstrates that there is a complex interplay between race, ethnicity, gender, age, and other matters for Black women at community colleges studying abroad. Overseas study offers numerous possibilities for growth for these women, "in terms of students' agency and empowerment, intercultural development, and in some cases, their sense of calling and self-actualization" (Willis 2015, 225).

A Narrow View

The spotlight on barriers has also led to an increased fixation on raw numbers. The bulk of research on underrepresentation and access in education abroad, including my own, has centered on participation rates, demographics, and, to some extent, funding (López McGee, Comp, and Contreras 2018). In other words, the field has been preoccupied with counting people and counting dollars. On the one hand, these efforts have been important because demographic changes matter and increasing representation of all students in education abroad is a central goal for social justice and equal access. On the other hand, the narrow focus leaves an incomplete picture.

There were no national records accounting for the race of students studying abroad until 1995. The Institute of International Education (IIE) added a question for study abroad students about their race/ethnicity in the 1994–95 *Open Doors* survey. That year, the *Open Doors* data showed that there were 76,302 total students abroad, of which 84 percent were White, 5 percent were Hispanic American, 5 percent were Asian American, 3 percent were multiracial, 3 percent were African American, and less than 1 percent were Native American (IIE 2005). By comparison, the total fall enrollment at all U.S. colleges and universities in 1994 was 14,304,800, and 75 percent of these students were White, 11 percent were Black, 8 percent were Hispanic, 6 percent were Asian or Pacific Islander, and less than 1 percent were Native American (National Center for Education Statistics 1996). In recent years, 71 percent of the students studying abroad were White, while 29 percent of the participants came from underrepresented groups (IIE 2018). In 2018, 52 percent of the students enrolled in U.S. higher education were White. More precisely, "[O]f the 16.6 million undergraduate students enrolled in fall 2018, some 8.7 million were White, 3.4 million were Hispanic, 2.1 million were Black, 1.1 million were Asian, 647,000 were of Two or more races, 120,000 were American Indian/Alaska Native, and 45,000 were Pacific Islander" (NCES 2020). These figures indicate that there was no parity between the proportion of underrepresented students studying abroad and those enrolled in U.S. higher education in general, dating back to the mid-1990s. This view of demographics is important because it obscures many elements of the education abroad experience for students of color.

By reframing the view, the field might better assist students on the margins in understanding the nuances of finding the distinct goodness of their learning experiences and identity formation. Questions that interrogate the intersectional identities and unique learning experiences of all students would change the discourse in beneficial ways, as Willis (2015) and others have shown. Sensoy and DiAngelo (2012, 145) remind those doing work in the service of social justice that "[w]e must be able to think critically about knowledge." This critical perspective in education abroad is needed to shift the paradigm toward equity. Some of the initial impulses that set the dominant view may have been laid out with the best of intentions and may have even been laudable endeavors to find solutions to problems, but the result is a paradigm view that focuses on negativity instead of goodness.

Voice

The second *V* in the framework is equally important for advancing social justice in education abroad. Lawrence-Lightfoot (2017) introduced the voice frame, by urging

> the development and amplification of voices that bridge the great divide between theory and practice; that take advantage of the different perspectives of researchers and practitioners; that recognize the richness of the counterpoint that gets produced when disciplined inquiry is grounded in, shaped, and constrained by the social and historical context. This means of course that we need to dismantle the hierarchy between the thinkers and the doers, the intellectuals and the activists, and create a symmetry of voices that values each perspective.

Beyond the need to listen to the collective voices of different adults, Lawrence-Lightfoot urged the room to listen to the "wise, authoritative, and critical" voices of students, which are often attentive to adults' contradictions.

Ultimately, she noted that the conversations around equity and social justice are most productive when all voices are honored and presented in language that is not exclusive or esoteric, but understandable and encouraging of more people joining in the conversation. The notion of amplifying voices is essential for advancing social justice in education abroad because, as Lawrence-Lightfoot (2017) put it, it allows for educators to "resist the hierarchies of power and language that get in the way of authentic and inclusive representations of a humanistic education." If the social justice aims of education abroad are to serve the widest array of students from all backgrounds—including those that have been underserved, under-resourced, and overlooked—then it is indeed beneficial to heed Lawrence-Lightfoot's advice and listen to the widest range of voices.

Examples of Voice from the Field of Education Abroad

In recent years, the field of education abroad has made good strides in both listening to and amplifying more voices. Several institutions and organizations have been leading these efforts. For example, NAFSA: Association of International Educators has been engaging in more work to promote a multiplicity of voices in broad and specific ways. In a broad sense, the very values of the organization advocate for inclusion. In 2015, NAFSA approved a Diversity and Inclusion Statement that affirmed the association's commitment to this work and stated, in part, "NAFSA encourages international educators to develop practices reflecting a commitment to diversity, inclusion, access, and equity. We encourage institutions and organizations to embrace these principles as well" (NAFSA 2015). In March 2018, NAFSA published its Strategic Plan for 2018–2020, which highlights inclusion at the outset in the articulation of NAFSA's core values:

> *NAFSA believes that international education advances learning and scholarship, fosters understanding and respect among people of diverse backgrounds and perspectives*, is essential for developing globally competent individuals, and builds leadership for the global community. We believe that international education lies at the core of an interconnected world characterized by peace, security, and well-being for all. *NAFSA believes that diversity in our classrooms, our communities, and our workplaces is our strength.* (NAFSA 2018, 1; emphasis added)

Highlighting the centrality of inclusion is a way of acknowledging a variety of voices at all levels and demonstrates a commitment to this endeavor at the highest levels of leadership, the NAFSA Board of Directors and the executive director and CEO of the organization.

Yet the high-level commitment would be hollow without specific examples of how this work is executed on the ground. As Lawrence-Lightfoot notes, the importance of amplifying voices is to ensure that all voices are heard. NAFSA has done this with its Education Abroad Knowledge Community, which includes an active Subcommittee on Diversity and Inclusion in Education Abroad. The subcommittee is led by volunteer leaders from across the spectrum within the field who help to seek out voices to present in a variety of platforms (online chats, regional and annual conferences, workshops, and other arenas). The subcommittee has also brought together the resources and voices available for this work on NAFSA's website: www.nafsa.org/eadiversity. In terms of amplifying voices, from 2017 until 2020, the web page hosted a "Diversity Expertise Log" with nearly 200 entries from individuals within the field who have a certain degree of expertise in a wide range of areas of underrepresentation. Finally, this very book on social justice in international education is yet another example of a successful amplification of voices since it includes authors from different, often underrepresented, backgrounds.

DIVERSITY ABROAD

Another example of amplified voices is the work done by Diversity Abroad, which was founded in 2006 by Andrew Gordon and has been both a leading voice for equitable education abroad and an organization that has highlighted and introduced new voices over its history. The organization operates under the principle that all students deserve "equitable access to global educational opportunities" (Diversity Abroad n.d.). Diversity Abroad has sought to dismantle hierarchies between educators and students by featuring student voices on its student-focused website, diversityabroad.com, and presenting staff voices on its professional service site, diversitynetwork.org. In both cases, Diversity Abroad intentionally showcases a multiplicity of voices in blog postings, formal reports, and articles.

The *Global Impact Exchange* is a recent example of this work. The quarterly online publication launched in 2018 and focuses on advancing the conversation around diversity, inclusion, and equity in global education (www.diversitynetwork.org/page/GlobalImpactExchange). Beyond the digital efforts made by Diversity Abroad, the annual Diversity Abroad conference has been a forum for voices since 2013, with high-quality sessions and increasing attendance. The Minority Serving Institution Global Education Summit, the Chief Diversity Officer and Senior International Officer Strategic Leadership Forum, and the Global Student Leadership Summit each offer a level field for those distinct groups to be heard and accepted. These intellectually stimulating, professionally engaging, and equity-focused programs have become the hallmarks of Diversity Abroad.

PUBLICATIONS

Beyond the work that NAFSA and Diversity Abroad have done, there have been other institutions striving to feature and amplify a multiplicity of staff and student voices. On the publishing front, the 2018 book *Promoting Inclusion in Education Abroad: A Handbook of Research and Practice*, edited by Heather Barclay Hamir and Nick Gozik and copublished by Stylus Publishing and NAFSA, includes 12 chapters from more than 20 authors throughout the field. The editors of the book assembled a diverse assortment of authors in terms of their institutional affiliations, positions, gender, race, and ethnicity. Beyond the prima facie composition of the contributors to the book, many of the authors shared more nuanced aspects of their intersectional identities in the "Editors and Contributors" section of the book.

Additionally, *Frontiers: The Interdisciplinary Journal of Study Abroad* released a special Virtual Issue on Diversity and Inclusion in Education Abroad in June 2019 that assembled "key scholarship on diversity, equity, and inclusion that has appeared in *Frontiers*" over its 24-year history (Contreras et al. 2019, 2). Related to this retrospective look, *Frontiers* also sought to bring to light new scholarship from a diverse group of scholars, practitioners, and scholar-practitioners. To recruit new voices, the guest editors reviewed newly published dissertations and invited authors to submit articles.

STUDENT VOICES

With regard to student voices, Michelle Tolan Tomasi at the Institute for Study Abroad, Butler University (IFSA-Butler) developed a digital platform called "Unpacked: A Study Abroad Guide for Students Like Me," which is a website dedicated to sharing authentic student voices and experiences under a number of different categories, such as faith communities, gender abroad, racial and ethnic identity, LGBTQIA+, first generation, students with special accommodations, and more (www.ifsa-butler.org/unpacked/). "Unpacked" provides a powerful platform for students of various groups to share their experiences and for students from similar groups to read about these experiences and see themselves in the shoes of the "Unpacked" writers.

As another example, State University of New York (SUNY) at Oswego launched a successful campaign called "I, Too, Am Study Abroad," which shares the study abroad experiences of underrepresented students at SUNY Oswego (Hulstrand 2016). Based on the "I, Too, Am Harvard" campaign—which sought to illustrate the experiences of Black students at Harvard—SUNY Oswego aims to show that education abroad is possible for all students by inviting returning students to lead panel discussions on topics such as "race and gender identity, financing study abroad, and marketing the study abroad experience" (Redden 2016). These are just some of the many examples of efforts made by those in the field to amplify additional voices.

Visibility

The final *V* of "visibility" is also instructive for achieving greater social justice in education abroad. To introduce this frame during her AERA Distinguished Lecture, Lawrence-Lightfoot told a story about her daughter Tolani. When she was 4 years old, Tolani woke up one morning and stretched out her arms as if to hug (or be hugged by) the world, and then she began to sing the song "You Are So Beautiful." In her four-year-old voice, the lyrics resonated in a different way. At AERA, Lawrence-Lightfoot recreated the moment by singing Tolani's version of the lyric, which she had changed to "I am so beautiful to you" Lawrence-Lightfoot finished singing with a smile and nodded her head affirmatively, "Yes, Tolani! Yes, to see and feel beauty, we must be visible" (Lawrence-Lightfoot

2017). As a stark contrast to the visibility of her beautiful daughter, Lawrence-Lightfoot quoted Ralph Ellison's ([1947] 1995, 3) book *Invisible Man*:

> I am an invisible man. No, I am not a spook like those who haunted Edgar Allan Poe; nor am I one of your Hollywood-movie ectoplasms. I am a man of substance, of flesh and bone, fiber and liquids—and I might even be said to possess a mind. I am invisible, understand, simply because people refuse to see me. Like the bodiless heads you see sometimes in circus sideshows, it is as though I have been surrounded by mirrors of hard, distorting glass. When they approach me they see only my surroundings, themselves, or figments of their imagination—indeed, everything and anything except me.

The prejudice of invisibility that was painfully yet beautifully described by Ellison in 1952 still exists today. The two sides of this coin of visibility and invisibility are particularly poignant to the work of education abroad with regard to social justice. As Lawrence-Lightfoot (2017) noted, "Diversity and authentic inclusivity are primarily about visibility." If visibility fosters inclusion, and invisibility is the catalyst for exclusion, then the important and hard work of enhancing visibility is necessary to support social justice and is essential for inclusive efforts in education abroad.

Greater Visibility

Rather than enumerate examples of visibility in the field, this section offers some suggestions for achieving greater visibility in education abroad. First, advocacy plays an important role in enhancing visibility. In education abroad, this means advocating that certain student populations who are on the margins are invited to the center. If there is a group that is not receiving equitable resources or is underserved or neglected, then it is incumbent upon professionals at all levels to utilize their voices to advocate that others are visible.

Since institutions of higher education are so diverse in terms of their size, scope, and mission, it is essential that we as educators understand our own institutions and see what groups or individuals are the most neglected on our campuses and in our institutions. As Lawrence-Lightfoot (2017) explained in her talk, "Observation and criticism must become daily habits of our lives as educators, as practitioners and researchers, as advocates and analysts." Advocacy in education abroad requires that we observe who is *not* at the table, then speak up in a *critical* way for those individuals to be present. Criticism does not have to be antagonistic or caustic; instead, it can be collaborative and situated in the context of constructive dialogue.

SELF-VISIBILITY IN EDUCATION ABROAD

Advocating for visibility is not only about seeing others; it is also important to ensure that our own identities are understood, articulated, and made visible. This is a type of self-advocacy that is essential, but also fraught with potentially challenging introspection, vulnerability, and risk. As much as we look outward, we must also look inward. Here again, Lawrence-Lightfoot's (2017) words are instructive: "As we support fairness and justice everywhere, goodness in education means learning to risk visibility, it means learning to bare public witness." In this way, we have to acknowledge our own levels of privilege and oppression. As a cisgender, light-skinned, Latinx male, I understand that my gender and pale phenotypic skin tone grant me distinct privileges within the United States. Yet I also fully experience, on a regular basis, imposter syndrome and stereotype threat within the field of education abroad and within my own predominately White institution. In this way, I acknowledge my unearned privileges while still negotiating my own visibility vis-à-vis those around me in dominant groups on my campus and in the field of higher education in general.

Understanding the subtle nuances of one's own identity can be an avenue to appreciating and advocating for the visibility of others. Thus, visibility in education abroad can be enhanced by both critical advocacy for others and introspection and visibility for ourselves.

Pathway to Action

Now that Sara Lawrence-Lightfoot has retired, her university has acknowledged her extraordinary service by naming the endowed chair that she held after her. She is the first African American woman in Harvard's history to have an endowed professorship named in her honor. Her liberating framework of View,

Voice, and Visibility is a powerful tool in the ongoing project of achieving social justice in education abroad. With this in mind, I offer the following questions as a guide to employing View, Voice, and Visibility in education abroad.

- View: In what ways can we reframe the view of critical social justice in education abroad? What is good, what is healthy, what is possible *for all students* in education abroad?

- Voice: How can we amplify the widest array of voices in education abroad so that we dismantle hierarchies and support educational equity and equal access?

- Visibility: How can we advocate for students to ensure that all students are visible? How can we interrogate our own biographies and advocate for ourselves so that we, too, are visible?

Lawrence-Lightfoot closed her talk by echoing the words of Jean Toomer: "'Whoever lifts himself/ Makes that great brown river smile'" (Jones and Latimer 1988, 50). She added: "So as I look out at you beautiful people…I want to celebrate the struggle, I want to honor the dissonance.…But mostly, I want to urge us to get busy, together, let's make the great brown river smile." I echo this call to action and encourage all colleagues in the field to use their privilege (as employed professionals with agency and heart) to use these frames to influence their own spheres of influence. As Beverley Daniel Tatum noted, it is important for us all to move beyond fear, anger, and other emotions to inspire others to "influence positive social change" (Jaschik 2017). In this regard, I hope this call will resonate within the field of education abroad, with the community responding with great vigor, because we are a group that values social justice, believes in honoring the individual dignity in all, and understands hard work.

References

Cole, Johnnetta Betsch. 1991. "Black Students and Overseas Programs: Broadening the Base of Participation." *Proceedings of CIEE 43rd International Conference on Educational Exchange: International Education: Broadening the Base of Participation.* Charleston, SC: Council on International Educational Exchange.

Contreras, Eduardo, Jr., Trixie Cordova, and Sara Spiegler. 2017. "The New F Word(s): Rethinking Access in the 21st Century." Presentation at the Forum on Education Abroad Annual Conference, Seattle, WA.

Contreras, Eduardo, Jr., Lily López-McGee, David Wick, and Tasha Willis. 2019. "Introduction: Virtual Issue on Diversity and Inclusion in Education Abroad." *Frontiers: The Interdisciplinary Journal of Study Abroad*, June 2019:1–6.

Diversity Abroad. n.d. "About Diversity Abroad." Diversity Abroad. https://www.diversityabroad.com/about.

Ellison, Ralph. (1947) 1995. *Invisible Man*. Reprint, New York: New York: Random House. Citations refer to the Random House edition.

Hamir, Heather Barclay, and Nick Gozik, eds. 2018. *Promoting Inclusion in Education Abroad: A Handbook of Research and Practice*. Sterling, VA: Stylus Publishing and NAFSA: Association of International Educators.

Hulstrand, Janet. 2016. "Increasing Diversity in Education Abroad." *International Educator* 25, 3:56–60.

Institute of International Education (IIE). 2005. *Open Doors, 1948–2004, Report on International Educational Exchange*. Institute of International Education.

Institute of International Education (IIE). 2018. "Student Profile." *Open Doors Report on International Educational Exchange*. Institute of International Education. https://www.iie.org/en/Research-and-Insights/Open-Doors/Data/US-Study-Abroad/Student-Profile.

Jaschik, Scott. 2017. "Updated Classic on Race Relations." *Inside Higher Ed.* September 6, 2017. https://www.insidehighered.com/news/2017/09/06/beverly-daniel-tatum-discusses-new-version-why-are-all-black-kids-sitting-together.

Jones, Robert B., and Margery Toomer Latimer, eds. 1988. "The Blue Meridian." In *The Collected Poems of Jean Toomer*. Chapel Hill, NC: University of North Carolina Press.

Lawrence-Lightfoot, Sara. 1983. *The Good High School: Portraits of Character and Culture*. New York, NY: Basic Books.

Lawrence-Lightfoot, Sara. 2017. "'Let the Great Brown River Smile.' Liberating Frames and Educational Discourses: On View, Voice, and Visibility." Distinguished Lecture at the American Educational Research Association Annual Meeting, San Antonio, TX. Published June 16, 2017. YouTube video, 47:33. https://www.youtube.com/watch?v=0qbGoo0N0lU.

López McGee, Lily, David Comp, and Eduardo Contreras. 2018. "Underrepresentation in Education Abroad: A Review of Contemporary Research and Future Opportunities." In *Promoting Inclusion in Education

Abroad: A Handbook of Research and Practice, eds. Heather Barclay Hamir and Nick Gozik. Sterling, VA: Stylus Publishing and NAFSA: Association of International Educators.

NAFSA: Association of International Educators. 2015. "NAFSA Diversity and Inclusion Statement." Washington, DC: NAFSA: Association of International Educators. http://www.nafsa.org/About_Us/About_NAFSA/Mission_and_Vision/NAFSA_Diversity_and_Inclusion_Statement.

NAFSA: Association of International Educators. 2018. *Strategic Plan 2018–2020*. Washington, DC: NAFSA: Association of International Educators. https://www.nafsa.org/about/about-nafsa/strategic-plan.

National Center for Education Statistics (NCES). 1996. "Table 202. Total Fall Enrollment in Institutions of Higher Education, by Type and Control of Institution and Race/Ethnicity of Student: 1976 to 1994." Washington, DC: National Center for Education Statistics Institute of Education Sciences. https://nces.ed.gov/programs/digest/d96/d96t202.asp.

National Center for Education Statistics (NCES). 2020. "Undergraduate Enrollment." Washington, DC: National Center for Education Statistics Institute of Education Sciences. https://nces.ed.gov/programs/coe/indicator_cha.asp.

The National Commission on Excellence in Education. 1983. *A Nation at Risk: The Imperative for Educational Reform*. Washington, DC: The National Commission on Excellence in Education.

Redden, Elizabeth. 2016. "'I, Too, Am Study Abroad.'" *Inside Higher Ed*. May 9, 2016. https://www.insidehighered.com/news/2016/05/09/suny-oswego-sees-success-diversifying-its-study-abroad-population.

Sensoy, Özlem, and Robin DiAngelo. 2012. *Is Everyone Really Equal? An Introduction to Key Concepts in Social Justice Education*. New York, NY: Teachers College Press.

Swaffield, Sue. 2017. "Reframing Views, Lifting Up Voices and Ensuring Everyone Is Visible?" *Professional Development in Education* 43, 4:493–496.

West, Charlotte. 2019. "Breaking Barriers to Study Abroad." *International Educator* 28, 4:30–35.

Willis, Tasha Y. 2015. "'And Still We Rise…': Microaggressions and Intersectionality in the Study Abroad Experiences of Black Women." *Frontiers: The Interdisciplinary Journal of Study Abroad* 26:209–230.

7

Social Justice-Centered Education Abroad Programming
Navigating Social Identities and Fostering Conversations

MALAIKA MARABLE SERRANO, MA

There are several definitions and interpretations of social justice. The definition that defines my work is "full and equal participation of all groups in a society that is mutually shaped to meet their needs. Social justice includes a vision of society that is equitable, and all members are physically and psychologically safe and secure" (Adams, Bell, and Griffin 2007, 1). In an education context, social justice sits at the center of inclusive pedagogy, which

> invites us to consider our choices around both the content we teach and the means through which we deliver it. Additionally, inclusive pedagogy argues that the social identities of both student and teacher have a direct impact on the learning experience. Self-awareness is therefore an important point of entry into inclusive pedagogical practice. (Georgetown University n.d.)

Working from this definition, it is clear that the social identities of all stakeholders—students, study abroad administrators, and faculty program leaders—influence education abroad program design, marketing and recruitment, orientation, program implementation, reflection, and reentry. Consequently, the students' identities and context of the program directly impact their education broad experience. No two students will have the same experience, and it is imperative for all stakeholders to recognize this reality.

Likewise, the identities of the teacher (or study abroad administrator) are central to the learning process and outcomes for the student. In 2018, Diversity Abroad issued a State of the Field Survey to assess the demographics and experiences of faculty and professionals who deliver international education experiences for higher education students. Seventy-one percent of the survey respondents identified as White and the remaining 29 percent identified as Black/African American, Hispanic/Latinx, Asian, Middle Eastern/Arab, or multiracial (Lopez-McGee 2018). These numbers closely mirror national statistics on the race and ethnicity of students who study abroad (Institute of International Education 2018). Social identities and the need for continuous self-reflection and awareness, as well as the discussions surrounding them, are the tenants of inclusive pedagogy.

This chapter begins with foundational definitions and theoretical frameworks around social justice, social identities, intersectionality, and deficit model thinking, as well as why those concepts are crucial to contemporary education abroad. The chapter then moves into the practice of creating brave spaces for students, faculty, and staff to engage in honest conversations around identity. Finally, it discusses inclusive program design considerations.

Storytelling is a tool that I use to model vulnerability and connect social justice and identity theories into my practice. Throughout the chapter, I share my experiences as an African American education abroad administrator and faculty program director. In keeping with the tenants of inclusive pedagogy, I believe that teachers and administrators need to be doing more of this: telling their stories through a diversity, equity, and inclusion lens. Of critical importance is the need to lift up and amplify the voices of international educators from minoritized social identities.

Identities

Names and naming stories can provide windows into our social identities—that is, a person's sense of who he or she is based on group membership(s). One of my favorite icebreaker classroom activities is to ask students to share the story of their name: What is your full name? Who named you and why? What is the meaning of your name? I then share the story of my name: In 1970, my father studied abroad for his junior year at the University of Nairobi in Kenya. While he was there, he heard a song called "Malaika" and said to himself, "If I ever have a daughter, I'm going to name her Malaika." I like to share the story of my name because it is rooted in, and ignited within me, a lifelong passion for discovering new people, places, ideas, and beliefs.

My Story

My social justice journey began nearly 20 years ago as a graduate student on a short-term faculty-led study abroad program. The course was on Afro-Brazilian culture, and we spent a month in Salvador, Brazil, learning basic Portuguese, meeting artists, practicing *capoeira* ("a Brazilian dance of African origin that incorporates martial arts movements"), and *candomblé*, ("an African-Brazilian religion combining African, Roman Catholic, and indigenous Brazilian elements") (Merriam-Webster 2019). In addition, we participated in a pre-Carnival celebration and *intercambios* (language and cultural exchanges) with local students.

From the minute I landed in Brazil until the moment I left, my race was no longer classified as "Black"; I had become "mulata." This was earth-shattering for me because for the first 22 years of my life, I had always self-identified as Black/African American. This racial identity was assigned to me before I was born and is prominently placed on my birth certificate. My "Blackness" is a source of pride, reinforced by my parents and family with messages of "Black is beautiful." It has also, however, been a source of pain in the form of microaggressions—being told, for example, that I was "very articulate for someone of my heritage." But in Brazil, suddenly my race had changed.

I desperately wanted to understand and process this experience with my professors and peers. Out of the 16 students on the program, only three of us self-identified as African American. I found great comfort in speaking about this shifting racial construction with my colleagues of color, for they too were going through a similar experience. However, when we brought this up during class, many of our classmates were dismissive and we received little support from our professors.

In retrospect, I now know that the entire class needed stronger preparation by the faculty program leaders around issues related to social identity construction in Brazil, in order to engage in conversations about race. My words are not meant to be disrespectful of the faculty members who led the program.

It is because of this program that I fell in love with Latin America and spent the following year teaching English in Venezuela. My story illustrates a serious issue that is not often discussed in the field of international education: Faculty members and study abroad administrators are often not adequately prepared or trained to engage in some of the difficult conversations related to social identities and the dynamics and changing nature of social identities in different contexts. This chapter intends to advance discussions on the need and opportunities for creating, promoting, and advocating for social justice-centered education abroad programs.

Social Justice and Education Abroad

The face of U.S. college students is rapidly changing. Today's college students do not fit the pervasive narrative of a "typical" college student. Nearly 45 percent of postsecondary students self-identify as students of color, nearly 40 percent receive Pell Grants, more than 45 percent are 21 years of age or older, and less than 50 percent live on campus (Bill and Melinda Gates Foundation 2019). The profile of study abroad participants is shifting as well and requires institutions to rethink their approaches to education abroad.

Study Abroad Participant Profile

Social justice-centered education abroad resonates strongly with Generation Z (Gen Z), who were born between 1997 and 2012 and are many of today's college students (Dimock 2019). Gen Z is the most racially and ethnically diverse generation in the United States (Parker, Graf, and Igielnik 2019). Gen Zers are likely to have friends from all over the world and have spent time researching their own identities abroad (e.g., Black in China, LGBTQ in Morocco, women in South Africa). They are more likely to know someone who uses gender-neutral pronouns and are generally more supportive of LGBTQ marriage and interracial relationships than previous generations (Parker, Graf, and Igielnik 2019). Many of these students are also coming to campus equipped with the language, agency, and expectations to have frank conversations around identity. This awareness is essential, given that students' identities have a direct impact on their learning experience, in the classroom and abroad.

The new reality of the changing college student population in the United States presents an urgent need to reevaluate the way education abroad programs have historically been constructed and how processes have traditionally been executed. Images of predominantly White or racially ambiguous, heterosexual, cisgender, upper-middle class, traditional-age students leave little room for alternative narratives. A social justice-centered approach to education abroad programming, however, will counter this mismatched narrative. To set the foundation for productive programs, education abroad administrators and faculty should begin integrating discussions around social identities into recruitment and predeparture orientations.

Social Identities

Social identities contribute to the formation of a person's sense of self, based on the individual's group membership(s) (Tajfel and Turner 2004) along certain characteristics such as sexual orientation, age, race, religion or spirituality, immigration status, first language, and other characteristics. People are told which group(s) they belong to, from the earliest stages of life onward. Group membership is reinforced by parents, family, neighbors, school, houses of worship, institutions, and the media, among other social and societal structures. Identities are, thus, socially constructed.

How identities "present" in a U.S. context might be different in another country and context—a divergence that many students may confront for the first time when they go abroad, as I did in Brazil. For example, identities that are most salient in the United States may not have the same level of salience in a different space. This difference in reception and emphasis can be particularly jarring to students, regardless of their racial or ethnic background, who visit or study in countries where their sense of racial and/or ethnic identity is challenged (e.g., a Korean American student is consistently told that they are Chinese or a White student in the Dominican Republic experiences becoming a racial minority for the first time). For international educators, understanding social identities can provide a holistic view of students who are from underrepresented backgrounds and their experience abroad.

In my own experience, my first awakening to the fluidity of social identity construction occurred during a semester abroad in Australia. Up until that point in my life, I had been told and socialized to believe that "all-American" was synonymous with "White, blond, and blue-eyed." However, when I landed in Australia, suddenly I was identified by my U.S. nationality first, and my race second. It was revolutionary, and from that point forward, I began to see and recognize my nationality as a salient identity in Australia.

I also lived in Venezuela from 2001 to 2002, during which time my national origin presented as Trinidadian, not someone from the United States. Why? Because in a Venezuelan context, a person with *café con leche* complexion and braids was not "all-American." I had people argue with me in confusion and disbelief that I was from the United States because my existence had disrupted their construction of the "American" image. These two examples underscore the impact of study abroad and international travel, not only for the participant but members of the host community as well.

Self-Reflection

Social identity exploration is the foundation of an inclusive mindset. For international educators, this means grounding our practice and attitude in an inclusive space. Before we can adequately advise students, we must start with ourselves and begin "unpacking" our social identities. Next, we must identify those affiliations that are most salient, the ones that frequently affect daily life. This identification is truly a process of continuous self-reflection. Tools such as the "Social Identity Wheel" (University of Michigan n.d.) or "My Multicultural Self" can be used by education abroad professionals, faculty, and students alike. Once the "unpacking" has taken place, we need to determine which of these identities are "visible" (e.g., race, gender) and which of these identities are "invisible" (e.g., sexual orientation, religious or spiritual affinity).

It can be tremendously impactful to both the faculty members and students, and boost their agency as they navigate a new context, if they have a better understanding of their own social identities, the identities that are both visible and invisible, the identities that are most salient in a U.S. context, and, finally, how all of these identities may "present" in the education abroad location. Faculty program leaders and in-country staff who support education abroad programs should engage in self-reflective work alongside the students. This recognition will create a feeling of openness, trust, and support for students, as well as foster an experience that is learner centered.

Figure 1. Identity in Global Contexts

Source: Serrano et al. (2019).

Figure 1 illustrates the social construction of race, ethnicity, and national origin. Each of these identities have been ascribed to me at one point in time: as a study abroad student, as a professional teaching English abroad, as a study abroad adviser participating on international site visits, and as a faculty program director in the Dominican Republic and Colombia. A similar exercise can be performed by study abroad administrators, students, and faculty program leaders to illustrate the fluidity and social construction of identities, which may be a new concept for many.

Intersectionality of Identities

Social identity theory opens the door to "intersectionality," which is a framework for conceptualizing a person, a group of people, or social problems that are rooted in historical and systemic oppression. Legal scholar Kimberlé Crenshaw (1989) coined the term "intersectionality" as a framework to describe the oppression of Black women, but it can be applied to other groups of people as well. A person's constellation of identities (figure 1) frames and shapes his or her interactions with the world and how the world views the individual. This theory acknowledges overlapping identities and experiences to understand the complexity of prejudices that people—in the case of Crenshaw, Black women—may face.

Marginalized identities are the ones we tend to think about most often, whereas privileged identities—"unearned benefits afforded to powerful social groups within systems of oppression"—are the ones we think about less often (Case, Iuzzini, and Hopkins 2012). Our marginalized and privileged identities shift depending on context. For example, in a U.S. context, my race (African American) and gender (cis woman) are my most salient identities. However, as a study abroad student in Australia, my nationality (American) quickly rose to become one of my most salient identities. My identities shifted again when, years later, I visited an exchange partner in South Africa. There, I learned that people with my complexion, generally those who have mixed-race ancestry, are assigned the racial category of "coloured," not "Black" as I had been accustomed to being labeled in the United States.

This was a lightning bolt moment for me. I had traveled and lived abroad on several continents, but I had never encountered a reclassification of my race before. Immediately, my mind started reeling. How am I preparing students for this reality? Other than my firsthand experience, what other resources are available? Is the wider education abroad community engaging in these types of discussions and reflections?

Support from the Field

Conversations about navigating social identities abroad have progressed in international education spaces. Additionally, national governments and higher education leaders alike are paying more attention to social identity dimensions and the underrepresentation of students from historically marginalized communities in education abroad (Aurora Universities 2018; Centennial College 2018; de Wit and Jones 2018; Institute of International Education 2018; Lincoln Commission 2005). NAFSA: Association of International Educators, the Diversity Abroad Network, the Forum on Education Abroad, and the

Institute of International Education (IIE) are just a few organizations that have made diversity and inclusion a priority in international education. These and other organizations support educators in preparing students to deal with issues surrounding their marginalized and privileged identities abroad.

NAFSA, Diversity Abroad, and others are also taking an inward look at the profession by exploring the identities of education abroad practitioners and faculty as well as lifting the question, "How can we diversify the profession?" In acknowledging that the demographics of the profession mirror the students who are going abroad, it invites dialogue around why over/underrepresentation exists and how to identify strategies to diversify the field. Intentional action around fostering more inclusivity in the education abroad profession will increase diversity of thought and experiences, which will positively benefit all students.

Deficit Model

Deficit model thinking is a framework that has been used in primary and secondary educational contexts for decades (Anzul et al. 2001; Han and Thomas 2010; McKay and Devlin 2016). Deficit thinking places the "blame of underachievement" on historically marginalized populations, without considering structural and institutional racism. With their own unconscious biases, some teachers and administrators may see only the "deficit" and discount and ignore the assets that marginalized and historically disadvantaged students have developed over a lifetime. Examples of deficit thinking in education abroad include the following:

- An adviser thinking, "If only the student's parents valued the study abroad experience…"

- A program director thinking, "If only the student didn't wait until the last minute, he or she could have found courses that fit with his or her major…"

- A financial aid administrator thinking, "If only the student started saving up sooner, he or she wouldn't have to drop out of the program due to financial constraints…"

Current discourse in education abroad around historically marginalized populations tends to center around students' deficits (e.g., financially disadvantaged, lacking family support, etc.). By framing the issue from a deficit perspective, it dismisses culpability from the institutions (e.g., about transfer credit, on using financial aid, etc.). However, when we are cognizant of deficit thinking and instead engage in critical assessment, we can reframe our programs and policies from a deficit model to a social justice-centered perspective. With this new frame, not only will the barriers to entry for education abroad participation be lowered for historically underrepresented populations, but all students will benefit from increased diversity of thought, life experiences, and expressions in conversations on the education abroad experience. Understandably, it may be an adjustment for some faculty, education abroad administrators, and other key stakeholders to adapt to this new way of thinking about underrepresented students in education abroad. However, if international education professionals maintain a learner-centered focus and position, it will truly be in the best interest of all students as they prepare for their international education experiences.

Social Justice Dialogue

Program directors and facilitators can create spaces for students to engage in respectful and honest social justice–centered dialogue in predeparture orientations, reentry workshops, and other forums. Arao and Clemens (2013, 139–140) offer a theoretical framework of ground rules for engaging in social justice dialogue that can be applied in education abroad spaces:

> authentic learning about social justice often requires the very qualities of risk, difficulty, and controversy that are defined as incompatible with safety....For agent group members, facing evidence of the existence of their unearned privilege, reflecting on how and to what degree they have colluded with or participated in oppressive acts, hearing the stories of pain and struggle from target group members, and fielding direct challenges to their world-view from target group members, and fielding direct challenges to their world-view from their peers can elicit a range of emotions, such as fear, sorrow, and anger...agent group impulse to

classify challenges to one's power and privilege as actions that detract from a sense of safety is, in itself, as manifestation of dominance.... People of color are then expected to constrain their participation and actions to confirm to White expectations of safety—itself an act of racism and White resistance and denial.

Arao and Clemens (2013) illustrate how detrimental a "safe space" can be for participants from historically underrepresented groups if it is formed without intentional thought. When ill-conceived, conversations in those spaces can actually reinforce dominance, in which case, rather than making progress toward understanding different experiences and points of view, a safe space can then potentially cause more harm to underrepresented students. Instead, international educators need to create brave spaces that open up dialogues on how social identities are socially constructed and fluid. In particular, in some contexts, students may be labeled and identified by the local contexts in ways that are unfamiliar to them.

In Arao and Clemens's (2013) Brave Spaces framework, the participants must adhere to the following conditions to engage in social justice-centered dialogue that is empowering for all students:

- Controversy with civility: Participants enter the conversation with an understanding that another party may say something they disagree with, but the discussion will be civil and respectful.

- Intentions and impact: Participants recognize and accept their contributions rather than not "taking things personally."

- Challenge by choice: Participants choose how far to challenge themselves; if participants are holding back, facilitators will respect their position and ask them to examine what is holding them back from challenging themselves.

- Respect: Participants are asked to describe what respectful dialogue looks like to them.

- No attacks: Participants are asked to describe what an attack might look like to them.

Facilitators can ask the group members whether they feel that the guidelines are appropriate and feasible. This shared agreement is fundamental for creating and maintaining trust. Facilitators may also want to open with a personal story or anecdote that supports the wider topic of discussion. By modeling vulnerability and demonstrating openness, facilitators can draw participants in and encourage them to share honestly, without fear of reprisal or being shamed.

Activation

International educators must develop social justice-centered education abroad programs with an inclusive mindset. When the community takes up a cause, the results can be profound. For example, not too long ago, science, technology, engineering, and mathematics (STEM) students were considered underrepresented in education abroad. The international education community rallied with conferences, workshops, countless sessions, articles, and other resources to educate administrators and faculty about the needs of serving this student population. The results have been amazing, with the percentage of STEM students going abroad at a record high of 25.5 percent in the 2016–17 academic year (IIE 2018). The education abroad community should rally around other historically marginalized groups in a similar way to see greater numbers going abroad.

Inclusive Program Design Considerations

When developing inclusive education abroad programs, faculty program directors should incorporate the following considerations into curricular and cocurricular, student recruitment, preparation, and reflection activities (Ledesma and Serrano 2019):

- Who is the education abroad program intended to serve? Will the program be accessible to all students? Does the program design effectively communicate respect for the diversity of identities represented among students, program leader(s), and the local community?

- What is the recruitment and outreach plan? Will the approach be collaborative? How are essential program requirements communicated? With whom?

- How will students' families be engaged during the study abroad application and predeparture orientation process?

- How will the program abroad foster community among participants, before, during, and after the experience?

- Does the course content reflect diversity in the local context? Are diverse authors reflected and cited in the required course reading? Do speakers represent a diversity of identities, perspectives, and viewpoints?

- Do cocurricular activities incorporate diverse experiences and learning environments? Are excursions accessible for all students?

- Will the program create a welcoming and affirming space for all students as they navigate shifting social identities in a cross-cultural environment? How will students be guided through emotionally intense learning experiences? Who will guide them?

Furthermore, to establish social justice-centered experiences, there are several questions education abroad professionals should consider from the outset regarding the student experience:

- What is the status of race/ethnic relations in the host country? How should students be prepared for differences in relations?

- What are the cultural attitudes toward sexual orientation and gender identity in the country?

- What are the implications of studying in a location that is (or is closely linked to) a student's family's country of origin? How will "heritage" students be perceived by the host culture?

- Are there required excursions that require a certain level of physical mobility to access?

- Is the cost of living higher, lower, or the same as the United States?

- How will students finance the program? What funding resources are available, and when are applications due?

- How will meals by taken? Are there opportunities for students to prepare their own meals?

- How difficult will it be to bring or obtain prescription medications?

- How difficult will it be to obtain products for all hair and skin types?

Case study exercises for inclusive program design that touch on these and other considerations can be found in Appendix A.

Program Implementation

I tried to incorporate these concepts in a study abroad program that I led to the Dominican Republic in 2014. The course was designed to examine social and racial inequalities from multinational perspectives: the Dominican Republic, Haiti, and the United States. Prior to arriving in the Dominican Republic, the students participated in two required predeparture orientation sessions, where they created group norms, engaged in several team-building exercises, and discussed social identities—first in a U.S. context and then the Dominican Republic context. The students spent a week engaging in literature and online discussion forums around several social justice issues, including poverty, education, race, and health care.

There was a connected strategy to the development of the program itself. By contracting with a study abroad provider who had an established partnership with community-based organizations in the Dominican Republic, service-learning was central to the course. The students applied scholarship to practice, used critical reflection to explore how one's experiences and identities inform approaches to addressing a wide range of social issues, and were introduced to asset-based strategies for combating social inequalities. From the predeparture discussions to the reflection work done in-country, the students and I created a community of trust that was critical to the success of the program and opened the door for important and, sometimes, difficult conversations around identity.

Conclusion

Social justice work is ongoing and can sometimes be intense. It is important for both facilitators and students to unpack and name the identities that are salient and recognize how these may shift in various contexts. Educators must show up fully, model vulnerability, and work toward fostering brave spaces in the classroom, at work, and in everyday life. This intentionality will foster a deep sense of trust between the facilitators and the students, as well as create psychologically safe environments to engage in healthy social justice dialogue.

References

Adams, Maurianne, Lee Anne Bell, and Pat Griffin, eds. 2007. *Teaching for Diversity and Social Justice, Second Edition*. New York, NY: Routledge.

Anzul, Margaret, Judith F. Evans, Rita King, and Dora Tellier-Robinson. 2001. "Moving Beyond a Deficit Perspective with Qualitative Research Methods." *Exceptional Children* 67, 2:235–249.

Arao, Brian, and Kristi Clemens. 2013. "From Safe Spaces to Brave Spaces: A New Way to Frame Dialogue Around Diversity and Social Justice." In *The Art of Effective Facilitation: Reflections from Social Justice Educators*, ed. Lisa M. Landreman. Sterling, VA: Stylus Publishing.

Aurora Universities. 2018. "Inclusive Internationalisation." Aurora Universities Network. https://aurora-network.global/project/inclusive-internationalisation.

Bill and Melinda Gates Foundation. 2019. "Today's College Students." Seattle, WA: Bill and Melinda Gates Foundation. https://postsecondary.gatesfoundation.org/what-were-learning/todays-college-students.

Case, Kim A., Jonathan Iuzzini, and Morgan Hopkins. 2012. "Systems of Privilege: Intersections, Awareness, and Applications." *Journal of Social Issues* 68, 1:1–10. http://dx.doi.org/10.1111/j.1540-4560.2011.01732.x.

Centennial College. 2018. *Inclusive Internationalization Summit: The Future of Transformative Learning*. Toronto, Ontario, Canada: Centennial College. https://p.widencdn.net/icactq/inclusive-internationalization-summit-program.

Crenshaw, Kimberlé. 1989. "Demarginalizing the Intersection of Race and Sex: A Black Feminist Critique of Antidiscrimination Doctrine, Feminist Theory and

Antiracist Politics." *University of Chicago Legal Forum* 1989, 1:Article 8. https://chicagounbound.uchicago.edu/cgi/viewcontent.cgi?article=1052&context=uclf.

de Wit, Hans, and Elspeth Jones. 2018. "Inclusive Internationalization: Improving Access and Equity." *International Higher Education* 94:16–18. https://ejournals.bc.edu/index.php/ihe/article/view/10561.

Dimock, Michael. 2019. "Defining Generations: Where Millennials End and Generation Z Begins." Washington, DC: Pew Research Center. https://www.pewresearch.org/fact-tank/2019/01/17/where-millennials-end-and-generation-z-begins.

Georgetown University. n.d. "Inclusive Pedagogy." Washington, DC: Georgetown University. https://commons.georgetown.edu/teaching/design/inclusive-pedagogy.

Han, Heejeong Sophia, and M. Shelley Thomas. 2010. "No Child Misunderstood: Enhancing Early Childhood Teachers' Multicultural Responsiveness to the Social Competence of Diverse Children." *Early Childhood Education Journal* 37, 6:469–476.

Institute of International Education (IIE). 2018. "Profile of U.S. Study Abroad Students, 2005/06–2016/17." *Open Doors Report on International Educational Exchange.* http://www.iie.org/opendoors.

Ledesma, Erica, and Malaika Serrano. 2019. "Inclusive Program Design and Pedagogy for Faculty-Led Programming." Presented at the WorldStrides ISA Custom Programs Summit, Chicago, Illinois.

Lincoln Commission. 2005. *Global Competence and National Needs: One Million Americans Studying Abroad.* Washington DC: Commission on the Abraham Lincoln Fellowship Program.

Lopez-McGee, Lily. 2018. *Survey of Diversity & Inclusion Among International Educators.* Berkeley, CA: Diversity Abroad. www.diversitynetwork.org/resource/resmgr/files/survey_of_diversity_among_in.pdf.

McKay, Jade, and Marcia Devlin. 2016. "Low Income Doesn't Mean Stupid and Destined for Failure: Challenging the Deficit Discourse Around Students from Low SES Backgrounds in Higher Education." *International Journal of Inclusive Education* 20, 4:347–363.

Merriam-Webster. 2019. "Candomblé." *Merriam-Webster Dictionary.* Retrieved from https://www.merriam-webster.com/dictionary/candomblé.

Merriam-Webster. 2019. "Capoeira." *Merriam-Webster Dictionary.* Retrieved from https://www.merriam-webster.com/dictionary/capoeira.

Parker, Kim, Nikki Graf, and Ruth Igielnik. 2019. "Generation Z Looks a Lot Like Millennials on Key Social and Political Issues." Washington, DC: Pew Research Center. https://www.pewsocialtrends.org/2019/01/17/generation-z-looks-a-lot-like-millennials-on-key-social-and-political-issues.

Serrano, Malaika, Sara Dart, Micaela Mathre, Suzanne Fils-Aime, Candace Ricks, and Lamar Shambley. 2019. "New Directions in Education Abroad: Talking Gen Z, Diversity and Inclusion and Career Readiness." Presented at the NYC International Educators April Meeting, New York, NY.

Tajfel, Henri, and John C. Turner. 2004. "The Social Identity Theory of Intergroup Behavior." In *Political Psychology: Key Readings*, eds. John T. Jost and Jim Sidanius. New York, NY: Psychology Press.

University of Michigan. n.d. "Social Identity Wheel." Ann Arbor, MI: College of Literature, Science, and the Arts University of Michigan. https://sites.lsa.umich.edu/inclusive-teaching/2017/08/16/social-identity-wheel.

Appendix A: Case Studies for Discussion in Faculty and Staff Workshops

Case study exercises for inclusive program design that can be used by education abroad advisers to facilitate interactive activities for faculty program leader workshops.

- A political science professor taking students to South Africa discovers that two openly gay students experienced street harassment when they were seen leaving a local establishment that is LGBTQ+ friendly. The students have expressed frustration with their classmates who can't understand why they're making a big fuss. How would you respond and why?

- The only African American student on a program in Argentina comes to her faculty member in tears due to the sexual harassment she is receiving from local men. A White, blond-haired, blue-eyed student overhears this and adds that she, too, has been the recipient of *piropos* (pickup lines) and the African American student just needs to "get over it." How would you respond and why?

- On a program in Spain, a history professor decides to give his students an impromptu four-day weekend. A group of students immediately make plans for a weekend getaway to Morocco. The professor notices one student standing off in the distance and asks if the student plans to join the others. The student sadly shakes his head and says that he cannot afford it. How would you respond and why?

8
Social Justice and Study Abroad at Historically Black Colleges and Universities
A Case Study of Howard University

TONIJA HOPE NAVAS, MA

When one enters the term "social justice" into the search field of the Howard University website, 10 pages of "hits" are revealed. Social justice is mentioned repeatedly on the web pages of the School of Social Work, the College of Divinity, and the School of Law. The term is included in the title of countless conferences and symposia hosted on campus, as well as in the online profiles of many faculty and staff members. It is intertwined into the fabric of the institution in explicit and implicit ways. What, then, does social justice mean at a historically Black college or university (HBCU)? And specifically, what does it mean at Howard University? In a 1973 address, the 13th president of Howard University, James Cheek (1973, 8), stated:

> If social justice means equity and parity in access to all of the opportunities, rewards, benefits and powers of the American society—and that is the test I apply—then this year the number of Black students enrolled in higher education would be approximately one million; but last year it was not even half a million.

President Cheek spoke of access to higher education as a measuring stick on issues of social justice for the country. Cheek (1973, 4) said, "Institutions such as Howard were founded to help this nation fulfill its promise as one nation, under God, indivisible, with liberty and justice for all. The task this university was founded to accomplish remains an unfinished task primarily because the promise this nation was created to keep remains an unfulfilled promise." According to Cheek, education was the vehicle to establish a more fair and just society in the United States, and failure to provide access to higher education for more African Americans signified that there was much more work to be done and that HBCUs should be at the forefront of that challenge.

Cheek's definition from the 1970s still rings true today and is echoed in more recent descriptions of social justice. Other educators and leaders throughout history have emphasized the link between social justice and access to education. Lee Anne Bell (2007, 1–2), professor emerita and former Barbara Silver Horowitz Director of Education at Barnard College, Columbia University, defines social justice as follows:

> [It is] both a process and a goal. The goal of social justice is full equal participation of all groups in a society that is mutually shaped to meet their needs. Social justice includes a vision of society in which the distribution of resources is equitable and all members are physically and psychologically safe and secure....The process for attaining the goal of social justice, we believe, should be democratic and participatory, inclusive and affirming of human agency and human capacities for working collaboratively to create change.

In an article from 2002, Joseph O. Jewell, a professor of sociology at Texas A&M University, stated:

> Beyond emancipation, access to education, particularly higher education, would forever transform the status of African Americans through the development of leadership and the articulation of a distinct social and political voice that placed a high value on matters of social justice and human equality. (Jewell 2002, 9)

During the era of slavery, teaching enslaved people of African descent to read and write was strictly prohibited. Thus, upon emancipation, most people of African descent sought an education. Scholar James D. Anderson, in his seminal piece *The Education of Blacks in the South, 1860–1935,* writes, "Virtually every account by historians or contemporary observers stresses the ex-slaves' demand for universal schooling" (Anderson 1988, 5). HBCUs are the result of African Americans' desire for higher education.

Historically Black Colleges and Universities

The term "historically Black college and university," or HBCU, was created by the Higher Education Act of 1965, a landmark piece of U.S. legislation, and defined as colleges and universities created prior to 1964 with the express purpose of educating people of African descent. As President Cheek stated, education provides access to all the opportunities, rewards, and benefits of American society, and HBCUs provide the access that can prepare individuals for positions of leadership across disciplines to lift the marginalized—whether their marginalization is due to their race, gender, religion, or, more recently, sexual orientation. From their founding, many HBCUs welcomed students from around the world. Howard University, for example, received students from China as early as 1870 (Logan 1969) and has maintained an international student population of between 7 and 15 percent over the years. Some of Howard University's most notable alumni were born abroad, including Kwame Toure (born Stokely Carmichael), Nnamdi Azikiwe, and its current president, Wayne A. I. Frederick.

With this history in mind, how do HBCUs translate their historical commitment to advancing social justice into a twenty-first-century paradigm? Pan-Africanism was born in the late nineteenth century and relied on the idea that Black people all over the world constitute a single nation and have a common destiny (Kasanda 2016). In the twenty-first century, it is not enough to think of social justice exclusively in the context of the United States; rather, social justice must be thought of in a global context as well, especially at an HBCU. The last part of Howard University's mission states that it is

> committed to the development of distinguished, historically aware, and compassionate graduates and to the discovery of solutions to human problems in the United States and throughout the world. With an abiding interest in both domestic and international affairs, the University is committed to continuing to produce leaders for America and the global community. (Howard University 2019)

This chapter examines Howard University's Ralph J. Bunche International Affairs Center's (RBC) approach of using global learning opportunities to address issues of social justice.

Ralph J. Bunche International Affairs Center

The RBC was founded in 1993, with former foreign service officer Julius Coles at the helm, followed by longtime director Horace Dawson, who also served as U.S. ambassador to Botswana. The RBC was primarily focused on programming around U.S. foreign policy and supporting the development of a more diverse group of future foreign service officers for the U.S. Department of State, ultimately leading to the creation of the Charles B. Rangel International Affairs Fellowship Program in 2002. The study abroad aspect of programming was incorporated into the work of the RBC years later. Today, the RBC houses not only the Rangel Fellowship but also the Thomas R. Pickering Foreign Affairs Fellowship and the Donald M. Payne International Development Graduate Fellowship, which serves the United States Agency for International Development. Additionally, thanks to a generous donation from Howard alumna Patricia Roberts Harris, the first Black female ambassador and the first Black female cabinet member, the RBC is able to offer the Patricia Roberts Harris Public Affairs Fellowship to Howard University students interested in a career in public affairs. Finally, the RBC organizes a range of global programming, often in collaboration with different departments, schools, and colleges, to complement classroom learning with presentations, symposia, conversations, and panels featuring experts, practitioners, and scholars from numerous fields.

A New Mission

When I arrived at the RBC in summer 2015, it had been without a director for almost four years. The foundation that had been built prior to my arrival provided a sturdy platform upon which to reimagine the RBC for a new generation of Howard University students. This new generation was connected via social media and had many and varied academic and professional interests. While the RBC's original mission of 1993 focused on international affairs specifically, nearly 20 years later, we wanted the new mission to reflect a more interdisciplinary approach to our work. The entire staff of the RBC worked with the university's executive director for strategic initiatives to develop a five-year strategic plan for the RBC, including a revised mission. Recognizing that there is no discipline that is not strengthened by the incorporation and appreciation of global perspectives, we set out to highlight the international efforts already under way across the university and provide support and coordination for increased global engagement with a revised mission for the Center. Collectively, the RBC team decided on the following mission statement:

> To serve as the hub and catalyst for enhancing international engagement for the benefit of the HU community. In doing so, the Center integrates global perspectives into the HU experience, promotes education abroad, facilitates deeper scholarship on global issues, supports cross-cultural dialogue and respect for cultural diversity, and prepares leaders who can find solutions to global problems. (Howard University n.d.)

The RBC continues to support the development of a more diverse group of future foreign service officers through the fellowship programs, but it also provides international programming that speaks to all disciplines across the institution through an annual lecture series and a robust programming calendar that reflects the current global landscape. The RBC aims to prepare students to navigate the increasingly interconnected world, with social justice at the forefront of our programs and activities. With this focus, the RBC set out to ensure that our global programs reflect our institution's values of access, equity, community, and social justice.

Global Perspectives

As international educators at an HBCU, we are acutely aware of global issues and challenges, particularly those affecting people of African descent around the world. We are, therefore, cognizant of the importance of providing broader and more enhanced perspectives through study abroad and on-campus global programming on these global issues and challenges to our students so they are well equipped to address them as they journey down their own paths. The opportunity to meet, interact with, and learn with and from those living amid some of these challenges provides our students with the proper context with which to seek the most appropriate resolutions. Providing our students with the chance to live and learn abroad is essential to their preparation as citizens of the twenty-first-century global community.

At the RBC, we often receive feedback from our students about feelings of exclusion from the predominantly Eurocentric nature of the curriculum on semester-long study abroad programs offered by other institutions and some study abroad providers. Often, our students choose to attend an HBCU because they are looking for a sense of inclusion that can come from courses that better reflect their own identity in an environment that celebrates their Blackness. Studying abroad through a program provider often means our students leave an HBCU environment and essentially enroll in a predominantly white institution for the semester or year. In a video produced for the RBC in 2018 (RBC 2018), some of our returned Howard University students spoke about their experiences on programs abroad with regard to their interactions with other students from the United States and how they felt they had to defend their identities to their white peers, educate them about African Americans and other people of color, and look beyond their program to find a sense of belonging. When studying abroad, our students must not only navigate a new country, unfamiliar cultural norms, and perhaps a new language; they also must navigate the racial dynamics among other U.S. students who may have had limited interaction with African Americans.

Howard University-CET Program

This feedback and the recognition of our students' challenges led us to conceive new programming ideas that would more fully address the needs and desires of Howard University students abroad. In designing our own study abroad program, we are responding to our students' interest in studying Blackness and social justice issues in a global context. For students to accomplish these dual goals, they need to have two sets of skills: (1) a social justice theoretical framework, and (2) language fluency to integrate fully into the host environment. Recognizing that we would benefit from a partner in developing this new program, RBC staff first met with CET Academic Programs leadership in spring 2016. CET is a prominent study abroad organization that occasionally partners with institutions to expand their education abroad options for students. CET leadership was open and enthusiastic about collaborating with Howard University to design a program that would interest to our students, as well as students from their other partner institutions. We invited Howard University faculty from various disciplines to discuss what a study abroad program inspired and designed by our university, an HBCU, would look like. The result was the Howard University-CET program Race, Ethnicity and Identity in Colombia, based in Cali, Colombia. The program is a semester-long, academic credit-bearing program that combines classroom and experiential learning. Students have the opportunity to engage with Afro-Colombian and Indigenous communities, thus complementing their classroom learning by allowing them to hear directly from members of those communities about their lives, successes, challenges, goals, and objectives.

Our priority was to develop an experience abroad centered around students' expressed interest in a program that highlights the Black experience of their host country. An environmental scan revealed that there were few study abroad providers operating programs in Colombia, and none with an Afro-Colombian focus. The second strategic priority was that Afro-Colombian professors would teach the core courses. It was important that a Howard University-designed program feature Black professors from the host country for two main purposes: First, we wanted students to learn from members of the Afro-Colombian community directly. Second, we wanted to draw more attention to the fact that there is a dearth of Black professors in Colombian higher education, in hopes that it would spark a conversation and lead to increased hiring of Black faculty.

Colombia in Context

Howard University chose Colombia as the host country for two main reasons. First, we wanted a country with a significant Black population since the goal was to center the Black experience. Second, we wanted a country whose official language was not English to allow students to strengthen their foreign language skills. Colombia offered both of these things and more.

Like the United States, Colombia (and the rest of Latin America) was an active participant in the transatlantic slave trade. It has been estimated that between 5 and 10 million Africans were forcefully brought to the Spanish and Portuguese colonies between the sixteenth and nineteenth centuries (Andrews

2004). According to 2005 census data, 10.6 percent of the population in Colombia self-identified as Afrodescendant (World Bank 2018). As with many countries in Latin America, it is difficult to accurately calculate the number of Black people in the population because of varying definitions of identity. Luis Gilberto Murillo Urrutia, the former governor of the state of Choco, said in a 2007 article for *Dollars and Sense* that "Afro-Colombians make up 36-40% of Colombia's people although the government says it's only 26% (or about 11 million people)" (Bacon 2007). An accurate accounting of the Black population is crucial to ensuring that resources are made available to Black communities, opportunities are equitably available, and education and healthcare reach those who traditionally have been excluded.

Almost every indicator points to disparities between Afrodescendants and the white/mestizo population in Colombia. For example, Afrodescendants make up 22 percent of the population living in Colombia's slums, compared with only 8 percent of whites/mestizos (World Bank 2018). The unemployment rate for Afrodescendants is 8.3 percent, compared with 6.4 percent for whites/mestizos, and only 35.5 percent of Afrodescendants complete secondary school, compared with 42.4 percent of whites/mestizos (World Bank 2018). In Colombia, completing tertiary education can reduce the likelihood of Afrodescendants being poor by between 21 and 31 percent; however, only 6.2 percent of Afrodescendants complete tertiary education, compared with 10.6 percent of whites/mestizos (World Bank 2018).

Cali, Colombia, is one of the cities in South America with a majority Black population and serves as the epicenter of Afro-Colombian culture for the Pacific coast. The civil war that engulfed Colombia for more than 50 years disproportionately affected people of African descent in rural areas. As a result, many Afro-Colombians have moved to Cali from other parts of the Pacific coast to escape the conflict in the more rural areas of the region. It is in this setting, in a city that is overwhelmingly and characteristically Black, that we wanted to create a study abroad program for mutual exchange and learning that centers the experience of Afro-Colombians.

With these considerations, we identified Universidad del Valle (UniValle), a public institution, considered one of the best in Colombia, as the host university. In 2014, then-president Juan Manuel Santos mandated that all public universities should seek to internationalize to improve the competitiveness of their universities (La W Radio 2014). As such, when our Howard-CET partnership approached UniValle about establishing a program, we were received warmly. Administrators and professors at UniValle were enthusiastic and worked with us to design a program that met our expectations.

Challenges of Developing the Program

Even with the best intentions, we faced two significant challenges in designing and establishing the program. First, much like in the United States, faculty from diverse backgrounds are difficult to find in Colombia. We had challenges identifying English-speaking, Black faculty to teach the core courses. Second, we had envisioned the program as a fully immersive program with U.S. and Colombian students in classes together. For that to be a reality would require that either the Colombian students speak English or the U.S. students speak Spanish at sufficient levels to take a class. We were unable to enroll U.S. students with a high level of Spanish proficiency, and few Colombian students speak English at the necessary level.

Faculty Leaders

A 2015 study coauthored by Afro-Colombian scholar Carlos Augusto Viáfara Lopez of UniValle reported that Afro-Colombians are overrepresented in primary and secondary education at a rate of 82 percent, compared with just 30 percent of non-Afro-Colombians. In higher education, however, Afro-Colombians represent only 9.7 percent, compared with 27 percent for non-Afro-Colombians (Viáfara and Serna 2015). With low representation in higher education, the proportion of Afro-Colombian university professors is also low, which created a challenge in finding an Afro-Colombian professor with a doctoral degree who could teach a full semester in English.

The push for an Afro-Colombian professor was also an effort to get UniValle to realize that it needed more Black professors on its faculty. UniValle leadership had only one person in mind for consideration, but that professor's English language skills were limited. We did eventually find a professor external to the university who was available and happened to have just received his PhD from Howard University in 2018. Other professors taught in the program and received positive student feedback. The absence of Afro-Colombians in the classroom was addressed by including more interactions outside the classroom through programming in and around Cali and beyond.

Language Barriers

A second challenge in the development of the program was related to language fluency. Initially, our goal was to recruit students with advanced levels of Spanish proficiency to allow for the U.S. and Colombian students to engage in deep, intellectual conversations about the Afro-Colombian experience and, conversely, the Black experience in the United States. We wanted to have one class where Afro-Colombian students and our North American students could learn together in Spanish. However, we were not able to enroll enough U.S. students with advanced Spanish proficiency. Similarly, learning English in Latin America is usually reserved only for those who can afford private lessons; therefore there was also a barrier for Colombian students to participate. To meet our overall goals and address this language issue, we decided to lower the prerequisite Spanish level to make it accessible to more U.S. students.

As international education professionals, we work to provide opportunities for our students to live and learn abroad because we believe that the interactions with individuals from the host country will provide firsthand understanding of their lived experiences. But what happens if there is a language barrier, as is often the case with education abroad? North Americans are widely known for being monolingual. According to the American Community Survey, between 2008 and 2010, English was the primary language spoken in the home by 79.7 percent of U.S. residents (Commission on Language Learning 2017).

Recognizing that many students from the United States do not have the advanced levels of Spanish that we had hoped, the Howard-CET Cali program was created to allow for immersive language learning hosted in a predominantly Black city through a program that centers the Black experience. The overarching thought is that recognizing and understanding that there are Black people in Colombia with similar challenges, successes, opportunities, and limitations who speak Spanish will encourage our students to invest in improving and mastering their Spanish language skills to be able to work together across national boundaries to support each other in the future.

Collaboration Across Barriers

The ability to communicate with people around the globe in their own language will become increasingly important as societies become more interdependent and interconnected. For people of African descent, who are dispersed around the world and who often speak many languages other than English, learning another language will be a vital tool in the work of collective and continued uplift. Eight of the 10 countries outside of Africa with the largest populations of people of African descent are in the Western Hemisphere, the largest being Brazil; only three of the 10 countries are Anglophone countries (Migiro 2018). To develop a more comprehensive understanding of the issues and concerns facing people of African descent around the world, it is imperative to communicate directly with them, wherever they are.

What are the benefits that arise from active communication among people of African descent? As an example, Black Lives Matter is a social justice movement born in the United States that has a global reach. Its mission is "to build local power and to intervene in violence inflicted on Black communities by the state and vigilantes" (Black Lives Matter n.d.). Statistics show that in the United States, Black people receive longer prison sentences than white people, and Black men are 2.5 times more likely than white men to be shot by police (Edwards, Lee, and Esposito 2019). The Black Lives Matter movement seeks to bring more attention and justice to these issues. Though originating in the United States, the reach of the movement has surpassed national boundaries, and students in the program who were engaged with UniValle's Black student organization, CADUBHEV, regularly discussed common issues and movements, such as Black Lives Matter.

People of African descent around the world working on issues that affect their local communities have shown solidarity with this U.S. movement because the same issues can be found where they live. The impact of Black people from North America coming together with Black people from Latin

America in a more formal, coordinated way to address these shared disparities could be significant, but language barriers can inhibit this solidarity. North Americans of African descent do not speak Spanish or Portuguese in significant numbers and, similarly, people of African descent in Latin America do not speak English in significant numbers because of cost-prohibitive English language instruction. There exists an opportunity to build solidarity around these common concerns, but people must be able to talk to each other directly and without intermediaries to find commonalities across different sectors of life, including health, education, and business.

Cultural Context in Language

Technical language fluency alone is not enough; the context of language is equally important. On a recent Howard University faculty-led program to Cali, Colombia, the group worked with an American woman to translate during the program. Although she was not a professional interpreter, the woman had been living in Cali for several years and was somewhat familiar with Afro-Colombian culture. She was fluent in Spanish, but as a cultural outsider, she was not aware of the specific, racialized vocabulary that is part of the local dialect. During a meeting, for example, she interpreted "*cimarron*" as "cinnamon, the spice." In actuality, "*cimarron*" is the Spanish word used to describe Africans who had escaped from being enslaved. In the Afro-Colombian community, this word is well known and it would not have been interpreted that way by someone who is more familiar with Afro-Colombian history and culture. The ability to communicate directly with cultural context is key.

Because of the low numbers of African American foreign language majors in the United States, there is also a lack of professional interpreters of African descent. It is important for our students to learn a language with relevant cultural context. The Howard-CET Cali program is intended to entice students of color, primarily, to study abroad and truly engage with host country nationals in Spanish to get a full understanding of what it means to be a person of African descent in Colombia. The stronger the communication among Colombian and U.S. students, the more profound their connections will be.

We hope that connection will, in turn, encourage them to work collectively toward more equitable and just societies in both countries.

Program Successes

For the program's inaugural spring 2019 semester, there were seven participants: two from Howard University and the others from Princeton, the University of Massachusetts-Amherst, and Yale. All of the participants were students of color, either African American or Latinx. During the fall 2019 program, there were seven participants again, but this time, there were four African American students and three white students. Among them were five women and two men, and all four African American students were female. White students were always welcome and in fact desired. They were part of the original vision. To achieve the goal of social justice, we must have white allies. We envisioned this program as a way to build allyship with white students so they better understand some of the issues that Black people face, both in the United States and abroad. The program would give them a sense of being the "other," an experience that Black students face regularly.

Despite some of the challenges that we experienced in setting up the program, Gyselle Garcia, part of the Howard University class of 2020 and a member of the inaugural program cohort, found great value in the program. She wrote:

> I didn't just learn in the classroom; I didn't just learn on campus. I learned on the bus, waiting for the bus, on the street, at the mall. I didn't just learn from professors, I learned from women and men selling *chontaduro* on corners, from the "assistants" to bus drivers who hang out of side doors rallying customers then counting bus fare once they've boarded. Learning was constant and I was grateful. Because little by little I went putting pieces together, and was able to connect with *Caleños* in an entirely different way. When I listened, everything was in communication with me. What I heard convinced me Cali wants people to know and feel the deep history of the space. It truly is an epicenter and I woke up most days extremely eager to get out because I knew even after creating a routine, no day would be the same.

When we designed the Howard-CET Cali Program in Colombia, we did so with the understanding that the learning would happen in the classroom from professors, but also through students' interactions with their host national roommates, the women who braid hair and sell sweets, the student leaders at the university, and the people selling *chontaduro* on the corners, just as Garcia describes. We wanted students to begin to understand what life is like for a person of African descent in another setting, in a country like Colombia. We wanted them to make connections between issues that people of African descent in both the United States and Colombia face and to see where there are synergies for support and solidarity across borders. Ultimately, the road to social justice is paved with understanding, and this experience provided a heightened level of understanding for the U.S. students on the program as well as for the Colombian students with whom they engaged.

By the end of her first semester back at Howard University, Garcia had maintained contact with her classmates at UniValle. As president of Chango, the Afro-Latin student organization at Howard University, Garcia collaborated on a proposal for an exchange to enable Afro-Colombian students from UniValle—namely, the members of CADUBHEV, the Black student organization there—to spend a month at Howard University in 2020. She believes that the students' experience in Washington, D.C., and at Howard University specifically, will contribute greatly to their development as students, activists, and professionals and promote further cross-cultural learning and understanding across groups.

Takeaways

We were pleased that CET Academic Programs was open to collaborating with us to develop this program. As an HBCU, we work with students of color every day to encourage participation in programs abroad and to improve their experience once there. But our approach, centering the experience of historically marginalized peoples, can be applicable to program designers at predominantly white institutions (PWIs) as well as other program providers. When developing programs with students of color in mind, it is important to be conscious of the unique history of racism and discrimination in a host country and how and by whom that history is shared in a classroom. At Howard University, for this program, we were intentional about seeking Afro-Colombian professors to ensure that our students hear authentic local voices to reinforce the goals of the program.

As PWIs and program providers continue to seek to diversify study abroad, they should identify who is missing from participants and talk to them. Find out what types of programs would interest them. But beyond that, ask students who have returned from study abroad about issues to address to improve the experience. Use that information to design a program for those people. Consider partnering with an HBCU or other minority-serving institutions (MSI) to design and implement a program. HBCUs and other MSIs have unique expertise in working with communities of color that could be beneficial to PWIs that may lack diversity in their study abroad offices but are looking to be more inclusive of their students of color.

Conclusion

"Social justice" is a term that is used in a variety of contexts and has different meanings for different people. At Howard University, in the context of study abroad, "social justice" means providing access and opportunities for our students and students at the host institution to share their experiences and broaden their perspectives so they can coordinate and collaborate to collectively advance issues of equity, access, and inclusion in both countries.

Programs like the Howard University-CET collaboration shine a light on the importance of cultural context in program development and the need for stronger language learning. The challenges and outcomes of this particular program demonstrate the importance of language education and cultural context for people of African descent in both countries. It also demonstrates to the university community worldwide the need for more faculty of African descent. Ultimately, we hope this program will build lasting bridges between the two countries that will allow students on both sides to identify new ways of working, growing, and prospering together.

References

Anderson, James D. 1988. *The Education of Blacks in the South, 1860–1935*. Chapel Hill, NC: The University of North Carolina Press.

Andrews, George Reid. 2004. *Afro-Latin America: 1800–2000*. Oxford, United Kingdom: Oxford University Press.

Bacon, David. 2007. "Blood on the Palms." *Dollars and Sense* 271. http://www.dollarsandsense.org/archives/2007/0707bacon2.html.

Bell, Lee Anne. 2007. "Theoretical Foundations for Social Justice Education." In *Teaching for Diversity and Social Justice: A Sourcebook, Second Edition*, eds. Maurianne Adams, Lee Ann Bell, and Pat Griffin. New York, NY: Routledge.

Black Lives Matter. n.d. "About." Black Lives Matter. https://blacklivesmatter.com/about/.

Cheek, James E. 1973. "In Pursuit of Social Justice: The Unfinished Business of the Nation and the Unfinished Business of Howard." *The Writings of James Cheek*. https://dh.howard.edu/cheekwrit/1/.

Commission on Language Learning. 2017. *America's Languages: Investing in Language Education for the 21st Century*. Cambridge, MA: American Academy of Arts and Science. https://www.amacad.org/sites/default/files/publication/downloads/Commission-on-Language-Learning_Americas-Languages.pdf.

Edwards, Frank, Hedwig Lee, and Michael Esposito. 2019. "Risk of Being Killed by Police Use of Force in the United States by Age, Race-Ethnicity, and Sex." *Proceedings of the National Academy of Sciences of the United States of America* 116, 34:16793–16798.

Howard University. n.d. "About Ralph J. Bunche Center." http://global.howard.edu/ralph-j-bunche/about-ralph-j-bunche-center-2.

Howard University. 2019. "Mission & Core Values." https://www2.howard.edu/about/mission.

Jewell, Joseph O. 2002. "To Set an Example: The Tradition of Diversity at Historically Black Colleges and Universities." *Urban Education* 37, 1:7–21.

Kasanda, Albert. 2016. "Exploring Pan-Africanism's Theories: From Race-Based Solidarity to Political Unity and Beyond." *Journal of African Cultural Studies* 28, 2:179–195.

La W Radio. 2014. "Santos acogió propuesta sobre la política de educación superior para 2034." La W Radio. April 8, 2014. https://www.wradio.com.co/noticias/actualidad/santos-acogio-propuesta-sobre-la-politica-de-educacion-superior-para-2034/20140804/nota/2352991.aspx.

Like, Robert C., Theresa J. Barrett, and Jeffrey Moon. 2008. "Educating Physicians to Provide Culturally Competent, Patient-Centered Care." *Perspectives: A View of Family Medicine in New Jersey* 7:10–20.

Logan, Rayford W. 1969. *Howard University: The First Hundred Years, 1867–1967*. New York, NY: NYU Press.

Migiro, Geoffrey. 2018. "Where Is the African Diaspora?" *WorldAtlas*. May 24, 2018. https://www.worldatlas.com/articles/where-is-the-african-diaspora.html.

National Center of Education Statistics. 2018. "Table 302.60. Percentage of 18- to 24-Year-Olds Enrolled in College, by Level of Institution and Sex and Race/Ethnicity of Student: 1970 Through 2017." *Digest of Education Statistics*. Washington, DC: U.S. Department of Education. https://nces.ed.gov/programs/digest/d18/tables/dt18_302.60.asp.

Ralph J. Bunche International Affairs Center (RBC). 2018. "Howard Student Voices: The Intra Group Experience of Study Abroad Final." https://www.youtube.com/watch?v=A_8mALsbRmg&t=13s.

Viáfara, Carlos, and Nini Serna. 2015. "Desigualdad de oportunidades educativas en la población de 15 a 29 años en Brasil y Colombia según autoclasificación étnico-racial." *Sociedad y Economía* 29:151–174.

The World Bank. 2018. *Afro-Descendants in Latin America: Toward a Framework of Inclusion*. Washington, DC: World Bank. https://www.worldbank.org/en/region/lac/brief/afro-descendants-in-latin-america.

9
Supporting Deaf Students in Education Abroad[1]

BECCA ABURAKIA-EINHORN, MPA

According to the Institute of International Education's (2019) *Open Doors Fast Facts* report, "341,751 U.S. students participated in study abroad programs for academic credit, a 2.7 percent increase over the previous year." Although this number may seem small in the context of the U.S. population, 16 percent of U.S. students pursuing a bachelor's degree will participate in study abroad during their undergraduate experience, and according to data from the *Open Doors* report, this percentage continues to grow each year (IIE 2019). As international experiences become essential building blocks of a global mindset desired by many employers, it is all the more important that these beneficial international opportunities become accessible to *all*.

Deaf people do travel, both on their own and with Deaf travel agencies that take Deaf Americans to international locations and provide accessible tours. But when it comes to the type of sojourns we traditionally understand as part of education abroad—receiving credit, traveling abroad with a faculty member or program provider, and enrolling directly at a foreign college, among others—these formal opportunities are generally inaccessible.

I manage the education abroad and international fellowship program at Gallaudet University, the premier institution of learning, teaching, and research for deaf, deafblind, and hard of hearing (d/db/hoh) students. Most of our students identify as deaf, deafblind, and hard of hearing, and it is my responsibility and honor to find international education opportunities that are accessible to our students.

There is significant diversity among the Deaf community as well as different ways of understanding and talking about deafness. Throughout this chapter, I use the word "deaf" with a lowercase *d* as well as "Deaf" with a capital *D*. According to Padden and Humphries's (2003, 2) *Deaf in America: Voices from a Culture*, "We use the lowercase deaf when referring to the audiological condition of not hearing, and the uppercase Deaf when referring to a particular group of deaf people who share a language—American Sign Language (ASL)—and a culture." For a complete guide to the definitions for some of the terminology used by the diverse members of the Deaf community, I recommend the National Association of the Deaf's (2020) "Community and Culture—Frequently Asked Questions."

Some deaf individuals do not consider deafness to be a disability; rather, deafness is a cultural identity. However, from a legal perspective, a deaf or hard of hearing student is considered to have a disability, and generally needs to be registered with the office of students with disabilities to obtain accommodations on campus. For a basic explanation of the different models of deafness, I recommend the Canadian Hearing Services's explanation of Models of Deafness (Canadian Hearing Services 2015).

Although we do have a number of deafblind students at Gallaudet, I use the term "deaf and hard of hearing (d/hoh) students" throughout the chapter, acknowledging that not all of the suggestions below will suffice for a deafblind student.

While I work daily with d/hoh students, I am a hearing person. I cannot truly understand the Deaf experience. I can, however, provide advice to hearing advisers, like myself, who find themselves in a position to support one or more Deaf students on their campuses. Recognizing our own identities and acknowledging that they are different from those of our students is an essential part of the advising process. When our students hold an identity that is different from one we hold ourselves, it means that listening must be our first step and we should learn how to practice responsible allyship. With a social justice framework, at times we can best

> contribute by creating space for students of marginalized identities to step into opportunities to which they did not previously have access. In my work at Gallaudet, I seek to increase access to education abroad programs for deaf, hard of hearing, and deafblind students so that in turn they can take their experience and use it to open doors and build more opportunities designed and directed by their own community.

Although the current education abroad opportunities available to d/hoh students are few and far between, there are concrete things that we as education abroad advisers can do to support these students and build bridges with study abroad program providers to increase accessible opportunities. In this chapter, I provide advice for advisers who are working with a d/hoh student, perhaps for the first time. By understanding Deaf students' needs and strengths, providing them with additional resources and support, and finding ways to pay for reasonable accommodations (e.g., adjustments, services, adaptations, modifications necessary for equal access), we can make study abroad more inclusive and equitable and bring a social justice lens into our work as educators.

Social justice is often defined in terms of equal access to opportunities. For education abroad, that would mean ensuring that all students can apply for and participate in a broad array of programs. While increasing the number of programs that d/hoh students can join would be a welcome change, we have to think broader than "equal access." To truly bring a social justice framework to our work in education abroad, we must build programs in which all students have an equal opportunity to succeed.

Opportunities for Change

My experience trying to find programs for students at Gallaudet has opened my eyes to the many obstacles that limit accessibility to education abroad programs, but it has also shown me that there are tremendous opportunities for change in the field. To bring about this change, we must understand the challenges facing d/hoh students, realize the strengths that make these students uniquely suited for education abroad, and learn more about what we can do to support their participation in programs.

As the percentage of students who study abroad increases alongside the demand for professionals with global experience, it is critical that d/hoh students are given the opportunity—as a matter of equity and career preparation—to fully participate in international programs. My experience working with students at Gallaudet has shown that with some creativity and adaptation, most overseas education programs can, in fact, be made accessible and valuable to these students.

When working with any student from an underrepresented group, it is understandable that some advisers may be nervous about supporting such a student to study abroad and may also underestimate the student's potential adaptability. The insights and practical recommendations in this chapter are designed to help advisers and study abroad program providers serve the d/hoh student community. However, while d/hoh students will always make up a relatively small portion of the students who study abroad, the content in this chapter can be useful for advising any student from a marginalized background who may not be served by existing processes and structures in the field of education abroad. By employing these tactics and changing our perspectives as advisers, we can bring about more social justice in international education.

Barriers to Accessibility

Currently, there are few education abroad programs accessible to d/hoh students, and the majority of students and advisers are unfamiliar with the ones that do exist. Moreover, most advisers are hearing people and receive, at most, a handful of applications from d/hoh students cross their desks throughout their careers. The average education abroad adviser's knowledge of this community's specific needs is sparse or nonexistent.

While there is a good (although still insufficient) amount of advice regarding supporting students with disabilities generally, the research, data, and articles that specifically focus on education abroad for d/hoh students are virtually nonexistent. This is a problem because d/hoh students need particular accommodations, which require specialized knowledge, and the costs of interpreters and speech-to-text services are higher than accommodations needed for many other disabilities. Moreover, examples of successful initiatives or approaches are scarce; there are exceedingly few universities offering programs designed for ASL users or ASL learners, or study abroad program providers who are willing or able to pay for the full on-site accommodations that d/hoh students need to participate and succeed academically.

Increasing access to education abroad for d/hoh students requires additional research (with the full participation of individuals from the Deaf community) in several areas, from advising approaches to program design to cost. The existing literature focuses too broadly on working with students with disabilities as if they are a homogeneous group—not distinguishing between different disabilities and the accommodations needed by certain students. A social justice approach requires us to recognize that even the subgroups we are working with (students of color, students with disabilities, etc.) are themselves made up of a diversity of sub-identities with unique backgrounds and needs.

Typically, education abroad offices begin to research access only when a specific student approaches them (sometimes with an eye on a specific program). This means that study abroad advisers and departments are focused on the "needs of a particular student applying for a particular study abroad site," rather than institutionalizing lessons learned or planning ahead for increased general access (Soneson and Cordano 2009, 270). Education abroad offices and program providers are then playing a game of "catch up" rather than attempting to design programs with the expectation that programs will inevitably include a diverse group of students with a variety of unique needs.

There are a number of reasons why the typical design of an education abroad program makes it inaccessible for many d/hoh students. Students who predominantly use ASL to communicate will find few education abroad opportunities accessible to them. This is in part because many education abroad programs are designed for foreign language learning. While d/hoh students can indeed learn other written and spoken languages (as opposed to other sign languages), they generally need a more specialized environment for this type of learning. Even when programs are offered in English (and do not require applicants to possess foreign language abilities), a d/hoh student who communicates predominantly in ASL will require one or two ASL interpreters in the classroom (depending on the number of hours of interpretation needed).

Outside the United States, beyond a handful of international interpreting agencies, it is difficult to find ASL interpreters since almost every country has one or more of its own unique sign languages and local interpreters are trained in local sign languages. If interpreters cannot be found locally, they must be provided from the United States and require housing and food, alongside interpreters' payment. Additionally, interpreters and speech-to-text services cannot realistically be provided 24 hours a day. In practice, such services are often limited to the classroom, which means that d/hoh students may lack access after-hours or feel uncomfortable adventuring out on their own. These are just some of the programmatic and financial questions that advisers, program planners, and students need to address together when d/hoh students embark on education abroad experiences.

The financial implications for both the institutions and the students can often affect accessibility as well. While it can be relatively costly to accommodate d/hoh students who go abroad, it is far from impossible. The cost should not be the main reason that prevents d/hoh students from studying abroad (as opposed to issues of safety, mental health, and degree fit, among other reasons).

Accommodations on Overseas Programs

One reason why study abroad remains elusive for d/hoh students is that the legal protections they have in the United States do not extend to overseas programs. All institutions receiving federal funding are required, under Section 504 of the Rehabilitation Act of 1973, to be accessible to d/hoh students. Although obtaining accommodations can still be a difficult or imperfect process for students at higher education institutions, it is legally required inside the United States. Students who prefer to learn in ASL can request interpreters in the classroom, while other students may request speech-to-text services if they prefer to learn in English but cannot hear the professor or their classmates perfectly. These are two of the main accommodations d/hoh students may request, but there are plenty more options, including note takers, captioned videos, and certified deaf interpreters, among others.

While d/hoh students have access to these accommodations in the United States, there has yet to be a definitive court case demonstrating that the Americans with Disabilities Act (ADA) and the Rehabilitation Act apply broadly and, in all respects, to education abroad programs sponsored by U.S. colleges and universities (Charney and Whitlock 2012). This means that d/hoh students are not guaranteed access to interpreters or speech-to-text services (as well as other accommodations) for abroad programs, even when operated by U.S. colleges and universities (Close 2001). Moreover, even when colleges or program providers are willing to make arrangements for accommodations, these services can be so prohibitively expensive to obtain (and often the student is asked to shoulder the financial burden) that the program is still inaccessible for many d/hoh students. When some students have to pay significantly more just to gain basic access to a program, it is an issue of social justice. As Holben and Malhotra (2018, 111) state:

> Regardless of where evolving laws stand, it is imperative for institution administrators to strategize how they will fully include students with disabilities in international education, motivated not only by a desire to comply with basic legal requirements for nondiscrimination but also by a stronger desire to be thought of as leaders and innovators supporting the most underserved students so that all students are given an opportunity to reach their full potential.

Limitations of Accommodations

A d/hoh student without full accommodations does not reap the full benefits that we know an education abroad program can bring to an individual's personal and professional growth. For these students, it is not enough to help them apply for and enroll in a program and provide the minimum accommodations that allow them to participate academically and socially. We must ensure they have the same opportunity their hearing peers have to thrive abroad.

However, given the high cost of providing interpreters and speech-to-text services for a study abroad program, as well as the difficulty of finding ASL interpreters abroad, sometimes d/hoh students settle for accommodations that do not provide enough communication access for them to be successful. For example, speech-to-text services, though still costly, are easier to provide than interpreters because these services can be done by on-site staff or remotely. There are often instances in which a deaf student is provided speech-to-text services for a study abroad program, even though the student uses ASL interpreters on the home campus and the student's preferred language of communication is ASL. Additionally, a deaf ASL user who is studying abroad without an interpreter may not have access to communicate with his or her peers at night in the dormitories, respond to a doctor during an emergency, or participate in a last-minute excursion due to a lack of advance planning. This exclusion fundamentally alters the study abroad experience. Sometimes, some of the deepest learning on an education abroad program takes place outside the classroom, in unexpected moments and on spontaneous adventures. It is our responsibility as educators and advisers to give all students the opportunity to engage in those learning moments across different settings.

Bridging the Gap in Information

Making study abroad more accessible to d/hoh students will certainly require additional resources and training. The dearth of practical information on accommodation approaches can be addressed by focusing on ways in which such students are accommodated in the United States, identifying and studying international programs that are already accessible, and learning from colleges and universities that provide strong disability support in the education abroad advising process.

Blogs and vlogs that d/hoh study abroad alumni have published about their experiences are useful for sharing with other d/hoh students as examples of successful experiences. However, these pieces are often focused on the student's perspective, which does not always provide enough information for universities and program providers to tackle the details of arranging and paying for accommodations.

At Gallaudet, we are currently gathering data from the last five years about d/hoh students who have studied abroad. This research is funded through a grant from the Increase and Diversify Education Abroad for U.S. Students (IDEAS) program, run by the U.S. Department of State with funding provided by the U.S. government and supported in its implementation by World Learning. Our goal is to get concrete information about what accommodations were provided, how they were arranged or obtained, and how they were funded. We plan to analyze the data and suggest several models that might work depending on the nature of the institution and the program.

For example, the solution for a two-week program will be different than the solution for a semester-long program. Moreover, the solutions will vary based on host country (and local laws), partner institution, and financial abilities of the sending institution. To gain a complete picture, we are collecting data from d/hoh participants as well as their program providers and universities. Once collected, analyzed, and published, this information will help more universities and study abroad program providers build into their programs the realistic costs of accommodations and find innovative ways to cover these costs.

While concrete information about interpreter availability and cost, for example, would be useful, advisers and program providers can employ many other tactics and practices to make their advising processes and programs more accessible for d/hoh students.

Through listening to my students as well as my Deaf colleagues at Gallaudet, I have learned some ways to best support d/hoh students so they can join an education abroad program as full and equal participants. The recommendations below are not exhaustive, nor are they immune to criticism. Moreover, like any advice, these insights come from a mix of learning from those who came before me, borrowing from other knowledgeable scholars in the field, and applying my own experiences working with students at Gallaudet. The advice can help ensure that more d/hoh students can experience the life-changing magic of education abroad.

Expect and Plan for Diversity

While there are study abroad programs focused on different academic subject areas, most programs are designed for nondisabled students. When we have the opportunity to design programs or even design our advising process, we should do so expecting that a diverse group of students will walk through our doors each semester.

One simple way to make an education abroad office more welcoming for d/hoh students is to caption all videos and webinars and provide transcripts of video content in the video's description. This not only allows d/hoh students to access the content but also signals to students that education abroad staff recognize there are d/hoh students within the school. To further support communication channels, at larger universities with known d/hoh populations, ASL interpreters should be requested for large presentations or made available upon request for study abroad fairs. While these requests are typically made through the disability services office (or equivalent), the education abroad office can note on their promotional flyers that accommodations can be made, again signaling an ability to work with students with disabilities.

Program providers should preemptively research speech-to-text services that can operate abroad and overseas interpreting agencies, so when a student applies for a specific program, the provider is ready with the resources to fulfill those needs. The National Deaf Center has detailed information about the different types of accommodations that d/hoh students may request (e.g., detailed descriptions of the various types of speech-to-text services). The University of Minnesota's Access Abroad initiative (University of Minnesota n.d.) also features a number of helpful resources, such as a detailed accommodations request form specifically for hearing disabilities.

In general, advisers and program providers need to think about "universal design," a concept that describes building environments or programs such that anyone, regardless of their identity or abilities, can access them. In addition to serving d/hoh students, adjustments made toward universal design often have unintended additional benefits. For example, many students for whom English is a second language also benefit and learn from captioned videos. Most important, making these adjustments without prompting from a student means less scrambling and may in fact attract more students to the education abroad office.

Meet Students Where They Are

Advisers must take the first step when it comes to outreach to d/hoh students. There are some students who know that they want to study abroad from the moment they step foot on campus. However, for many students from marginalized backgrounds, studying abroad may be a foreign concept.

Too often, we as advisers use our energy to promote opportunities to students who would already be coming to our office. However, this strategy also means that we miss out on engaging bright and motivated students who do not even know that an education abroad office exists.

This first step could be reaching out to the ASL club or faculty and staff in the deaf studies program, if either exists on campus. Another great outreach opportunity is to drop off education abroad flyers and brochures at the disability services office (University of Pittsburgh Study Abroad Office 2007). Education abroad advisers can also make connections with staff in the disability services office so they are fully aware of the range of opportunities available to students. Disability services staff should be provided with enough information about education abroad programs to be able to serve as advocates. Not only will this connection help recruit students with disabilities, but it also will be useful when a student requests accommodations. Indeed, in some cases, disability services offices sometimes will provide funding for interpreters even though it is not legally required, and this outcome is more likely if the two departments work closely together.

Avoid "Hearing-People Face"

As advisers, we must be cognizant of when we unknowingly allow our biases to color our first interactions with students. At conferences, I often present on the topic of "hearing-people face": the face hearing people make when they meet a d/hoh person, insofar as it reflects their immediate panic. Professors, baristas, cashiers, and even study abroad advisers (including me when I first started working at Gallaudet) often make this face. When students of certain marginalized backgrounds and identities (e.g., d/hoh students) walk into our offices, we sometimes get anxious thinking about how difficult it will be to find a program for them, and we may even get "sticker shock" when we start to think about the cost of accommodations.

The truth is that we actually make accommodations for all of our students, regardless of their backgrounds and abilities. As advisers, we must not panic when students with disabilities walk through our doors—in the same way we rarely panic when a college athlete asks for a program that will not interfere with his or her practice schedule. This shift in perspective can help us recognize that we may already have the skills necessary to serve diverse groups of students and help them make the most of their experiences.

Avoid "hearing-people face" is not just a feel-good suggestion to keep an open mind and a positive attitude; it is a call to advisers to recognize our biases, acknowledge our privileges, and understand the ways that these come into play when we advise students who hold identities that we do not.

Advise from a Strengths-Based Perspective

Strengths-based advising uses students' talents as the basis for educational planning; by employing this approach, advisers start with the assumption that students bring certain strengths to the academic environment (Schreiner and Anderson 2005). Focusing on a students' strengths can help advisers and study abroad program providers ensure successful experiences. More important, when students are aware of their strengths, they are often more motivated to achieve their goals and make positive choices.

Unfortunately, due to a lifetime of education in a biased society, when students from marginalized backgrounds come into our advising offices, our brains often jump straight to a deficit mindset. Most of the conference presentations and written information regarding students from marginalized backgrounds tends to focus on the additional support and additional resources that these students need. It is vital that study abroad advisers also recognize that students from marginalized backgrounds bring their own strengths and benefits to study abroad.

For example, advisers often panic while trying to find ASL interpreters abroad, as it can be a daunting task. But d/hoh students who use ASL are expert communicators. They live every day in a country where their language is the minority, and they always figure out how to order a coffee or get directions. Their communication skills and their resilience to figure things out and make themselves understood are exactly what make them especially prepared for study abroad. D/hoh students generally have strong gestural skills, which are also a benefit in countries where nonverbal communication (gestures) often accompanies spoken language.

Additionally, Deaf students are often able to find travel benefits simply because of their shared identity with other Deaf people. From a practical standpoint, d/hoh students who are connected to the larger Deaf community are often able to tap into community resources when traveling. It is not uncommon for an individual to find a place to stay, a local tour guide, or an interpreter by networking through the Deaf community.

For some students whose main identities are represented among the majority of students on their campus and community, a study abroad program may be one of the first times in their life when they are thrown into a new and different environment. D/hoh students generally have experience being the only d/hoh person in a room. Although situations like that are often challenging and can have detrimental effects on the student, it also often means these students have certain capacities for resilience that many of their peers may not.

Using a strengths-based advising approach to frame our work as international educators and program providers, we can structure our advising and program development to challenge students' growth and build on their strengths.

Understand Students' Learning and Communication Preferences

D/hoh students have a variety of needs and preferences, and they come into the education abroad office with different experiences behind them. They may prefer to communicate using English or ASL, or they may feel equally comfortable using both languages in everyday communication and in the classroom. They may have varying levels of comfort with being the only d/hoh person in a classroom or on a program. They may have some ability to hear, or they may not be able to hear anything at all. They may use technology to help them hear (e.g., hearing aids or cochlear implants) or no technology at all.

No one background leads to a specific preference. I have worked with Deaf students from Deaf families who want to study abroad in a Deaf environment, as well as other students from similar backgrounds who are ready to experience a "mainstream" (public) education environment for the first time. Listening first and letting go of our assumptions can go a long way toward understanding our students.

Study abroad advisers should engage students in honest conversations about their needs and preferences. Students with disabilities are not required to disclose their disabilities during the application process or during an international exchange program (MIUSA n.d.[a]). However, students do need to disclose their disability to obtain necessary accommodations. Mobility International USA (MIUSA) has developed a useful guide for building trust in the advising process so that students feel comfortable disclosing this information to advisers. Sometimes students with disabilities fear that by disclosing their disability and their accommodation requests, they will be shut out of programs and opportunities.

In my experience, for example, sometimes d/hoh students will say that speech-to-text services are sufficient when they would prefer ASL interpretation because they know speech-to-text services are easier to arrange and cost less. Without a trusting environment, students may withhold important information and, in the end, not receive the support they need to succeed. An additional benefit of employing universal design when building programs is that the burden on individual students to disclose their specific needs is decreased. Having students complete a pre-advising form that allows them to identify concerns they have about education abroad (e.g., financial issues, disability, sexual orientation) before an advising appointment signals to students that they are not the only ones thinking about these aspects of their identity and provides an avenue for them to disclose.

Think About the Environment

Study abroad programs are 24-hour-a-day experiences, and advisers and program providers should consider all aspects of a program when determining accommodations. This includes thinking about accommodations needed for the information environment, the physical environment, the legal environment, and the attitudinal environment. Thinking about the different environments can help us ask the right questions to ascertain what accommodations are needed.

The information environment refers to classes, extracurricular activities (such as museum visits), and orientations in which students take in information in formal ways. For example, if a tour guide is hired for a museum visit, how will d/hoh students be able to participate? The physical environment refers to things like the dorms and the physical classroom space. Do d/hoh students need a lighted emergency alarm added to their rooms? Can the classroom be rearranged in a circular or u-shape so the d/hoh student can easily see all of their classmates?

The legal environment, which refers to policies and laws in the host country, is particularly important for d/hoh students. When a d/hoh person goes to a hospital in the United States, the hospital is required (under the ADA) to provide an effective means of communication for both d/hoh patients, as well as d/hoh family members visiting patients. This is not the case around the world. Study abroad advisers should make sure students understand that laws and policies are different around the world, and encourage students to research their specific host country before traveling.

Students should be encouraged to look through their itinerary to determine what activities or trips may require additional accommodations for their participation. The program director or study abroad adviser should do the same; in some cases, it may be useful for someone at the host location to physically check a dorm or a method of public transportation, for example. Finally, when a student identifies a part of the itinerary that may be an issue, accommodations should be provided or activities should be modified or swapped to allow participation.

The attitudinal environment refers to the way the student is treated. As Katz (2010) explains, "Although many countries already have disability laws, experienced advisers do not characterize a country as accessible or inaccessible solely on the basis of legislation or technological advancement. The cultural values of a country can be a strong determinant of the experience a student with disabilities may have." Additionally, a student's experience is affected not only by the host country residents but also by their peers enrolled in the same program.

In summer 2019, a deafblind student participated in a Gallaudet program in Madrid, Spain. To increase the inclusivity of the program, we held a workshop with four deafblind trainers before the students left the United States. The goal was for the other students to learn some basic pro-tactile sign language (a language used by deafblind individuals), as well as more about deafblind communication and culture, to facilitate communication among the group members, especially in anticipation of informal excursions and moments during the program.

Consult the Experts

When working to provide accommodations for a student with a disability, advisers should recognize the knowledge they bring to the table while also acknowledging their gaps in expertise. In 2007, the University of Pittsburgh Study Abroad Office debuted a video called *Making It Happen: Study Abroad for Students with Disabilities*, which demonstrates that by bringing together the student, the study abroad adviser, and someone from the disability services office, the student's needs can be better met for study abroad programs. The issue is that "typically most study abroad advisers don't have an in-depth knowledge of disability and appropriate accommodations and that most disability specialists don't have in-depth knowledge of study abroad" (University of Pittsburgh Study Abroad Office 2007). It requires collaboration on all parts to address issues of accessibility adequately.

A student with a disability is the expert on his or her own capabilities and needs. For d/hoh students, that means they know best their capabilities, preferred communication styles, and needed accommodations. Advisers should look to students to lead on the decisionmaking process when it comes to accommodations and, when working with a d/hoh student, recognize their hearing privilege and how it affects their perception of the student.

At the same time, students often do not know how to think about their capabilities, preferences, and needs in an international context. For example, in certain countries, emergency systems use just sound as an alarm. For a d/hoh student traveling abroad, any emergency systems in classrooms and dorms must have both lights and sound. Students with hearing aids might not realize that the batteries they need could be hard to find abroad. These are things that many d/hoh students may not know to check for or plan for in advance, especially if this is their first time traveling internationally. Study abroad advisers can help by providing information about what a study abroad program will be like and researching information about the student's future environment.

The disability services office is the third part of the puzzle, providing expert information about accommodations. Disability services staff also often already have a rapport with students and can build the trust needed for students to fully disclose their needs and concerns. To establish avenues of collaboration and communication, study abroad advisers should connect with staff in the disability services office at the beginning of each academic year to ensure everyone is ready to work together (Soneson and Cordano 2009).

Moreover, disability services staff will be able to provide resources that can be sent to study host institutions or study centers to help program faculty and staff learn more about how they can support d/hoh students. For example, *Make a Difference: Tips for Teaching Students Who Are Deaf or Hard of Hearing: Handbook* is a publication from the University of Arkansas at Little Rock that provides concrete recommendations for teachers who have d/hoh students in the classroom (Downs, Owen, and Vammen 2000). These resources can help study abroad program providers prepare before a student arrives in the host country (e.g., by instructing teachers to refrain from speaking to the class while writing on the whiteboard with their back facing the students).

Collaborate, Negotiate, and Compromise

The ADA only applies inside U.S. borders; as a result, there is not usually a straightforward process for a university or a study abroad program provider to pay for services and resources needed to accommodate students with disabilities while abroad. The best of intentions often fall apart due to an inability to pay for the accommodations needed or a lack of knowledge and planning about who should arrange and pay for the accommodations.

Success stories happen when home universities, program providers, and host universities (if applicable) collaborate on arranging accommodations and paying for them. For example, in some cases, universities will agree to pay for the ASL interpretation or speech-to-text services abroad, while the provider agrees to pay for the housing and food for the interpreter. If universities are already paying for these accommodations on campus, study abroad advisers should check the cost difference for providing them abroad. If the difference in payment is negligible, the study abroad office should advocate for the home university to cover this cost abroad.

Additionally, some host universities may be willing to share the costs or able to help with arrangements for accommodations. Students studying abroad are protected by the local laws in their host country and, thus, may be able to access some accommodations through the disability services office at their host university.

Of course, even if interpreters are available at a local host institution, they may only be able to interpret in the local sign language. Karen Keen at the Disability Resource Center at the University of California-Santa Cruz found that when sending a deaf student to Scotland, the University of Edinburgh's Disability Office would be able to provide notetakers, but that an interpreter with proficiency in ASL would not be easy to find locally (Keen n.d.). However, if local interpreters have experience with International Sign (IS),[2] this may be another solution for providing communication access for students who are not comfortable with English speech-to-text services.

One way to reduce the need for accommodations is to provide opportunities for a d/hoh student to study a foreign sign language or intern with a Deaf organization or company. Many Gallaudet students do internships abroad with Deaf organizations, which minimizes the need for interpreters. Moreover, d/hoh students who use ASL are often eager to learn foreign sign languages. If language courses are offered in a program, adding a course in a foreign sign language can be substituted for a spoken language course. This would also attract more d/hoh students to apply to programs as well as hearing students who are studying ASL in the United States.

Above all, universities and program providers should develop a budget or a fund for accommodations in advance so they are ready when students need them. For example, the University of Illinois at Urbana-Champaign developed a scholarship called Enabled Abroad that provides funding that can be used toward expenses incurred from a student's disability while participating in a study abroad program. If scholarships (from a university or an organization) are intended to help students of limited means afford programs, then giving them to disabled students with the purpose of paying for accommodations is inherently inequitable because a d/hoh student may also need funds to help them pay for the basic program costs, let alone accommodations (which can be extremely costly). It is important to remember that these monies will be used to provide equity by paying for accommodations that, if the program were in the United States, would be paid for by the university or the U.S. government (not by the student).

Be Transparent and Realistic

Living abroad involves students adapting to new and different circumstances, ranging from small inconveniences to substantial shifts in habits and expectations. For many students, these experiences are lessons (both small and large) in humility and gratitude.

While we as advisers should seek to do our best to provide the accommodations necessary for d/hoh students to thrive on a study abroad program, we usually cannot guarantee the same level of access that students are used to on their home campus. This is not necessarily a bad thing; study abroad is meant to be an opportunity for students to stretch themselves and step outside their comfort zone. Often the hardest part for advisers is knowing the difference between pushing students to adapt to new circumstances and pushing them into risky or inequitable situations.

Providing transparency about accommodations gives students agency. With the proper information, students are able to determine independently whether they want to participate in a program. It is important that advisers "talk with the individual about their comfort level and 'stretch zone,' their sense of adventure, and their ability to succeed in less than perfect access conditions" (Roth-Vinson 2013). "Challenge by Choice" is a term often used in various learning environments that means that students get to choose their level of challenge, the level of support they want from others, and how deeply they participate. A major proponent of the "Challenge by Choice" philosophy is the National Clearinghouse on Disability and Exchange (NCDE), which is administered by MIUSA. NCDE aims to increase the participation of people with disabilities in all types of travel with a purpose. Adopting the "Challenge by Choice" approach means providing students with appropriate and detailed information about what type of access they can expect, but ultimately allowing them to make the decision about whether they are comfortable participating.

Unfortunately, sometimes we truly cannot obtain the ideal accommodations for a student, often due to cost, lack of time, or an inability to find the proper resource (e.g., an ASL interpreter in another country). Sometimes a program may be accessible while an activity within a program is not. In these cases, it is imperative to be transparent with students. In some situations, a student may decide that the benefits exceed the drawbacks and that they will be able to succeed with the given accommodations even if they are not ideal. Advisers should help students establish realistic expectations so they can make productive, intentional decisions regarding their participation in programs or activities within programs.

A Path Forward

With the increase in the number of students studying abroad and the increase in the number of students with documented disabilities, education abroad offices and program providers must learn how to make the recruitment, application, and advising processes accessible to students with disabilities, including d/hoh students. Despite the lack of clarity regarding the ADA's application to students studying overseas, U.S. universities can make programs all over the world accessible to d/hoh students through partnerships with foreign institutions and study abroad providers.

One of the most rewarding parts of being a study abroad adviser is hearing about students' experiences upon their return. A positive study abroad experience often leads students to apply for other professional opportunities abroad, like the Fulbright U.S. Student Program or Peace Corps, which can lead to even more personal growth and long-term career preparedness. For d/hoh students who have often experienced being locked out of programs, events, and activities, opening the door to study abroad programs can have a huge effect on their futures.

The recommendations in this chapter can help study abroad advisers and program providers learn how they can better serve d/hoh students in a genuinely inclusive, progressive, and far-sighted way. According to the National Deaf Center, an estimated 1.3 percent (more than 200,000 individuals) of college students are d/hoh (Garberoglio, Palmer, and Cawthon 2019). Those students deserve the opportunity to go abroad to experience and encounter new cultures alongside their hearing peers. With increased support from study abroad advisers and program providers, d/hoh students will have a portfolio of study abroad options to choose from (like their hearing peers already do), instead of the narrow set of opportunities they are currently offered.

I have often heard the saying that diversity is being invited to the party, inclusion is being asked to dance, and equity is when you have the opportunity to plan the party in the first place. Paying lip service to equal access is not enough—we must provide the resources needed so that d/hoh students can participate in study abroad programs and use their experiences as springboards for personal development and professional success. An increase in d/hoh participation would also likely lead to more d/hoh individuals entering the field of international education. Were this to occur, with Deaf input and co-creation on program design and advising processes, study abroad providers and universities would increase access in a transformative way such that d/hoh students would have ever-increasing opportunities to thrive on study abroad programs.

References

Canadian Hearing Services. 2015. "Models of Deafness." *Canadian Hearing Services*. https://www.chs.ca/models-deafness.

Charney, Allison D., and Josh D. Whitlock, McGuireWoods LLP. 2012. "Federal Disability Laws: Do They Translate to Study Abroad Programs?" *NACUA Notes* 10, 7:1–9.

Close, Thomas. 2001. Letter to Dr. Lattie Coor, President, Ariz. State Univ., from L. Thomas Close, Office for Civil Rights, U.S. Department of Education, Region VIII.

Downs, Sharon, Christy Owen, and Anna N. Vammen. 2000. *Make a Difference: Tips for Teaching Students Who Are Deaf or Hard of Hearing: Handbook*. Little Rock: University of Arkansas at Little Rock. https://www.umaryland.edu/media/umb/oaa/campus-life/disability-services-/documents/Tips-for-Teaching-Students-Who-Are-Deaf-or-Hard-of-Hearing.pdf.

Garberoglio, Carrie Lou, Jeffrey Levi Palmer, and Stephanie Cawthon. 2019. *Undergraduate Enrollment of Deaf Students in the United States*. Washington, DC: U.S. Department of Education, Office of Special Education Programs, National Deaf Center on Postsecondary Outcomes. https://www.nationaldeafcenter.org/sites/default/files/Undergraduate%20Enrollment%20%20of%20Deaf%20Students%20in%20the%20United%20States.pdf.

Hamir, Heather Barclay, and Nick J. Gozik. 2018. *Promoting Inclusion in Education Abroad: A Handbook of Research and Practice*. Sterling, VA: Stylus Publishing and NAFSA: Association of International Educators.

Holben, Ashley, and Monica Malhotra. 2018. "Commitments That Work: Removing Barriers for Students with Disabilities in Education Abroad." In *Promoting Inclusion in Education Abroad: A Handbook of Research and Practice*, eds. Heather Barclay Hamir and Nick J. Gozik. Sterling, VA: Stylus Publishing and NAFSA: Association of International Educators.

Institute of International Education (IIE). 2019. "Open Doors Fast Facts 2019." *Open Doors Report on International Educational Exchange*. https://www.iie.org/-/media/Files/Corporate/Open-Doors/Fast-Facts/Open-Doors-2019-Fast-Facts.ashx?la=en&hash=1FF4995155DE3E0F186A1E880D2CB6A0C7302C42.

Katz, Eve. 2010. "Students with Disabilities Studying Abroad." *International Educator*, September/October 2010, 52–57.

Keen, Karen. n.d. "Sending a Deaf Student Abroad: One University's Experience." *Mobility International USA*. http://www.miusa.org/resource/bestpractice/ucsc.

Mobility International USA (MIUSA). n.d.(a). "Disability Disclosure 101." *Mobility International USA.* https://www.miusa.org/resource/tipsheet/disabilitydisclosure101.

Mobility International USA (MIUSA). n.d.(b). "Disclosure and Building Trust." *Mobility International USA.* https://www.miusa.org/resource/tipsheet/buildingtrust.

National Association of the Deaf. 2020. "Community and Culture – Frequently Asked Questions." *National Association of the Deaf.* https://www.nad.org/resources/american-sign-language/community-and-culture-frequently-asked-questions/.

National Deaf Center. 2019. "Creating Access: Study Abroad." *National Deaf Center.* https://www.nationaldeafcenter.org/resource/creating-access-study-abroad.

Padden, Carol, and Tom Humphries. 2003. *Deaf in America: Voices from a Culture.* Cambridge, MA: Harvard University Press.

Roth-Vinson, Cerise. 2013. "Challenge By Choice." *Mobility International USA* (blog). November 6, 2013. https://www.miusa.org/blog/2013/challengebychoice.

Schreiner, Laurie A., and Edward "Chip" Anderson. 2005. "Strengths-Based Advising: A New Lens for Higher Education." *NACADA Journal* 25, 2:20–29.

Soneson, Heidi M., and Roberta J. Cordano. 2009. "Universal Design and Study Abroad: (Re-) Designing Programs for Effectiveness and Access." *Frontiers: The Interdisciplinary Journal of Study Abroad* 18, 1:269–288.

University of Minnesota. n.d. "Access Abroad Overview." *Learning Abroad Center.* https://umabroad.umn.edu/professionals/accessabroad.

University of Pittsburgh Study Abroad Office. 2007. *Making It Happen: Study Abroad for Students with Disabilities* (video). Pittsburgh, PA: University of Pittsburgh.

World Association of Sign Language Interpreters (WASLI). 2014. "International Sign Definition." *World Association of Sign Language Interpreters.* https://wasli.org/international-sign-definition.

Endnotes

[1] The following reviewers provided feedback on this chapter: Arlinda Boland, MA (Gallaudet University); Jarvis Grindstaff, MA (Gallaudet University); Justin Harford (Mobility International USA); and Rowena Winiarczyk, MA (Gallaudet University).

[2] "International Sign (IS) is a contact variety of sign language used in a variety of different contexts, particularly at international meetings such as the World Federation of the Deaf (WFD) congress, events such as the Deaflympics, in video clips produced by Deaf people and watched by other Deaf people from around the world, and informally when travelling and socialising. It can be seen as a pidgin form of sign language, which is not as conventionalised or complex as natural sign languages and has a limited lexicon" (WASLI 2014).

10
Integrating Refugees into U.S. Higher Education

BRYCE LOO, MA

Few groups on this planet are as vulnerable and marginalized as refugees and other displaced people, and unfortunately, there are a historic number of them. According to the United Nations High Commissioner for Refugees (UNHCR 2020), there are more than 70 million people displaced worldwide, with 25 million classified as refugees. These numbers rival World War II and its aftermath.

Among the many concerns for refugees is education, particularly for refugee youth. However, most efforts to provide education to refugees worldwide, particularly in refugee camps and first countries of asylum, focus on primary and secondary education (Dryden-Peterson 2010). Higher education typically receives much less attention. As of 2016, less than 1 percent of university-age refugees were able to access higher education (Ferede 2018). Many more are almost certainly eligible and need access to the world's universities and colleges, as higher education can provide economic mobility and social and cultural capital to those who attend and graduate.

Additionally, in the context of higher education in the United States, refugees should be included in discussions and actions around social justice, the drive to right historic wrongs and inequities for marginalized groups. While tremendous strides have been made over the past 60 or 70 years to include more racial and ethnic minorities, low-income students, and women in higher education, major gaps still persist. Migrants, and particularly refugees, who are mostly non-white and lower income (sometimes by circumstance), face many structural barriers—factors that frequently privilege native-born students—to accessing and succeeding in higher education.

For U.S. institutions, giving refugees the opportunity to attend their institutions when eligible should be an easy decision, though there are significant challenges and barriers. Like other international students, refugees can contribute to an institution's goals, such as internationalizing the curriculum and providing unique global perspectives for all students (see Knight and De Wit 1995; De Wit 2002). But in fact, as Streitwieser, Loo, Ohorodnik, and Jeong (2019) argue, institutions can realize another internationalization rationale, which they refer to as the "humanistic rationale." Under this rationale, institutions can fulfill their missions to serve the public good and contribute at both the global and local levels by helping integrate vulnerable but talented and capable refugee students into a local host community. Such efforts can be—and in some cases recently have been—student- or faculty-led. In this way, stakeholders across the entire campus community can fulfill the humanistic mission and goals, including working toward social justice, while giving refugees the opportunity to better their lives, whether they stay in the United States or return home to help rebuild post-conflict or post-disaster societies.

This chapter addresses challenges and possible solutions for integrating refugees into U.S. higher education. It begins with an examination of who refugees are, both in a global context and within the U.S., then provides an overview of the main challenges that displaced students face in accessing and integrating into U.S. institutions. Finally, it will discuss some possible solutions to many of these challenges.

Who Is a Refugee?

Defining who a refugee is can be surprisingly challenging in a general sense, but it can be even more fraught for U.S. colleges and universities often caught in the crosshairs of federal policy regarding international students and immigrants. Is a refugee an international student, for example? This section outlines who constitutes a refugee in both international and U.S. contexts, including the legal designations that refugees may receive.

The International Context

The primary global definition of a "refugee" comes from the 1951 *Convention and Protocol Relating to the Status of Refugees*, often known as the Refugee Convention (UN 2010). This is also the primary mechanism of international law governing the treatment of refugees. In 1967, the Convention was amended to remove any geographic barriers related to refugees, as the 1951 Convention specifically applied to Europe in the aftermath of World War II.

The Convention defines a refugee as one who "owing to well-founded fear of being persecuted for reasons of race, religion, nationality, membership of a particular social group or political opinion, is outside the country of his nationality and is unable or, owing to such fear, is unwilling to avail himself of the protection of that country" (UN 2010). A key component is that refugees are displaced *outside* of their home country.

Betts and Collier (2017), however, argue that the definition presented in the Convention is outdated and not reflective of the reality of most displacement situations. The Convention definition focuses heavily on persecution based on dimensions of identity, but Betts and Collier note that most of the world's refugees are fleeing general danger and mass violence, what they call "fragile state[s]" (p. 18). For example, Syria and Venezuela, two of the "fragile states" producing the largest numbers of external displacements, are the result of war in the first case and violent economic and political meltdown in the second. While "membership of a particular social group or political opinion" may be a reason that some flee, most leave because the situations in those countries have become unlivable due to violence, often as the result of or in combination with political strife and economic problems. Natural disasters, such as earthquakes and hurricanes, also produce large numbers of externally displaced people, and climate change threatens to displace even more (Sachs 2007).

The U.S. Context

Laws and policies guiding refugee status, admission, and settlement in the United States predominantly come from the Immigration and Nationality Act (INA) of 1965 and the Refugee Act of 1980. The main legal definition of a "refugee" comes from the INA and is, at its core, virtually identical to the

Refugee Convention. One important addition made to the INA through a 1996 amendment includes anyone "forced to abort a pregnancy or to undergo involuntary sterilization," or those "persecuted" in attempting to resist such efforts (INA 1965, (a)(42); Masson 2009). One result of this amendment is that numerous Chinese nationals have claimed asylum in the United States due to China's one-child policy (Masson 2009).

The term "refugee" often refers to someone resettled through the Refugee Resettlement Program, which was formalized by the Refugee Act of 1980 (American Immigration Council 2020). A resettled refugee is selected by the United States from abroad, often from a refugee camp, to be settled into the United States permanently. Generally, a U.S. embassy selects refugees, often family units, usually following referrals from the UNHCR. Following security and medical vetting, which can take years, refugees are brought over and settled in select locales around the country. Nine nonprofit, mostly faith-based agencies often known as VOLAGs (voluntary agencies) provide settlement services using money granted by the Office of Refugee Resettlement. Refugee adults are expected to get a job and become economically self-sufficient as soon as possible. The VOLAGs get refugees settled into housing and provide services such as employment counseling. After one year in the United States, refugees can apply for permanent residency (USCIS 2020c).

Another prime way in which refugees can settle in the United States permanently is through the asylum process. Asylum-seekers enter the United States through a variety of means, such as on a student or tourist visa. They can apply upon arrival at a U.S. port of entry—such as an airport, seaport, or border crossing—or within one year of arrival (USCIS 2020a). In applying for asylum, they are asking to be allowed to stay under the same criteria as a refugee. Asylees may apply for permanent residency one year after being granted asylum.

Once granted asylum, asylees are given permission to work, which they cannot do under most circumstances while waiting for their claim to be adjudicated (USCIS 2020a). An asylum-seeker can, in most circumstances, receive an education while waiting for their claim to be processed, but in many cases cannot receive in-state tuition or federal or state financial aid (discussed later).

Tobenkin (2006a) points out that students with a pending asylum application receive no special protection from the federal government until formally granted asylum, but many colleges and universities treat asylum-seekers the same as asylees in admissions applications. In general, for those yet to be granted asylum, legal status may be a constant source of anxiety.

The complex immigration system allows for others who may qualify as refugees under international law to come or stay under other statuses, both temporary or permanent in nature. An overview of the various "humanitarian" statuses granted by the U.S. government is available on the United States Customs and Immigration Services (USCIS) website (2020b; www.uscis.gov/humanitarian).

One other important consideration for higher education institutions is that an individual may meet the legal definition of a refugee but may come legally as an international student, or they may be undocumented. Displaced international students (who come on an F-1, J-1, or M-1 visa) hold only temporary status, a possible issue for students from countries that may be dangerous for them to return to once they complete their degree program. While they will face similar challenges to most international students, they may face some that are unique to refugees and other displaced people, such as issues with academic documentation. Those who are undocumented are often also fleeing violence and traumatic situations in their home countries like other refugees.

The term "refugee" can be problematic, as it may be applied to a specific legal designation (a resettled refugee) or used in the more universal sense. Throughout this chapter, the terms "displaced student" or "displaced individual" will be used where possible to be more inclusive of people in refugee-like circumstances. For those working with displaced students, the key is to understand that specific circumstances and experiences, rather than simply legal status, determine who is a refugee. Many will never have been officially labeled as a refugee (by UNHCR, the U.S. government, or another official entity). It is also worth noting that many students may not wish to be labeled a refugee for various reasons (Murray 2016), notably any negative connotations associated with the word or because of actual or perceived prejudice and discrimination.

The Right to an Education

A series of international conventions and agreements outlines refugees' and displaced people's right to education, including higher education (Unangst 2019). Watenpaugh (2016, 14) perhaps best articulated the principles behind these frameworks in a U.S. context: "American higher education—from its great universities, liberal arts institutions to community colleges—can and must play a role in addressing that reality of permanent exile by working through multiple means to aid in the reconnection of young refugees to education. Doing so, we also defend the basic human right to education, and lay the foundations for addressing this and the other refugee crises that will surely follow." Perhaps most notable among these conventions is Article 26 of the Universal Declaration of Human Rights, which notes that higher education is the right of all "on the basis of merit" (quoted in Unangst 2019).

Barriers to Higher Education Access and Integration

Compared with other major host nations of refugees and asylum-seekers—such as Australia, Canada, and many European countries—there is a relative dearth of literature on refugee access to and integration into higher education in the United States. The lack of scholarship may be related to the relatively small numbers of refugees who enroll in higher education or that they often "disappear" when entering higher education because they are generally permanent residents, rather than separately classified international students (Felix 2016, 60). Despite the lack of extensive research, there are clear barriers to access for displaced students, drawn both from the U.S. literature and that of other major predominantly English-speaking host nations, such as Canada.

In looking at these challenges, one must keep a few things in mind. First, displaced students may be applying from different locations and contexts (which relates to the topic of legal status, discussed shortly). Some may have settled in the local U.S. community of the institution, while others may be applying from other locations in the U.S. Some may, however, be applying from abroad, whether from a refugee camp, in an urban setting in a first country of asylum (e.g., a Syrian refugee living in Istanbul), or even from their home country in the midst of crisis (i.e., someone who has not yet fled). In the latter case, most will likely be applying to come to the United States as international students. A student's current circumstances will determine, in large part, the type of support services they need in terms of admissions, arrival, and integration.

A second consideration specifically relates to those who have already resided in the United States for longer timespans as refugee and asylee youth. These individuals who have received at least some schooling in the United States likely will face fewer challenges than those who arrived recently (Felix 2016). For example, refugee students who have completed high school in the United States will likely have stronger English skills, including better comprehension of vernacular American English, and will have a better understanding of the U.S. education system, including the application process for colleges and universities.

Third, challenges and appropriate solutions will naturally vary by level and type of program. The challenges and supports needed will be different for an 18-year-old entering college for the first time than they are for a doctoral candidate or medical student. Additionally, certain programs need to maintain specific accreditation status and may have less flexibility to adapt policies, though there likely are ways to adapt practices to meet such policies.

For institutions, these challenges may seem overwhelming, with many students needing accommodations. But as Stanton (2016) notes, institutions should be able to "adjust their processes, not lower their standards." Most prospective students are bright, capable, and motivated but face unique challenges. In most cases, offices do not need to rewrite policies completely but should use creativity and flexibility to find solutions.

The remainder of this section discusses the main barriers that displaced students often face when attempting to access higher education and integrate successfully into the campus.

Legal Status

There is a bewildering array of legal statuses under which displaced students can enter the United States, which can cause confusion in the admissions process for both students and institutions and myriad challenges for students. As will be discussed later, a student's legal status has real ramifications when it comes to financing their education, as those with permanent status can access virtually all federal student aid, while those on temporary status or who are undocumented cannot. Furthermore, for some, the issue of legal status can be a major source of anxiety, particularly if that status is precarious.

At most institutions, displaced students with permanent status apply through the domestic applicant stream and face few or no problems related to their legal status. However, two states, Alabama and South Carolina, do not allow undocumented students to enroll in public colleges or universities (NCSL 2019). The University of Georgia system also prohibits students without legal status from enrolling, a policy initiated by the Board of Regents in 2010 (Vasilogambros 2016; Georgia Tech 2020). Otherwise, most states and public systems have no bar on the admission of undocumented students (NCSL 2019). In some cases, depending on the state, public universities or colleges may either be required to ask about a student's status or be prohibited from asking. However, likely in most cases, that decision is left up to individual institutions (College Board 2020).

In many instances, it may not be clear that an applicant is a refugee (or "displaced"), and many displaced students may not want to self-identify as a refugee. As a result, it is sometimes hard to know when a displaced student has shown up at your doorstep until there is a conversation about the individual's circumstances. Resettled refugees and asylees will "appear" in the application system as permanent residents, and thus, it may be difficult to target appropriate support to them. Complicating matters, many staff at colleges and universities may not understand the various statuses that prospective students may hold, or the documentation of such statuses (Tobenkin 2006a). What does it mean, for example, for a student to be a Special Immigrant Visa holder[1]? The paperwork demonstrating status for many displaced individuals, particularly asylees, can be inconsistent and cause confusion for admissions staff. Medical schools, in particular, are less likely to admit a student that can easily be classified as a U.S. citizen or permanent resident, in large part because of state requirements (Tobenkin 2006a). It is also common for an admissions office to inappropriately classify a displaced student with permanent status as an international student (with nonimmigrant status) because the office misunderstands the applicant's status or the corresponding documentation, the applicant holds education credentials from another country, and other factors (Yi and Marquez Kiyama 2018).

Family Obligations

Displaced students generally come as part of larger family units, either with parents and siblings (or more), or with a spouse and children. Many college-age displaced youth need to help support their families, financially and sometimes in other ways (Shankar et al. 2016). This can present a barrier to students in terms of the time and money required to go to college.

The U.S. refugee system emphasizes self-sufficiency for those brought to the United States and those who have been granted asylum (Yi and Marquez Kiyama 2018). Resettled refugee adults are expected to get a job that financially supports their families within 180 days of arrival (Perry and Mallozzi 2011). A VOLAG may not advise capable refugees of enrolling in higher education after resettlement because the agency's funding is tied to economic self-sufficiency. Even refugee youth who come with parents often need to get work, in large part because their English skills may be stronger than those of older relatives. Displaced youth may have other obligations such as caring for younger siblings or their own children, caring for sick or disabled relatives, or running errands and translating for family members (Shakya et al. 2012).

Planning, Accessing Information, and Navigating U.S. Higher Education

One of the greatest differences between refugees and other internationally educated individuals entering U.S. higher education (such as international students and other types of immigrants) revolves around planning and information-gathering. Typically, refugees do not have the same ability to plan ahead and research U.S. higher education, including types of institutions, the application process, financing, and so forth (Tobenkin 2006a). Refugees typically come to the United States because they have little other choice. Most resettled refugees and asylees also lack the social and cultural capital of American students in that, in most cases, these students typically cannot rely on their parents for information and advice about U.S. higher education, even if the parents are well-educated (Felix 2016).

Additionally, students who have arrived as resettled refugees or asylees may find that university or college staff know little about such statuses, as mentioned earlier, and do not understand the backgrounds of these students (Tobenkin 2006a). As a result, students may be inappropriately advised to, for example, obtain a GED when they already have a postsecondary degree or college coursework, or they may be sent back through a degree program unnecessarily. It is common for refugee and asylee students to be placed at the wrong education level (Shakya et al. 2012).

Coupled with the issue of reduced ability to plan and gather information is the complexity of the U.S. higher education system and individual institutions (Shakya et al. 2012). These structural barriers, as AACRAO's (2019, 10) report on inclusive admissions for refugees puts it, revolve around "an unfamiliar and bureaucratic higher education system." Often, students do not know where to start in terms of asking questions and beginning the application process. In many other countries, the application process is much more personal, with stronger one-on-one advising, whereas the application process in the United States is mostly online and impersonal (Loo 2017). Students must also navigate the local community, often dealing with issues such as housing, transportation, and opening bank accounts (AACRAO 2019).

The Application Process and Requirements

The fact that most U.S. college and university admissions applications are online may be problematic for some refugees abroad. For applicants abroad, particularly in refugee contexts, access to the internet may be intermittent and weak. Mozina and Doyle (2016) recommend creative solutions focused on alternative applications. For example, an institution could develop a fillable PDF that can be downloaded and saved on a student's computer (or even their phone). Additionally, some institutions (Tooley 2016) have reported the difficulty that displaced students face in procuring a visa, including having to travel to a neighboring country to visit a U.S. embassy or consulate.

Many institutions have made the major standardized exams that are typically required for admission, such as the SAT and GRE, optional. That is certainly not the case for all institutions. However, for colleges and universities where such exams are requirements, some officials may be able to waive these requirements if refugees from or living in certain countries are not able to access them (Tooley 2016).

Additionally, English proficiency is a key requisite in admissions. Beyond the practical necessities of ensuring that applicants can do coursework in English, for those coming on an F-1 or J-1 visa, English proficiency is a regulatory requirement in that institutions must ensure that international students can meet all regular admissions requirements and be able to function well in the classroom. State governments and accreditation agencies might impose further requirements regarding language proficiency and assessment. Typically, major English proficiency examinations such as the Test of English as a Foreign Language (TOEFL) and International English Language Testing System (IELTS) have been the most common methods of assessment. However, for students in displacement situations, accessing such exams can be challenging (Mozina and Doyle 2016). For these applicants, institutions may consider other ways to assess and document applicants' English abilities, using methods such as online interviews and writing samples, so long as they meet regulatory requirements.

Academic Documentation

Once displaced students are ready to start the application process, many face the challenge of being able to produce official academic documents, such as transcripts (or mark sheets) and degree certificates, that can establish their academic credentials (Fricke 2016; Loo 2016, 2019). Many U.S. colleges and universities evaluate these documents themselves, while others outsource the job to a third-party credential evaluation service that has greater capabilities. These agencies produce a report that advises the institution on the equivalency of the prospective student's degree(s) from abroad to U.S. credentials. In either case, the prospective student is almost always required to request their home institution(s) from abroad send the documents directly to the institution or agency for evaluation. In some cases, the student may be allowed to submit official copies of the requisite documents, with which the institution or agency can then verify the authenticity of the documents directly with the issuing institution. These practices surrounding authenticity of documents allow colleges and universities, and the credential evaluation agencies, to minimize the possibility of fraud.

For refugees, these requirements can prove problematic for a number of reasons. The biggest challenges often come from the issuing institutions (Loo 2019). Universities, ministries of education, and other official issuing institutions often do not function normally in the midst of a conflict zone or a natural disaster. Some Syrian universities, for example, have been bombed, often multiple times, over the course of the civil war there. In a more slow-moving crisis, such as in Venezuela, universities may have simply run out of both money and personnel, many of whom may have fled the country. These institutions may not have the means to send documents abroad or verify them. In other cases, institutions may refuse to issue documents for a variety of reasons, including political motivations or as a matter of standard practice within that country. For example, there are known cases of young Syrian men being refused documents since they fled abroad to avoid mandatory military service to the Assad regime. In some cases, institutions can issue official documents, but only in person. This is clearly problematic for students who have already gone abroad, and it may be too dangerous for family or friends to go on their behalf to pick up the documents.

Refugees often need to flee suddenly, with little ability to take much with them. In cases where institutions overseas are unable to send official documents or verify, students can be left with few options. There is evidence, however, from some institutions and credential evaluation agencies that many refugees have the foresight to bring at least copies of important documents with them (WES 2018). The key is whether the institution is able to accept such documents that are not officially issued. If not, it leaves many students with little choice but to start over or repeat many courses if they have already completed a degree or at least some coursework (Perry and Mallozzi 2011).

One other important thing to keep in mind when assessing academic background: Depending on their circumstances, many refugees experience significant gaps in their formal education (Dryden-Peterson 2015), which may be difficult for them to explain or account for, at least based on written records. These gaps may be anywhere from a few weeks to several years. The main reasons typically are conflict, restricted access to education in first countries of asylum (per government regulations), constant migration, and lack of availability of schools in a particular locale (as is the case in many parts of Somalia). In cases where there appear to be educational gaps in a student's record, it is important to discuss the circumstances of those gaps, which may have been beyond the student's control.

Financing

The sheer cost of higher education can be a major barrier for many displaced students. Many refugees come to the United States with relatively few financial resources or lose their resources after fleeing (Kanno and Varghese 2010). As noted earlier, some will need to work to support themselves and their families. Economic needs may trump the need to return to school and advance a career. In a study of refugee pilot project participants in Canada conducted by World Education Services (WES), one Syrian refugee put it this way, in the context of employment, though this could also apply to education: "I have the motivation to do anything that could help me finding a job in my profession…but it is almost impossible to do…in parallel with my full time job. If I quit my current job, there will be no resource[s] to cover my life expenses. The type of help I am looking for is a temporary financial support that could allow me to quit from my current job and do one of the programs that may help me finding a job in my profession" (quoted in Loo 2017).

A student's status greatly determines what type of aid they can receive and, in the case of public institutions, the price tag of an education. Resettled refugees and those granted asylum, along with those on other permanent statuses, are eligible to apply for federal student aid in the form of low-interest loans, Pell Grants, and the like by filling out the FAFSA (Free Application for Federal Student Aid) form (Federal Student Aid n.d.). In many states, these students also qualify for in-state tuition at public institutions. Colorado law, for example, allows resettled refugees and those on Special Immigrant Visas (i.e., Afghans and Iraqis who worked for the U.S. military) to receive in-state tuition at public institutions (Colorado Department of Higher Education 2018). Displaced students who come as international students, those awaiting asylum decisions, those with temporary status, and undocumented students are not eligible. Depending on the state, those on temporary statuses or who are undocumented may be able to apply for state aid, though generally international students are not able to. Each state has different criteria and requirements for determining residency, affecting whether a student can access in-state rates (Tobenkin 2006b).

Students who do qualify for federal aid may need help filling out the FAFSA (Mozina and Doyle 2016). For most, the amount and complexity of documentation they will need to submit may be daunting, including documents showing their status and—for younger, dependent students—parents' financial records (Felix 2016; NASFAA 2018). Parents' financial records may be difficult or impossible to get or nonexistent for many refugees newly arrived in the United States.

Even when students are able to access aid, it may not cover all expenses. It may cover tuition and fees but not living expenses and other expenses such as books or computers. In general, funding a higher education degree can be one of the most vexing challenges for both student and institution.

English Proficiency and Cultural Integration

Even for displaced students who meet basic language proficiency requirements for admissions, English in both academic and daily contexts may be challenging (Kanno and Varghese 2010). Students may not have command of the English used in their specific disciplines. Additionally, colloquial American English may be unfamiliar to them, as they likely learned a more formal style of English abroad (Felix 2016). Research on international students shows that command of the local language is crucial for academic success and cultural integration (Andrade 2006; Zhang and Goodson 2011). The same holds true for displaced students.

Similar to other students from abroad, displaced students must integrate culturally and socially into the campus community and the broader community, within the American cultural context, to experience the most success. Displaced students are not unlike many American first-generation college students in that they need to learn the "culture of college," as Felix (2016, 141) puts it. Once on campus, these students must navigate the norms and practices of U.S. college campuses and classrooms.

Issues of identity also become salient for many displaced students. Like for other immigrant students, displaced students (at least those who have permanent status) must negotiate complex understandings of who they are in relation to their home country and their new country of settlement. Felix (2016, 131) explains it this way: "The higher education environment… act[s] as a breeding ground for the intensely personal process of constructing a bicultural identity and making meaning of the collection of experiences encompassing one's life story." For many displaced students, the label of "refugee" can be complex, and many students may not want to assume it or have their identity labeled in such a way. It is also important to remember that not all students will want to speak on behalf of other displaced people or individuals from their particular national, ethnic, religious, or other background (Murray 2016). Displaced students should only speak in such contexts when comfortable.

Prejudice and discrimination, whether overt or through subtler microaggressions, can also be a challenge for displaced students, particularly as many come from minority ethnic, racial, and religious backgrounds. In Shakya et al.'s study (2012) of refugee youth in Toronto, participants said they had encountered discrimination and biases on the part of teachers, administrators, community members, and others, including assumptions about intelligence and ability based on their national or refugee background or their command of English. Students deal with such prejudice and discrimination in a variety of ways, both active and passive, but research makes clear that discrimination can have "detrimental impacts…on academic performance, youth identity, and overall well-being" (Shakya et al. 2012, 72).

Institutional Solutions for Support

Displaced students are as capable of excelling in U.S. higher education as other international or immigrant students, but as discussed, they have unique needs (as well as many that are similar to other students), both in terms of initial access and in fully integrating into the institution academically, socially, and culturally. By providing such support, colleges and universities can clearly demonstrate serious commitment to their missions to serve the greater good by aiding marginalized and vulnerable students. Luckily, institutions likely have most of the resources they need to help such students. It is a matter of intentionality and creative reconfiguration of these resources. This section discusses possible steps that colleges and universities can take to help displaced students who come to their campus.

Help Students Access Information and Navigate U.S. Higher Education

As described earlier, displaced students often struggle to navigate U.S. higher education in general and individual institutions specifically. One recommendation is to designate a single office on campus where displaced students, once identified, can be referred for help. AACRAO (2019) provides this advice: "Institutions that have training, clear policies and procedures for getting displaced and vulnerable individuals to the right office or contact person no matter what 'door' they knock on (a 'no wrong door' policy) will go a long way to providing access and minimizing unnecessary distress" (53). One office with staff who are well trained on issues related to displaced students, including issues of status and how to help such students navigate the admissions process, can go a long way to help students get a foot in the door. All staff and faculty should know about this office and be able to refer prospective displaced students to it. This will help students avoid dead ends in their search for information and the start of the application process. Shankar et al. (2016) found that newly arrived refugees value developing a close relationship with an individual or an office, as they often find institutional providers hard to approach otherwise. A dedicated office can gently guide students through the process and help make introductions to other key offices. In the end, it likely does not matter which office (or group of individuals) serves this role, as long as they are trained, have strong knowledge of and relationships across the institution, and are willing to help.

For such an office, it is important to think about how to get displaced students connected around campus, from initial advising and the admissions process onward. These students will need to meet with and get to know a wide range of individuals and offices on campus, many of whom will have roles with which they are unfamiliar. Training for staff who work in this office, as well as other key offices, can help ensure that prospective and current displaced students are advised properly, based on their status and in ways that meet their needs. Faculty and staff from the countries or regions of concern may be good resources as well and may be able to help develop training for other faculty and staff (Stanton 2016).

As an adviser gets to know a student and understand their circumstances, it is important to think through and give as many options to students as possible based on those circumstances. For example, students who must work or who have other family responsibilities may need options and support services similar to "nontraditional" college students, such as older students with families. These could include offering alternatives to full-time, traditional programs, with advising about flexible scheduling of courses (including evening and weekend options) and part-time and online programs and courses.

Institutions can also use off-campus resources to help guide students, particularly those who are still abroad or otherwise not yet living in the local area. One such resource is EducationUSA (educationusa.state.gov), a branch of the U.S. State Department that helps provide information and advising to prospective international students. Their services are both online in the form of resources and online events and in person through advising centers located around the world. There are often no advising centers in countries experiencing a lasting crisis, but there are usually centers in nearby countries, including in many major first countries of asylum. For example, Venezuelans who have fled to Colombia, a top country of first asylum, can access one of 11 centers across Colombia (EducationUSA 2020).

Develop Alternative Forms of Credentialing

Best practices on working with displaced students and professionals with limited documentation have been collated worldwide since the 1990s. More recently, starting around 2015, the Syrian crisis opened a "policy window," incentivizing many institutions in the West and worldwide to rethink and retool their admissions policies regarding refugees and asylum-seekers, including in academic documentation (Loo 2019, 102–103). In that time, there have been numerous reports and other products that have synthesized best practices (e.g., Loo 2016; AACRAO 2019).

Most best practice reports discuss the need for admissions offices to think through their current policies and processes, including where there might be flexibility, how to mitigate risk, and the benefits of flexibility for displaced students. Then, the actual process of evaluating and recognizing credentials has been developed into various similar models with multiple steps or stages in working with a displaced student lacking full official or verifiable documentation. These steps, as detailed by AACRAO (2019, 53–61), are as follows:

1. "Identify Need and Determine Eligibility
2. Reconstruct the Applicant's Academic Background
3. Utilize Various Types of Standard and Supporting or [Corroborating] Documents
4. Utilize Resources and Expertise
5. Assess Learning
6. Conduct the Final Analysis and Reach a Decision"

To describe the full process succinctly, in the absence of full official documentation, an admissions office can reconstruct an applicant's academic history using oral or written information from the applicant (such as through an application, a written statement, or an interview) and whatever documentary evidence the applicant can provide. With the right in-house expertise and internal and external resources, including a database or library of previous documents from that country, the evidence from the applicant can be assessed. If more proof is needed, the applicant's competencies in their claimed field can be assessed using any variety of tools, including tests, interviews with professors, sample work, and so forth. The office can then make a final assessment and determine what level of recognition, if any, can be given to the individual's background, enough to make an admission and placement decision. In some cases, the office may not be able to recognize the full academic background claimed by the applicant, but they can recognize parts of it or admit the student with conditions, such as completion of a few extra courses or maintenance of a certain GPA within the first semester or year.

Many of these practices have been successfully implemented by U.S. institutions, including Monmouth College (Tooley 2016), the University of Colorado-Boulder's graduate admissions office (Loo 2016), and others. Monmouth College, for example, was able to use successful scores on placement exams to help some Syrian students backfill courses in fields such as foreign languages, math, and statistics. Taking a broader view, a 2018 AACRAO survey of 500 admissions officers from across the country found that 49 percent of respondents from public institutions and 41 percent of private nonprofit institutions had practices in place for working with displaced undergraduate applicants who could not meet normal admissions criteria. For graduate students, the rates were lower: 38 percent of public institutions and 25 percent of private non-profit institutions. These numbers indicate that a sizable number of colleges and universities are working on solutions to this challenge. Many admissions offices may not have the means to conduct such a process, particularly if they outsource much or all of their international credential evaluation work, but they can potentially rely on a U.S. credential evaluation agency.

Several of these agencies have developed some solutions. One of the largest such agencies, World Education Services (WES), used an alternative evaluation model to develop a pilot program for Syrian refugees in Canada, where the agency also works. Working with referral partners across Canada, WES produced credential evaluation reports by thoroughly assessing non-verified documents for 337 Syrian refugees (WES 2018). According to a follow-up study with pilot project participants (WES 2019), more than half used their credential evaluation report to apply to an educational institution in Canada, and around 71 percent of those who did were accepted. The project has since been scaled up into a program known as the WES Gateway Program, for which applicants from a broader range of countries are eligible. WES has stated plans to bring a similar program to the United States (Kalachova 2019).

Offer Financial Supports When Possible and Advise Students on Financial Options

The most straightforward solution to the financing challenge is for institutions to set aside funds for one or a few displaced students, which will demonstrate their commitment to internationalization and social justice (Streitwieser et al. 2019). Universities and colleges from around the United States and the world who have joined the Institute of International Education's (IIE) Syria Consortium for Higher Education in Crisis have made the commitment to do this specifically for Syrian refugee students (IIE 2020). As of February 2018, there were 69 U.S. institutions that were part of the consortium, representing a broad array of sizes, types, and locations of colleges and universities working to offer scholarships to deserving students.

Canada offers one unique model of financing that may have some applicability to U.S. higher education. The Student Refugee Program (SRP) from the World University Service of Canada (WUSC) uses Canada's unique private refugee sponsorship system to bring in eligible students predominantly from refugee camps in Africa and the Middle East to attend university in Canada and settle permanently (Peterson 2010; WUSC 2020). Most cogent for the purposes of this discussion, however, is its funding model. Local committees led predominantly by students on each campus are in charge of raising the funds for the refugees that come in through WUSC-SRP. They can do so in one of a variety of ways. Perhaps the most common method is through the use of student levies, in which a small fee, usually just a few dollars, is added onto the bill for all students each semester or year, which students can opt out of typically. The funds raised often allow a university to fund one or a couple of students for at least one year and sometimes for the duration of their studies. For example, Simon Fraser University in British Columbia funds its WUSC-SRP students through a levy of $2.50 for full-time undergraduates and $1.00 for graduates every term (Borean 2020). Since 1981, the university has brought in 71 refugee students under this model. Currently, WUSC lists 171 institutions participating in the program, including some of Canada's top universities (WUSC 2020), which indicates the success that this program has found within Canadian higher education. U.S. institutions may be able to use one or all of the components of this model: student fundraising efforts or use of student levies, with significant buy-in from student groups.

Some institutions have also found success reaching out to the broader institutional community and the local community (e.g., Millner 2016). For example, an institution's board of trustees may be able to develop a scholarship program for displaced students. There are also numerous external resources and funding sources for refugee students. For example, the Michigan-based non-profit Jusoor (www.jusoorsyria.com) offers scholarships for Syrian students worldwide (Jusoor 2020). IIE has developed a large database of scholarship opportunities for refugees worldwide, including the United States, in its Platform for Education in Emergencies Response, or IIE-PEER (www.iie.org/Programs/IIE-PEER; IIE 2020).

Offer Support for Full Integration

Having adequate language skills is one of the biggest factors in terms of integrating. To help students improve their English, for both the classroom and daily life, institutions can use existing resources for international and immigrant students, particularly campus-based intensive English programs (IEPs) or third-party programs. Kanno and Varghese (2010), however, point out that issues can arise among immigrant students (including refugees) labeled as ESL (English as a Second Language) learners and placed in ESL classes. For one, these students may internalize the label, believing that their English is not good enough to participate in mainstream classes and to socialize with English-speaking students. As a result, they may get to know few of their American classmates. Also, ESL (or IEP) courses are often expensive for these students and usually do not carry academic credit. As a result, Kanno and Varghese (2010) recommend some alternatives, such as developing "a separate ESL track of the freshman composition course, integrating ESL students into regular composition classes with instructors who are aware of the needs of L2 [second language] writers, and optional ESL courses for specific skill areas for which ESL students can voluntarily sign up" (324).

That said, any other support services, such as the campus writing or tutoring center and conversational English programs for international students, can also be useful. When on-campus programs are insufficient, it may be worth looking to partner with community organizations. VOLAGs (in cities and towns with large resettled refugee populations), other immigrant-serving organizations, employment services, adult education schools, and more may have dedicated ESL classes. Some institutions have found creative solutions that involve the campus community. For example, the University of Toronto developed a successful program in which Syrian refugee students and local students "trade[d] languages," alternating practicing Arabic and English (Howells 2016), a good example of how displaced students can help internationalize the campus.

To help with integration, many of the same supports as for international students, immigrants, and first-generation students, such as new student orientation programs and cultural festivals that include the cultures of displaced students, will likely be helpful. It is also important to consider that for displaced students to be fully included and empowered within the institution, like for other traditionally marginalized groups of students and for international students, a broad range of the campus community, including staff, faculty, and current students, must participate. In fact, many efforts to assist refugees on U.S. campuses have been student- and faculty-led.

Students are particularly important in integration efforts. Again, WUSC provides a good example of how students can lead the way. As mentioned earlier, each institution that participates in WUSC's SRP has a committee that comprises mostly students. This committee is in charge of not only the funding of refugee students but also the integration and peer mentorship of these students, both academically and socially (McKee, Lavell, Manks, and Korn 2019). While these committees are aided by a national organization in

Canada, a similar concept could be introduced on U.S. campuses with interested students guided by faculty or staff advisors.

Standard student support offices, ranging from student activities to mental health services, can play a role in helping ensure that displaced students meet success. Planning and training to help this population of students are key. Mental health services with counselors or therapists who are culturally informed, incorporate culturally sensitive practices, and are trained in treating mental and emotion trauma are particularly pertinent (Burbage and Klein Walker 2018).

Partner with Organizations Assisting the Displaced and Network with Colleagues

Lastly, U.S. institutions do not need to go it alone. There are communities of like-minded institutions and individual faculty, staff, and students who meet and pool together best practices and resources. IIE (www.iie.org/en/Programs/Student-Emergency-Initiatives) particularly has been at the forefront of organizing responses from U.S. higher education to refugee crises, starting predominantly with the Syrian crisis but now with a broader scope. In particular, the Syria Consortium for Higher Education in Crisis has brought together more than 80 institutions from around the United States and the world to respond to the Syrian crisis, with institutions making the commitment to work on admitting and financing at least one Syrian refugee student. They also pool together resources in terms of best practices.

Another organization, the University Alliance for Refugees and At-Risk Migrants (2020), or UARRM (www.uarrm.org), is a recently formed community of mostly U.S. university-based scholars and practitioners working on issues related to refugee and other displaced students and scholars. Some of their main goals include mapping efforts that assist displaced students across the United States, communicating and disseminating information about efforts, and developing relevant initiatives.

For college and university leaders, there is the Presidents' Alliance on Higher Education and Immigration (2020; www.presidentsimmigrationalliance.org), another recently formed group composed of institution presidents and chancellors. The focus of the group is on all immigrant and international students, including displaced and undocumented students, in U.S. higher education. The group works on policy advocacy and collecting and disseminating best practices among their membership.

These organizations are just a few examples of coordinating efforts across the sector and creating communities of practitioners, researchers, and leaders.

Conclusion

IIE president Allan Goodman (2016) has argued that if each of the world's roughly 20,000 higher education institutions would take in just one refugee student, as well as one threatened scholar, it would "make a dent in preventing a global lost generation." Universities and colleges in the United States, which has one of the largest higher education sectors in the world, could make a significant contribution. The rationales for doing so are greater than not, despite the significant challenges. Perhaps the biggest reason for helping displaced students whenever possible is institutions' mission to serve a public good and the impetus toward social justice, often a core concern for students, faculty, and staff. American colleges and universities present a historic paradox: They both serve—at least in word—to improve the lives of students, including historically marginalized groups such as racial minorities, but have often reinforced privilege (Gidley, Hampson, Wheeler, and Bereded-Samuel 2010). Helping refugees and displaced students, even just a few, allows institutions to demonstrate their commitment to serving the underprivileged, as refugees are among the most marginalized people globally.

At the same time, the ability for refugees to access and integrate into U.S. higher education produces a multitude of benefits: for U.S. society, for the institution, and certainly for the refugee, as well as for the refugee's home country in some instances. These benefits include better economic and social integration in the United States, greater internationalization of the campus, and the ability for refugees to regain dignity and autonomy, as well as advance refugees' careers. With a bit of creative thinking and collaboration, institutions can overcome most or all the challenges that displaced students face and help at least a few become a full part of the campus community. Simply put: It's the right thing to do.

References

American Association of Collegiate Registrars and Admissions Officers (AACRAO). 2018. *Admissions Practice Snapshot: Results of the AACRAO November 2018 60-Second Survey.* Washington, DC: AACRAO. https://www.aacrao.org/research-publications/research/admissions-reports.

American Association of Collegiate Registrars and Admissions Officers (AACRAO). 2019. "Inclusive Admissions Policies for Displaced and Vulnerable Students." *AACRAO Pledge for Education.* https://www.aacrao.org/signature-initiatives/article-26-backpack-project/aacrao-pledge-for-education/.

American Immigration Council. 2020. "Fact Sheet: An Overview of U.S. Refugee Law and Policy." https://www.americanimmigrationcouncil.org/research/overview-us-refugee-law-and-policy.

Andrade, Maureen Snow. 2006. "International Students in English-Speaking Universities: Adjustment Factors." *Journal of Research in International Education* 5, 2:131–154.

Betts, Alexander, and Paul Collier. 2017. *Refuge: Rethinking Refugee Policy in a Changing World.* New York, NY: Oxford University Press.

Borean, Lauren. 2020. "Support SFU's WUSC Student Refugee Program." *Simon Fraser University News.* March 13, 2020. https://www.sfu.ca/sfunews/stories/2020/03/support-sfu-s-wusc-student-refugee-program-.html.

Burbage, Michelle L., and Deborah Klein Walker. 2018. "A Call to Strengthen Mental Health Supports for Refugee Children and Youth." *National Academy of Medicine.* August 27, 2018. https://nam.edu/a-call-to-strengthen-mental-health-supports-for-refugee-children-and-youth/.

College Board. 2020. "Advising Undocumented Students." https://professionals.collegeboard.org/guidance/financial-aid/undocumented-students.

Colorado Department of Higher Education. 2018. "Memorandum: Clarifying Senate Bill 18-087." November 1, 2018. https://highered.colorado.gov/Academics/Refugee-Students/SB18-087-Clarification-Memo.pdf.

De Wit, Hans. 2002. *Internationalization of Higher Education in the United States of America and Europe: A Historical, Comparative, and Conceptual Analysis.* Westport, CT: Greenwood Publishing Group.

Dryden-Peterson, Sarah. 2010. "The Politics of Higher Education for Refugees in a Global Movement for Primary Education." *Refuge: Canada's Journal on Refugees* 27, 2:10–18.

Dryden-Peterson, Sarah. 2015. *The Educational Experiences of Refugee Children in Countries of First Asylum*. Washington, DC: Migration Policy Institute (MPI). https://www.migrationpolicy.org/research/educational-experiences-refugee-children-countries-first-asylum.

EducationUSA. 2020. "Find an Advising Center." https://educationusa.state.gov/find-advising-center.

Federal Student Aid. n.d. "Eligibility for Non-U.S. Citizens." https://studentaid.gov/understand-aid/eligibility/requirements/non-us-citizens.

Felix, Vivienne R. 2016. "The Experiences of Refugee Students in United States Postsecondary Education." Doctoral dissertation, Bowling Green State University. https://etd.ohiolink.edu/!etd.send_file?accession=bgsu1460127419&disposition=inline.

Ferede, Martha K. 2018. *Higher Education for Refugees* (Background Paper Prepared for the 2019 Global Education Monitoring Report: Migration, Displacement and Education: Building Bridges, Not Walls). Paris, France: United Nations Educational, Scientific, and Cultural Organization (UNESCO). https://unesdoc.unesco.org/ark:/48223/pf0000266075.

Fricke, Adrienne. 2016. "Regional Opportunities and Challenges for Syrian Students." In *Supporting Displaced and Refugee Students in Higher Education: Principles and Best Practices*, ed. Nele Feldman and Courtney Lind. New York, NY: Institute of International Education (IIE). https://www.iie.org/Research-and-Insights/Publications/Supporting-Displaced-and-Refugee-Students-in-Higher-Education.

Georgia Tech. 2020. "Undergraduate Admission: Lawful Presence." https://admission.gatech.edu/lawful-presence.

Gidley, Jennifer M., Gary P. Hampson, Leone Wheeler, and Elleni Bereded-Samuel. 2010. "From Access to Success: An Integrated Approach to Quality Higher Education Informed by Social Inclusion Theory and Practice." *Higher Education Policy* 23, 1:123–147.

Goodman, Allan. 2016. "Three Ways Higher Education Can Respond to the Syrian Refugee Crisis." *Education Plus Development* (blog), *Brookings Institution*. May 13, 2016. https://www.brookings.edu/blog/education-plus-development/2016/05/13/three-ways-higher-education-can-respond-to-the-syrian-refugee-crisis/.

Howells, Laura. 2016. "Syrians and Canadians Trade Languages at Weekly U of T Workshop." *CBC News*. November 5, 2016. https://www.cbc.ca/news/canada/toronto/syrian-university-of-toronto-languages-1.3838658.
Immigration and Nationality Act (INA). 1965. 8 USC 1101. https://uscode.house.gov/view.xhtml?req=granuleid%3AUSC-prelim-title8-section1101&num=0&edition=prelim.
Institute of International Education (IIE). 2020. "Student Emergency Initiatives (SEI)." https://www.iie.org/Programs/Student-Emergency-Initiatives.
Jusoor. 2020. Jusoor Scholarship Program. https://jusoorsyria.com/programs/jusoor-scholarship-program/.
Kalachova, Alyona. 2019. "WES Gateway Program Named 'Promising Practice' in Settlement, Integration in Canada." *Global Talent Bridge Partner Blog* (blog), *World Education Services*. May 20, 2019. https://www.wes.org/partners/gtb-blog/canada-gateway-program-named-promising-practice-in-settlement-integration/.
Kanno, Yasuko, and Manka M. Varghese. 2010. "Immigrant and Refugee ESL Students' Challenges to Accessing Four-Year College Education: From Language Policy to Education Policy." *Journal of Language, Identity, and Education* 9, 5:310–328.
Knight, Jane, and Hans De Wit. 1995. "Strategies for Internationalization of Higher Education: Historical and Conceptual Perspectives." In *Strategies for Internationalization of Higher Education: A Comparative Study of Australia, Canada, Europe, and the United States of America*, ed. Hans De Wit. Amsterdam: European Association of International Education (EAIE).
Loo, Bryce. 2016. *Recognizing Refugee Qualifications: Practical Tips for Credential Assessment*. New York, NY: World Education Services (WES). https://knowledge.wes.org/wes-research-report-recognizing-refugee-credentials.html.
Loo, Bryce. 2017. "Early Insights from Canada: What Help Do Refugees Need to Enroll in North American Higher Education?" *WENR: World Education News and Reviews*. May 2, 2017. https://wenr.wes.org/2017/05/early-insights-from-a-canada-what-help-do-refugees-need-to-enroll-in-north-american-higher-education.
Loo, Bryce. 2019. "North American Policy and Practice: Refugee Qualifications and Access to Higher Education." In *Higher Education Challenges for Migrant and Refugee Students in a Global World*, ed. Khalid Arar, Kussai Haj-Yehia, David B. Ross, and Yasar Kondakci. New York, NY: Peter Lang.

Masson, Sean T. 2009. "Cracking Open the Golden Door: Revisiting U.S. Asylum Law's Response to China's One-Child Policy." *Hofstra Law Review* 37, 4:1135–1169.

McKee, Carolyn, Lee-Anne Lavell, Michelle Manks, and Ashley Korn. 2019. "Fostering Better Integration Through Youth-Led Refugee Sponsorship." *Refuge: Canada's Journal on Refugees* 35, 2:74–85.

Millner, Wesley. 2016. "Displaced Students Enriching the University of Evansville." In *Supporting Displaced and Refugee Students in Higher Education: Principles and Best Practices*, ed. Nele Feldman and Courtney Lind. New York, NY: Institute of International Education (IIE). https://www.iie.org/Research-and-Insights/Publications/Supporting-Displaced-and-Refugee-Students-in-Higher-Education.

Mozina, Megan E., and Gerald P. Doyle. 2016. "Defining the Challenges and Developing Solutions: Illinois Tech's Support for Syrian Students." In *Supporting Displaced and Refugee Students in Higher Education: Principles and Best Practices*, ed. Nele Feldman and Courtney Lind. New York, NY: Institute of International Education (IIE). https://www.iie.org/Research-and-Insights/Publications/Supporting-Displaced-and-Refugee-Students-in-Higher-Education.

Murray, Jennifer. 2016. "Bard College: Responding to Syrian Refugee Crisis in New York and Berlin." In *Supporting Displaced and Refugee Students in Higher Education: Principles and Best Practices*, ed. Nele Feldman and Courtney Lind. New York, NY: Institute of International Education (IIE). https://www.iie.org/Research-and-Insights/Publications/Supporting-Displaced-and-Refugee-Students-in-Higher-Education.

National Association of Student Financial Aid Administrators (NASFAA). 2018. *Tip Sheet for Refugee and Asylee Students*. https://www.nasfaa.org/uploads/documents/Tip_Sheet_Refugee_Asylee_Students.pdf.

National Conference of State Legislatures (NCSL). 2019. *Undocumented Student Tuition: Overview*. September 19, 2019. https://www.ncsl.org/research/education/undocumented-student-tuition-overview.aspx#.

Perry, Kristen H., and Christine A. Mallozzi. (2011). "'Are You *Able* to…to Learn? Power and Access to Higher Education for African Refugees in the USA." *Power and Education* 3, 3:249–262.

Peterson, Glen. 2010. "'Education Changes the World': The World University Service of Canada's Student Refugee Program." *Refuge: Canada's Journal on Refugees* 27, 2:111–121.

Presidents' Alliance on Higher Education and Immigration. 2020. "About the Alliance." https://www.presidentsimmigrationalliance.org/about/.

Sachs, Jeffrey. 2007. "Climate Change Refugees." *Scientific American*. June 1, 2007. https://www.scientificamerican.com/article/climate-change-refugees/.

Shakya, Yogendra B., Sepali Guruge, Michaela Hynie, Arzo Akbari, Mohamed Malik, Sheila Htoo, Azza Khogali, Stella Abiyo Mona, Rabea Murtaza, and Sarah Alley. 2012. "Aspirations for Higher Education Among Newcomer Refugee Youth in Toronto: Expectations, Challenges, and Strategies." *Refuge: Canada's Journal on Refugees* 27, 2:65–78.

Shankar, Saguna, Heather L. O'Brien, Elissa How, Yilei Wendy Lu, Millicent Mabi, and Cecilia Rose. 2016. "The Role of Information in the Settlement Experiences of Refugee Students." *Proceedings of the Association for Information Science and Technology* 53, 1:1–6.

Stanton, Andrea. 2016. "Best Practices: Making Use of Existing University Resources to Welcome and Integrate Refugee Students." In *Supporting Displaced and Refugee Students in Higher Education: Principles and Best Practices*, ed. Nele Feldman and Courtney Lind. New York, NY: Institute of International Education (IIE). https://www.iie.org/Research-and-Insights/Publications/Supporting-Displaced-and-Refugee-Students-in-Higher-Education.

Streitwieser, Bernhard, Bryce Loo, Mara Ohorodnik, and Jisun Jeong. 2019. "Access for Refugees into Higher Education: A Review of Interventions in North America and Europe." *Journal of Studies in International Education* 23, 4:473–496.

Tobenkin, David. 2006a. "Escape to the Ivory Tower." *International Educator*, September/October 2006. https://www.nafsa.org/professional-resources/publications/international-educator-septemberoctober-2006.

Tobenkin, David. 2006b. "Web Extra! Financial Aid Challenges for Political Asylee and Refugee Students." *International Educator*, September/October 2006. https://www.nafsa.org/professional-resources/publications/web-extra-financial-aid-challenges-political-asylee-and-refugee-students.

Tooley, Brenda. 2016. "Transforming Lives, Building Community: Active Engagement in the IIE Consortium Addressing the Crisis in Syria." In *Supporting Displaced and Refugee Students in Higher Education: Principles and Best Practices*, ed. Nele Feldman and Courtney Lind. New York, NY: Institute of International Education (IIE). https://www.iie.org/Research-and-Insights/Publications/Supporting-Displaced-and-Refugee-Students-in-Higher-Education.

Unangst, Lisa. 2019. "Human Rights Discourse and Refugee Higher Education." *Inside Higher Ed* (blog). June 23, 2019. https://www.insidehighered.com/blogs/world-view/human-rights-discourse-and-refugee-higher-education.

United Nations. 2010. *Convention and Protocol Related to the Status of Refugees.* Geneva, Switzerland: United Nations High Commissioner for Refugees (UNHCR). https://www.unhcr.org/en-us/3b66c2aa10.

United Nations High Commissioner for Refugees (UNHCR). 2020. "Figures at a Glance." https://www.unhcr.org/en-us/figures-at-a-glance.html.

United States Customs and Immigration Services (USCIS). 2020a. "Asylum." https://www.uscis.gov/humanitarian/refugees-and-asylum/asylum.

United States Customs and Immigration Services (USCIS). 2020b. "Humanitarian." https://www.uscis.gov/humanitarian.

United States Customs and Immigration Services (USCIS). 2020c. "Refugees." https://www.uscis.gov/humanitarian/refugees-and-asylum/refugees.

United States Department of State. 2020. "Special Immigrant Visas (SIVs) for Iraqi and Afghan Translators/Interpreters." https://travel.state.gov/content/travel/en/us-visas/immigrate/siv-iraqi-afghan-translators-interpreters.html.

University Alliance for Refugees and At-Risk Migrants. 2020. "About Us." https://www.uarrm.org/about.

Vasilogambros, Matt. 2016. "The Folly of Under-educating the Undocumented." *The Atlantic*, March 16, 2016. https://www.theatlantic.com/politics/archive/2016/03/the-folly-of-under-educating-the-undocumented/473877/.

Watenpaugh, Keith D. 2016. "Principles for the Protection and Support of Refugee University Students: A Global Imperative and the Definitive Challenge to the Human Right to Education." In *Supporting Displaced and Refugee Students in Higher Education: Principles and Best Practices*, ed. Nele Feldman and Courtney Lind. New York, NY: Institute of International Education (IIE). https://www.iie.org/Research-and-Insights/Publications/Supporting-Displaced-and-Refugee-Students-in-Higher-Education.

World Education Services (WES). 2018. *A Way Forward for Refugees: Findings from the WES Pilot Project.* New York, NY: World Education Services (WES). https://knowledge.wes.org/GlobalTalentBridge-A-Way-Forward-for-Refugees-Findings-from-the-WES-Pilot-Project.html.

World Education Services (WES). 2019. *Accessing Education, Licensure, Employment: Addendum to* A Way Forward for Refugees. New York, NY: World Education Services (WES). https://knowledge.wes.org/GlobalTalentBridge-A-Way-Forward-for-Refugees-Findings-from-the-WES-Pilot-Project.html.

World University Service of Canada (WUSC). 2020. "Student Refugee Program." https://srp.wusc.ca.

Yi, Varaxy, and Judy Marquez Kiyama. 2018. *Failed Educational Justice: Refugee Students' Postsecondary Realities in Restrictive Times*. Las Vegas, NV: Association for the Study of Higher Education (ASHE). https://cece.sitehost.iu.edu/wordpress/wp-content/uploads/2017/02/Failed-Educational-Justice-FINAL-2.pdf.

Zhang, Jing, and Patricia Goodson. 2011. "Predictors of International Students' Psychosocial Adjustment to Life in the United States: A Systematic Review." *International Journal of Intercultural Relations* 35, 2:139–162.

Endnote

[1] The Special Immigrant Visa (SIV) is for Afghans and Iraqis who worked for the U.S. military in those countries, usually as translators, who then find themselves threatened because of their work with the U.S. (United States Department of State 2020). An SIV holder may settle in the U.S. permanently.

11

Exploring the Intersection of Transnationalism and Critical Race Theory[1]

A Critical Race Analysis of International Students' Experiences in the United States

CHRISTINA W. YAO, PhD; CHRYSTAL A. GEORGE MWANGI, PhD; AND VICTORIA K. MALANEY BROWN, PhD

The past 2 decades have seen a major increase in the number of international students attending institutions of higher education in the United States. During the 2018–19 academic year, there were nearly 1.2 million international students studying in the United States, representing a 63 percent increase from 2008–09 and a 123 percent increase from 1998–99 (IIE 2019). These students are an increasingly heterogeneous population, originating from more than 200 countries (IIE 2019). The top 10 countries of origin for international students include six Asian countries, which send 63 percent of the total number of international students to the United States (IIE 2019). Other countries in the top 10 include Brazil, Canada, Mexico, and Saudi Arabia (IIE 2019).

In the U.S. context, many of these international students are considered to be racial and/or ethnic minorities, and they often face racism, nativism, and other forms of discrimination (Fries-Britt, George Mwangi, and Peralta 2014a; George Mwangi et al. 2016; Hanassab 2006). Yet much of the existing literature focuses on how international students can assimilate and cope with these issues rather than using a social justice-oriented lens to interrogate the systems of oppression that create negative student experiences. Using Critical Race Theory (CRT) as a framework, this chapter provides a critical review of literature on the role of structural systems affecting international students' experiences and the intersection of racism with other forms of marginalization.

First, we provide an overview of CRT as our theoretical framework and literature search process. We engage CRT to analyze extant scholarship on international students' entry into and experiences within the U.S. higher education system. We argue for the utility of CRT in understanding international student experiences in the United States and provide implications for practice, theory, and future research to contribute to Critical Race Praxis (Yamamoto 1997), which bridges the gap between theory and practice and is one of the central tenets of CRT.

Theoretical Framework

The concept of CRT emerged from activists and scholars during the 1970s who were interested in studying race, racism, and power in the U.S. legal system (Crenshaw 1988). Informed by the U.S. civil rights movements in the 1960s, CRT focuses on social justice, liberation, and economic empowerment (McCoy and Rodricks 2015). CRT argues for the centrality of race and racism as well as the importance of taking an activist stance to counter White hegemony, White supremacy, and claims of colorblindness and meritocracy (Matsuda et al. 1993). As a result of the interconnections between global cultures and society, CRT can be expanded beyond a U.S.-centric theory used only for understanding the experiences of domestic racial groups. International students to the United States, particularly those from non-White and non-English-speaking countries, are often othered and racialized using U.S. constructs of race. CRT can provide a lens for interrogating the racism and racialization they experience.

There are several core tenets that frame how CRT is applied, including

- the permanence and endemic nature of race and racism in U.S. society;
- sharing of the experiential knowledge that people of Color experience every day;
- interest in convergence theory, which occurs when the dominant culture tolerates advances for racial justice only when it suits its own personal interest;

- intersectionality, which situates experiences within the context of multiple, interlocking systems of oppression that are interrelated and shaped by one another;

- Whiteness as property, which benefits and privileges that which is associated with Whiteness and the protection of Whiteness as an asset;

- critique of liberalism and critique of meritocracy, which engages a rejection of colorblindness, a postracial society, and the belief that individual failure or success is driven by ability;

- an expansive and restricted view of equality where the expansive view advances the idea that equality can redress the effects of racial oppression and subordination; and

- a commitment to social justice (Delgado and Stefancic 2001; McCoy and Rodricks 2015).

Ladson-Billings and Tate (1995) introduced the use of CRT in education scholarship, which has led to its growing application in this field (e.g., Decuir and Dixson 2004; Solórzano, Ceja, and Yosso 2000). Since the development of CRT in the 1970s, it has evolved to include the experiences of other marginalized racial groups including AsianCrit (Liu 2009) and LatCrit (Perez Huber 2010).

CRT was developed as a response to U.S. systems of oppression, particularly as they relate to U.S. domestic people of Color, and until recently, it was used almost exclusively by U.S. scholars to examine U.S.-based research problems. However, CRT can be applied, revised, and expanded in a transnational context and used to understand and frame international students' experiences (Gillborn 2008). We situate international students' experiences within the U.S. context, while also engaging a global dimension that emphasizes the experiences of foreign-born people of Color in colleges and universities. Mills (1997, 3) states, "Racism is global White supremacy and is itself a political system, a particular power structure of formal and informal rule, privilege, socio-economic advantages." A stronger emphasis must be placed on international students' experiences in the United States from a systems perspective, and CRT can lend to this perspective due to its emphasis on countering systems of White hegemony, White supremacy, and claims of colorblindness and meritocracy that affect the lives of international students on predominantly White institutions (PWI) in the United States. Thus, we center our analysis and critique of scholarship on the experiences of international students within a context that emphasizes PWIs as highly globalized as well as highly racialized.

Literature Search

Our review included journal articles and reports published between 1996 and 2016 to focus on contemporary scholarship. We searched five bibliographic databases (Academic Search Premier, ERIC, Education Research Complete, PsycINFO, and Social Sciences Citation Index) using the following search term combinations: "international students" AND "United States" AND (race OR diversity). From the 185 articles and reports that were retrieved, we removed duplicates, inaccessible documents, and articles and reports that did not focus on the topic of inquiry (e.g., articles focused on international students in Australia or Canada or on U.S. students). This resulted in 53 articles and reports remaining for review. We reviewed the reference lists of these documents and added 10 articles and reports that were relevant but did not appear in our search. This provided a total of 63 articles and reports that we reviewed for this analysis.

Literature Analysis

We engaged CRT as a conceptual lens to analyze the literature and used the tenets most salient to the international student experience in the United States as a way to structure this chapter: permanence and centrality of race and racism, Whiteness as property and White supremacy, intersectionality, and meritocracy and interest convergence.

Permanence and Centrality of Race and Racism

The history of colonization and slavery in the United States along racial and ethnic lines led to the development of a racial hierarchy, with those considered to be "White" at the top and all other populations considered "of Color" positioned beneath (Bashi and McDaniel 1997; Smedley 1993). Racial positioning in the United States reflects this historical racial stratification and ultimately affects opportunities for social mobility and adjustment (Alba and Nee 2003; Waters 1994). The experiences and socialization of international students in the United States are situated within this racial reality, as well as in how their race is constructed in the U.S. context.

For many international students of Color, adjusting to a prescribed U.S. racial minority identity can be a new and perplexing experience, particularly for students who come from racially homogenous countries or countries where they are of the racial majority (Boafo-Arthur 2014; Bordoloi 2014; Constantine et al. 2005; George Mwangi and Fries-Britt 2015; George Mwangi et al. 2016; Wei et al. 2012). Some students may struggle adapting to differences in socialization around race from their home country with how they are racialized in the United States. For example, in studies on the campus experiences of foreign-born Black students, the findings suggest that because of the dissonance the participants experienced around race, they initially did not feel connected to race and racism in the United States and attempted to distance themselves from these issues (Fries-Britt, George Mwangi, and Peralta 2014a; George Mwangi and Fries-Britt 2015; George Mwangi et al. 2016). Yet, as CRT also suggests, the centrality of racism to the U.S. experience over time led to a number of campus racial encounters that forced students in these studies to consider their own racial status and identity in the U.S. context (Fries-Britt, George Mwangi, and Peralta 2014a; George Mwangi et al. 2016). This finding is also present in other research demonstrating that international students who have lived longer in the United States perceive more racial discrimination (Poyrazli and Lopez 2007).

A number of studies have demonstrated that international students of Color (primarily from Asia, the Middle East, Latin America, and Africa) often perceive that they experience more discrimination from U.S. students and faculty than do their White international student peers (Boafo-Arthur 2014; Bonazzo and Wong 2007; Hanassab 2006; Lee 2010; Lee and Opio 2011; Lee and Rice 2007; Lobnibe 2013; Poyrazli and Grahame 2007; Trice 2004). These students' experiences often included social isolation, being called racial slurs, and other forms of harassment (Bordoloi 2014; Constantine et al. 2005; Ee 2013; Fries-Britt, George Mwangi, and Peralta 2014a; Lee and Opio 2011; Lee and Rice 2007; The Civil Rights Project 2003). Hanassab (2006) also found that non-White international students often perceived experiencing racial discrimination from campus staff, potential employers, and members of the local community. Much of the literature is clear in finding that these racialized and racist experiences can negatively affect international students' college success and well-being, as discrimination is found to increase homesickness and decrease learning outcomes, self-esteem, and engagement, as well as lead to greater stress, academic withdrawal, and self-isolation (Fries-Britt, George Mwangi, and Peralta 2014a; Bordoloi 2014; Karuppan and Barari 2010; Poyrazli and Lopez 2007; Schmitt, Spears, and Branscombe 2002).

Although the literature demonstrates that race and racism are central to international students' educational experiences, less is discussed about universities' roles and responsibilities. Instead, much of the literature focuses on students' coping mechanisms, such as denial, silence, or the burden of trying to adapt (Boafo-Arthur 2014; Bonazzo and Wong 2007; Ee 2013; Lee 2007; Lee and Opio 2011). de Araujo (2011) explains that this focus on coping and adjustment has led many scholars and practitioners to emphasize ways of reducing stress for international students. For example, Constantine et al. (2005) offer counseling practitioners recommendations to help students cope with their experiences. Yet this solution does not challenge racist systems or provide mechanisms for greater change at an institutional or societal level, as Lee and Rice (2007, 385) describe: "We find that not all of the issues international students face can be problematized as matters of adjustment, as much research does, but that some of the more serious challenges are due to inadequacies within the host society." Scholarship related to international students and their racialized experiences should center on challenging systemic racism and oppression, as well as placing greater onus on universities to improve their campus racial climate.

Whiteness as Property and White Supremacy

White culture is considered normative in U.S. society, as illustrated in early immigration policies that privileged White people seeking entry into the

United States (Delgado and Stefancic 2001). Whiteness as property and the supremacy of Whiteness are apparent in three specific areas related to international students in the United States: the privileged positioning of White American values, the pervasiveness of English as the dominant language, and the assumption of assimilation and acculturation of foreign students.

As illustrated in previous literature, international students of Color often have very different experiences compared with international students from predominantly English-speaking, White cultures. As such, international students of Color may experience difficulties on campus due to different power dynamics, particularly related to their cultural backgrounds and language differences. American students who seek to maintain their position of supremacy may often view international students in a negative manner (Bordoloi 2014; Charles-Toussaint and Crowson 2010). For example, Charles-Toussaint and Crowson (2010) conducted a study of American students, which included White students and students of Color, at one U.S. institution to examine American students' prejudicial attitudes toward international students. Charles-Toussaint and Crowson (2010, 423) found that the American students viewed international students "as threatening their beliefs and values, while also posing threats to their social status and economic, educational, and physical well-being." The authors posit that their participants' prejudiced attitudes stem "from their desires for power and superiority" (Charles-Toussaint and Crowson 2010, 423).

Another example of White and Western supremacy is exhibited through the pervasiveness of English language dominance. English language proficiency has had a direct effect on international students' overall engagement and academic experience, indicating the hegemonic influence of the English language in U.S. academic spaces (Lefdahl-Davis and Perrone-McGovern 2015). Studies indicate that strong English language proficiency can mitigate discrimination (Chapman Wadsworth, Hecht, and Jung 2008; Di Angelo 2006; Karuppan and Barari 2010), as international students with higher English proficiency tended to have lower perceived discrimination. Yao (2016) found that limited English language proficiency can negatively affect international students' overall sense of belonging, leading to feelings of loneliness and isolation at a PWI.

Such negative experiences could lead to feelings of inferiority by international students who may feel the need to work harder to prove their worth on campus, while being positioned less favorably than their White American peers.

Much of the current literature (e.g., Boafo-Arthur 2014; Di Angelo 2006; Geary 2016; Frey and Roysircar 2006; Lefdahl-Davis and Perrone-McGovern 2015; Yan and Berliner 2011) includes recommendations that imply the need for international students to assimilate to dominant White norms rather than consider how host institutions can establish more accepting practices. Yan and Berliner (2011) suggest that Chinese international students should integrate to the larger campus culture as a way to successfully acculturate to the United States, and institutions must develop an integration strategy to assist Chinese students' transition to university life. This recommendation was repeated by Boafo-Arthur (2014), who suggests that institutions must assist Black African international students in their adjustment and acculturation to the United States to cope with prejudice and discrimination. As indicated by these studies, assimilation into the dominant campus culture is held up as the ideal for mitigating negative and discriminatory experiences, which contributes to the maintenance and reification of a White supremacist system.

Intersectionality

Delgado and Stefancic (2001, 51) define intersectionality as "the examination of race, sex, class, national origin, and sexual orientation, and how their combination plays out in various settings." International students can experience multiple points of privilege and oppression given their intersecting identities (e.g., nativity, race/ethnicity, religion, gender, socioeconomic status) at different points in time. Racialized experiences are further complicated by a foreign status that can also evoke xenophobia and nativism from U.S. peers and faculty. For example, African international students may experience discrimination for being African and for being Black (Boafo-Arthur 2014; Constantine et al. 2005), which was similar to the discriminatory experiences of international students based on race, nativity, and religion in Lee and Opio's (2011) study. Yet, multiple studies did not acknowledge the intersections of identities within their research design or analysis or even disaggregate international student data (e.g., Sherry, Thomas, and Chui 2010; Smith and Khawaja 2011). For example, in a study focusing on international students from Latin American and Asian countries who experienced psychological distress and difficulties adjusting to the United States, the authors did not seem to discuss intersectionality with regard to students' age and gender (Wilton and Constantine 2003). While the literature does acknowledge the intersections of social identities, several studies do not account for differences in countries of origin or how nativity influences perceptions of skin color and religious beliefs (Sherry, Thomas, and Chui 2010; Smith and Khawaja 2011).

An example of intersectionality includes international students often contending with instances of neoracism, which is a form of discrimination that is "attributed to skin color as well as culture, national origin, and relationships between countries" (Lee 2007, 28). In particular, students from Africa, East Asia, India, Latin America and the Middle East experienced more discrimination than students from Canada and Europe (Lee 2007). International students can often face neoracism based on their multiple social identities related to socioeconomic status, national origin, skin color, and cultural norms (Lee 2007). In another study, Lee and Rice (2007) found that in higher education, neoracism can occur in the form of rejection of admission, subjective academic evaluations, loss or lack of financial aid, negative comments from faculty or fellow students, and difficulties forming interpersonal relationships in the host country.

Meritocracy and Interest Convergence

Altbach and Knight (2007) describe the internationalization of higher education as an enterprise that is mostly driven by profit. International students are often used as opportunities for institutions to make a profit, most notably through high student fees and the utilization of international graduates for inexpensive research and teaching labor.

Increasing the number of international students matters to the United States because these students provide an opportunity to stay competitive in the global economic market (Douglass and Edelstein 2009; García and de Lourdes Villarreal 2014). As such, universities may admit international students based on their ability to fulfill economic, political, and diversity demands. In addition, the U.S. domestic supply of "native students, particularly those in STEM fields at the undergraduate level, is limited" (Douglass and Edelstein 2009, 12), and thus, international students are needed to fill the talent pool. As a result, interest convergence is at play to ensure the financial and workforce gains from international students' presence in the United States.

Interest convergence is perhaps the most visible tenet of CRT in international student-related research in the U.S. context. U.S. colleges and universities often recruit international students to serve the needs of the host campus and U.S. society. For example, in a report on the need to improve U.S. higher education access to international students, NAFSA: Association of International Educators (2003, 5) explains, "It is, therefore, worth restating the ways in which openness to international students continues to serve the fundamental interests of U.S. foreign policy, our economy, and our educational system—even more so in an age of global terrorism." Scholarship then mirrors this by describing the significance of research on international students' experiences as important to ensuring U.S. higher education's competitive edge as a major enrollment location (Altbach and Knight 2007; Douglass and Edelstein 2009).

The literature clearly positions international students to the United States as sources of economic gain (e.g., Altbach and Knight 2007; de Araujo 2011; George Mwangi 2013; García and de Lourdes Villarreal 2014; Lee and Opio 2011; Lee and Rice 2007; Peterson et al. 1999; Ritter 2016). International students are such a driving economic force because they pay higher tuition than domestic students and many pay out of pocket. George Mwangi (2013) demonstrates this argument by illustrating that there is higher international student enrollment when there is a decrease in state appropriations, suggesting these students may help increase revenue from tuition when state funding for higher education is reduced. International students are also discussed as a source for filling cultural diversity needs (e.g., Ault and Martell 2007; George Mwangi 2013; García and de Lourdes Villarreal 2014; Douglass and Edelstein 2009; de Araujo 2011; Lee and Opio 2011; Lee and Rice 2007; Rose-Redwood 2010; Tas 2013). Thus, the presence of international students can be part of institutional strategies for increasing the intercultural competency (Breuning 2007; Lefdahl-Davis and Perrone-McGovern 2015) and engagement of domestic students, as well as creating greater diplomacy between the United States and other nations (Lee and Rice 2007; Peterson et al. 1999).

Specific demographics of international students can be recruited to help fulfill other U.S. societal or university goals. Lee and Opio (2011, 629–630) discuss the issue of interest convergence related to international student athletes, stating, "The driving forces behind international student athlete flows have shifted in recent years from motives related to diplomatic exchange to competition for athletic title gains and institutional prestige. Indirectly, financial forces also come into play."

While many U.S. universities engage in comprehensive efforts to recruit international students, ensuring these students' positive adjustment and success would reflect socially just institutional practice. However, even when scholars point to the need to support international students, it is often situated within the larger premise serving the interests of broader U.S. society. Fries-Britt, George Mwangi, and Peralta (2014b, 459) demonstrate this in their problem statement:

> U.S. policymakers name the insufficient production of American graduates in STEM to meet occupational demands over the past 2 decades as a national crisis (National Science Board 2012). This lack of STEM participation led to the recruitment of foreign-born students and professionals to the U.S. in order to mitigate the gap in the STEM talent pipeline (National Science Board 2012)....Investigating the academic adjustment and success of foreign-born students is critical as they comprise a valuable component of the STEM pipeline.

Furthermore, implications from several studies reflect the need for improving the educational experiences of international students to benefit host universities' reputation and marketability (e.g., Karuppan and Barari 2010; Lee 2010; Yan and Berliner 2011). For example, Karuppan and Barari (2010) indicate that while the United States is still the major destination for international students, the country is losing its competitive edge to other nations, particularly since implementation of post-September 11 immigration restrictions. Karuppan and Barari (2010) argue that to attract more international students to the United

States, it is important that students have a positive educational experience so they will help recruit future students. These factors align with the concept of interest convergence in that international student recruitment appears to be driven by the interests of U.S. institutions, with less attention given to international students' campus experiences. Further, scholars who use this type of rationale to demonstrate the significance of their research reify interest convergence and the idea that negative international student experiences are only important to investigate as a means of serving the interests and benefit of universities.

Critical Race Praxis: Recommendations for Practice, Theory, and Research

CRT must be connected to action to realize its full potential. Without the connection to a real-world application, CRT exists only as a theoretical construct for examining educational issues. Thus, Critical Race Praxis (Yamamoto 1997), which attempts to bridge the gap between theory and practice, is essential to moving beyond a surface examination of international students' experiences. In this section, we offer suggestions for Critical Race Praxis through practice, theory, and research.

Implications for Practice

For most U.S. universities, when a student indicates that they are "international" on a college application or other university document, they are not asked their race or their race is not included in institutional data (George Mwangi 2014). The ramification of this practice is that international students are left out of support programming and services for racially minoritized students, further separating them from opportunities to process their racial identity and racism in the United States or obtain support around those issues. While international students may define their racial identity in a different way than might be defined in the U.S. context, and the way they perceive their racial identity in the United States may shift over time, our review of literature demonstrates that they are "raced" in the United States. We suggest that universities should capture and report both the race and the domestic or international status of their students. This transparency is a first step in acknowledging the complexity of race and racism on college campuses, the existence of race beyond a U.S. construct, and the need for support for all students of Color (domestic and international) related to racial identity.

Literature shows that international students are subjected to racism, prejudice, and discrimination throughout their educational experiences in the United State, often without targeted university support for navigating those experiences (Boafo-Arthur 2014; Bonazzo and Wong 2007; Chapman Wadsworth, Hecht, and Jung 2008; Lee 2007; Lee and Opio 2011; Tamale 1996; Yao 2018). There are a number of practices that universities can develop to remedy this. For example, when bias incidents happen to international students, institutions should not require students to explain these experiences in English if the student is more comfortable and confident using a different language. Offering translators and the option for international students to write reports of bias incidents in their native language is one way in which universities can acknowledge and resist English language dominance as an oppressive practice.

Universities should move away from models in which the responsibility for supporting international students is in one office. Institutions should not benefit from the diversity that international students of Color embody and, yet, lack substantial commitment to fighting racist-nativism and improving equity on their campuses (Ahmed 2012). It is imperative that universities ultimately move beyond services and programming (e.g., coping mechanisms) as a solution for challenges that international students experience on an individual level and work toward institutional transformation at a structural level. This is a social justice goal that should be integrated into universities' internationalization and diversity strategies to ensure the sustained success of international students.

Implications for Theory

This review demonstrates that international students' experiences in the United States are rife with othering, power inequities, and racialization that make CRT an applicable framework. Expanding CRT to examine international students' experiences in the United States contributes to better understanding the systems of oppression that affect international students as a racialized student group on campuses.

While we argue for the utility of CRT for understanding international students' experiences, we also contend that it can be extended to better encompass a global context that intersects the U.S. socio-historical contexts with student mobility. This is relevant given the rapidly increasing levels of transnationalism, migration, and mobility to the United States. Scholars have acknowledged the importance of a global context in the development of CRT branches including AsianCrit and LatCrit, which consider issues related to immigration, citizenship, language rights, accent, and discrimination based on national origin (Delgado and Stefancic 2001). Although several scholars have applied CRT to international contexts (e.g., Chakrabarty 2012; Kitching 2015; Lynn and Jennings 2009; Schroeter and James 2015; Warmington 2012), we did not see evidence in the literature that these theories had yet been applied directly to the experiences of international students in the United States.

Although greater numbers of non-White international students are enrolling in U.S. universities, our analysis illustrates that entry to the United States is often predicated on factors such as ability to pay for college or U.S.-home country relations, rather than solely on student merit or expanding educational opportunities. Immigration laws and policies can serve as an additional gatekeeping function (Lee 2006), particularly those related to student visas, which shape student mobility as an elitist activity. These factors can be used to restrict or exclude individuals and whole nations in their access to U.S. higher education. In alignment with CRT, we view international student enrollment in the United States as a racial project (García and de Lourdes Villarreal 2014; Omi and Winant 2015) in which international students are treated as economic and political commodities used to reify a White supremacist system. We encourage further expansion of CRT to focus on how policies related to international student mobility and temporary immigration (e.g., student visas, college enrollment, college financing) interact to perpetuate the existing racialized social structure and justify racial inequalities.

Just as CRT rejects an ahistorical and a-contextual lens (Delgado and Stefancic 2001), it is important to consider an international student's home country as well as that country's historical, political, economic, and cultural contexts. This is particularly important because the relationship between international students' sending and receiving countries can be situated within a dynamic of hegemony, coloniality, and dominance due to the movement of race through constantly changing global forces (Mishra Tarc 2013). The enrollment of international students in the United States can have major negative social and economic effects on Global South nations, such as when students do not return after attaining a degree (e.g., brain drain). Conversely, this often has a positive impact on the U.S. economy and workforce (e.g., brain gain; Knight 2008).

Many of the nations losing talent have majority populations of Color, which CRT demonstrates as an intentional reinforcement of racial subordination. This is reflected in the STEM talent pipeline in the United States, which is "leaky" and leads to the recruitment of international students to mitigate this issue. While a number of African international students are enrolled in STEM graduate programs in the United States, there are more African engineers in the United States than in all of Africa, illustrating a great loss of talent to that continent (Kaba 2009). CRT should be expanded to consider U.S. dynamics with sending countries, the impact of immigration to the United States on the sending country, and how these issues are situated within the context of racial privilege, hegemony, and colonialism. Researchers can also consider what happens when international students return to their home countries. The literature demonstrates the power of acculturative forces in U.S. higher education, the racialization process that exists, and the privileging of English and U.S. and Western ways of knowing. These experiences will ultimately affect international students and their engagement in their home societies when they return. CRT can be used to investigate the global nature and maintenance of White supremacy through the transnational movement of international students.

Implications for Research

Much of the literature emphasized students' psychological experiences, which are important; however, researchers also need to focus on the systemic and structural oppression that affect international students' experiences on campus. For example, how do institutions recruit international students? How can CRT be used to examine marketing practices?

In addition, we recommend that we shift the emphasis of research from international student recruitment to international students' experiences. Although enrollment and admissions are important, the experiences and motivations for student success could shift the narrative from international students as an economic force to international students as members of a collegiate community. This could address the interest convergence of international student recruitment to fulfill institutional and national financial needs.

Finally, we must commit to the centrality of experiential knowledge of students of Color in higher education scholarship and research. We recommend that research on international students' experiences be disaggregated, as we know that White international students and international students of Color have very different experiences given skin color, national origin, and language. In addition, moving beyond quantitative studies would allow for international students to share their personal voice and narratives related to their campus experience. This can demonstrate a commitment to action and social justice, leading to Critical Race Praxis for the benefit of all college students.

References

Ahmed, Sara. 2012. *On Being Included: Racism and Diversity in Institutional Life.* Durham, NC: Duke University Press.

Alba, Richard, and Victor Nee. 2003. *Remaking the American Mainstream: Assimilation and Contemporary Immigration.* Cambridge, MA: Harvard University Press.

Altbach, Philip, and Jane Knight. 2007. "The Internationalization of Higher Education: Motivations and Realities." *Journal of Studies in International Education* 1, 3–4:290–305.

Ault, David, and Kathryn Martell. 2007. "The Role of International Exchange Programs to Promote Diversity on College Campuses: A Case Study." *Journal of Teaching in International Business* 18:153–178.

Bashi, Vilna, and Antonio McDaniel. 1997. "A Theory of Immigration and Racial Stratification." *Journal of Black Studies* 27, 5:668–682.

Boafo-Arthur, Susan. 2014. "Acculturative Experiences of Black-African International Students." *International Journal of Advanced Counseling* 36, 1:115–124.

Bonazzo, Claude, and Joel Wong. 2007. "Japanese International Female Students' Experience of Discrimination, Prejudice, and Stereotypes." *College Student Journal* 41, 3:631–639.

Bordoloi, Samit. 2014. "On Being Brown and Foreign: The Racialization of an International Student Within Academia." *Sociological Imagination* 50, 3:50–66.

Breuning, Marijke. 2007. "Undergraduate International Students: A Resource for the Intercultural Education of American Peers?" *College Student Journal* 41, 1:1114–1122.

Chakrabarty, Namita. 2012. "Buried Alive: The Psychoanalysis of Racial Absence in Preparedness/Education." *Race Ethnicity and Education* 15, 1:43–63.

Chapman Wadsworth, Brooke, Michael Hecht, and Eura Jung. 2008. "The Role of Identity Gaps, Discrimination, and Acculturation in International Students' Educational Satisfaction in American Classrooms." *Communication Education* 57, 1:64–87.

Charles-Toussaint, Gifflene, and Michael Crowson. 2010. "Prejudice Against International Students: The Role of Threat Perceptions and Authoritarian Dispositions in U.S. Students." *The Journal of Psychology* 144, 5:413–428.

The Civil Rights Project. 2003. *Know Your Rights on Campus: A Guide on Racial Profiling and Hate Crime for International Students in the United States.* Cambridge, MA: Harvard University.

Constantine, Madonna, Gregory Anderson, Berkel LaVerne, Leon Caldwell, and Shawn Utsey. 2005. "Examining the Cultural Adjustment Experiences of African International College Students: A Qualitative Analysis." *Journal of Counseling Psychology* 52, 1:57–66.

Crenshaw, Kimberlé. 1988. "Race, Reform, and Retrenchment: Transformation and Legitimation in Antidiscrimination Law." *Harvard Law Review* 101, 7:1331–1387.

de Araujo, Abrahao. 2011. "Adjustment Issues of International Students Enrolled in American Colleges and Universities: A Review of the Literature." *Higher Education Studies* 1, 1:1–8.

Decuir, Jessica, and Adrienne Dixson. 2004. "'So When it Comes Out, They Aren't That Surprised That It Is There': Using Critical Race Theory as a Tool of Analysis of Race and Racism in Education." *Educational Researcher* 33:26–31.

Delgado, Richard, and Jean Stefancic. 2001. *Critical Race Theory: An Introduction.* New York, NY: New York University Press.

Di Angelo, Robin. 2006. "The Production of Whiteness in Education: Asian International Students in a College Classroom." *Teachers College Record* 108, 10:1983–2000.

Douglass, John, and Richard Edelstein. 2009. "The Global Competition for Talent: The Rapidly Changing Market for International Students and the Need for a Strategic Approach in the US." *Center for Studies in Higher Education, Research and Occasional Paper Series.* https://cshe.berkeley.edu/publications/docs/ROPS.JD.RE.%20GlobalTalent.9.25.09.pdf.

Ee, Jongyeon. 2013. "'Is He an Idiot!' Experiences of International Students in the United States." *Journal of International Students* 3, 1:72–75.

Frey, Lisa, and Gargi Roysircar. 2006. "South Asian and East Asian International Students' Perceived Prejudice, Acculturation, and Frequency of Help Resource Utilization." *Journal of Multicultural Counseling and Development* 34:208–222.

Fries-Britt, Sharon, Chrystal George Mwangi, and Alicia Peralta. 2014a. "Learning Race in the U.S. Context: Perceptions of Race Among Foreign-Born Students of Color." *Journal of Diversity in Higher Education* 7, 1:1–13.

Fries-Britt, Sharon, Chrystal George Mwangi, and Alicia Peralta. 2014b. "The Acculturation Experiences of Foreign-Born Students of Color in Physics." *Journal of Student Affairs Research and Practice* 51, 4:459–471.

García, Hugo, and Maria de Lourdes Villareal. 2014. "The 'Redirecting' of International Students: American Higher Education Policy Hindrances and Implications." *Journal of International Students* 4, 2:126–136.

Geary, Danielle. 2016. "How Do We Get People to Interact? International Students and the American Experience." *Journal of International Students* 6, 2:527–541.

George Mwangi, Chrystal. 2013. "The Impact of State Financial Support on the Internationalization of Public Higher Education: A Panel Data Analysis." *Higher Education in Review* 10:61–77.

George Mwangi, Chrystal. 2014. "Complicating Blackness: Black Immigrants and Racial Positioning in U.S. Higher Education." *Journal of Critical Thought and Praxis* 3, 2:1–27.

George Mwangi, Chrystal, and Sharon Fries-Britt. 2015. "Black Within Black: The Perceptions of Black Immigrant Collegians and Their U.S. College Experience." *About Campus* 20, 2:16–23.

George Mwangi, Chrystal, Sharon Fries-Britt, Alicia Peralta, and Nina Daoud. 2016. "Examining Intraracial Dynamics and Engagement Between Native-born

and Foreign-Born Black Collegians in STEM." *Journal of Black Studies* 47, 7:773–794.
Gillborn, David. 2008. *Racism and Education: Coincidence or Conspiracy?* London: Routledge.
Hanassab, Shideh. 2006. "Diversity, International Students, and Perceived Discrimination: Implications for Educators and Counselors." *Journal of Studies in International Education* 10, 2:157–172.
Institute of International Education (IIE). 2019. *Open Doors 2019.* http://www.iie.org/en/Research-and-Publications/Open-Doors/Data.
Kaba, Amadu. 2009. "Africa's Migration Brain Drain: Factors Contributing to the Mass Emigration of Africa's Elite to the West." In *The New African Diaspora,* eds. Nkiru Nzegwu and Isidore Okpweho. Bloomington, IN: Indiana University Press.
Karuppan, Corinne, and Mahua Barari. 2010. "Perceived Discrimination and International Students' Learning: An Empirical Investigation." *Journal of Higher Education Policy and Management* 33, 1:67–83.
Kitching, Karl. 2015. "How the Irish Became Crt'd? 'Greening' Critical Race Theory, and the Pitfalls of a Normative Atlantic State View." *Race Ethnicity and Education* 18, 2:163–182.
Knight, Jane. 2008. "The Internationalization of Higher Education: Complexities and Realities." In *Higher Education in Africa: The International Dimension,* eds. Damtew Teferra and Jane Knight. Chestnut Hill, MA, and Accra, Ghana: Boston College Center for International Higher Education and Association of African Universities.
Ladson-Billings, Gloria, and William Tate. 1995. "Toward a Critical Race Theory of Education." *Teachers College Record* 97:47–68.
Lee, Erika. 2006. "A Nation of Immigrants and a Gatekeeping Nation: American Immigration Law and Policy." In *Companion to American Immigration History,* ed. Reed Ueda. Oxford, England: Blackwell Publishers.
Lee, Jenny. 2007. "Neo-Racism Toward International Students: A Critical Need for Change." *About Campus* 11, 6:28–30.
Lee, Jenny. 2010. "International Students' Experiences and Attitudes at a U.S. Host Institution: Self-Reports and Future Recommendations." *Journal of Research in International Education* 9, 1: 66–84.
Lee, Jenny, and Thomas Opio. 2011. "Coming to America: Challenges and Difficulties Faced by African Student Athletes." *Sport, Education and Society* 16, 5:629–644.

Lee, Jenny, and Charles Rice. 2007. "Welcome to America? International Student Perceptions of Discrimination." *Higher Education* 53:381–409.

Lefdahl-Davis, Erin, and Kristin Perrone-McGovern. 2015. "The Cultural Adjustment of Saudi Women International Students: A Qualitative Examination." *Journal of Cross-Cultural Psychology* 46, 3:406–434.

Liu, Amy. 2009. "Critical Race Theory, Asian Americans, and Higher Education: A Review of Research." *InterActions: UCLA Journal of Education and Information Studies* 5, 2:1–12.

Lobnibe, Jane-Frances. 2013. "Different Worlds, Mutual Expectations: African Graduate Student Mothers and the Burden of U.S. Higher Education." *Journal of Education and Learning* 2, 2:201–209.

Lynn, Marvin, and Michael Jennings. 2009. "Power, Politics, and Critical Race Pedagogy: A Critical Race Analysis of Black Male Teachers' Pedagogy." *Race Ethnicity and Education* 12, 2:173–196.

Matsuda, Mari, Charles Lawrence, Richard Delgado, and Kimberlé Crenshaw. 1993. *Words That Wound: Critical Race Theory, Assaultive Speech, and the First Amendment.* Boulder, CO: Westview.

McCoy, Dorian, and Dirk Rodricks. 2015. "Critical Race Theory in Higher Education: 20 Years of Theoretical and Research Innovations." *ASHE Higher Education Report* 41, 3:1–117.

Mills, Charles. 1997. *The Racial Contract.* New York: Cornell University Press.

Mishra Tarc, Aparna. 2013. "Race Moves: Following Global Manifestations of New Racisms in Intimate Space." *Race Ethnicity and Education* 16, 3:365–385.

NAFSA: Association of International Educators. 2003. *In America's Interest: Welcoming International Students.* Washington, DC: NAFSA: Association of International Educators.

Omi, Michael, and Howard Winant. 2015. *Racial Formation in the United States, Third Edition.* New York, NY: Routledge.

Perez Huber, Lindsay. 2010. "Using Latina/o Critical Race Theory (LatCrit) and Racist Nativism to Explore Intersectionality in the Educational Experiences of Undocumented Chicana College Students." *Educational Foundations* 24:77–96.

Peterson, Dennis, Peter Briggs, Luiza Dreasher, David Horner, and Trevor Nelson. 1999. "Contributions of International Students and Programs to Campus Diversity." *New Directions for Student Services* 1999, 86:67–77.

Poyrazli, Senel, and Kamini Grahame. 2007. "Barriers to Adjustment: Needs of International Students Within a Semi-Urban Campus Community." *Journal of Instructional Psychology* 34, 1:28–46.

Poyrazli, Senel, and Marcos Lopez. 2007. "An Exploratory Study of Perceived Discrimination and Homesickness: A Comparison of International Students and American Students." *The Journal of Psychology* 141, 3:263–280.

Ritter, Zachary. 2016. "International Students' Perceptions of Race and Socio-Economic Status in an American Higher Education Landscape." *Journal of International Students* 6, 2:367–393.

Rose-Redwood, CindyAnn. 2010. "The Challenges of Fostering Cross-Cultural Interactions: A Case Study of International Graduate Students' Perceptions of Diversity Initiatives." *College Student Journal* 44, 2:389–399.

Schmitt, Michael, Russell Spears, and Nyla Branscombe. 2002. "Constructing a Minority Group Identity Out of Shared Rejection: The Case of International Students." *European Journal of Social Psychology* 33, 1:1–12.

Schroeter, Sara, and Carl James. 2015. "'We're Here because We're Black': The Schooling Experiences of French-Speaking African-Canadian Students with Refugee Backgrounds." *Race Ethnicity and Education* 18, 1:20–39.

Sherry, Mark, Peter Thomas, and Wing Chui. 2010. "International Students: A Vulnerable Population." *Higher Education* 60:33–46.

Smedley, Audrey. 1993. *Race in North America: Origin and Evolution of a Worldview*. Boulder, CO: Westview.

Smith, Rachel, and Nigar Khawaja. 2011. "A Review of the Acculturation Experiences of International Students." *International Journal of Intercultural Relations* 35:699–713.

Solórzano, Daniel, Miguel Ceja, and Tara Yosso. 2000. "Critical Race Theory, Racial Microaggressions, and Campus Racial Climate: The Experiences of African American College Students." *The Journal of Negro Education* 69, 1:60–73.

Tamale, Sylvia. 1996. "The Outsider Looks in: Constructing Knowledge About American Collegiate Racism." *Qualitative Sociology* 19, 4:471–495.

Tas, Murat. 2013. "Promoting Diversity: Recruitment, Selection, Orientation, and Retention of International Students." *Journal of International Education & Leadership* 3, 2:1–45.

Trice, Andrea. 2004. "Mixing It Up: International Graduate Students' Social Interactions with American Students." *Journal of College Student Development* 45, 6:671–687.

Warmington, Paul. 2012. "'A Tradition in Ceaseless Motion': Critical Race Theory and Black British Intellectual Spaces." *Race Ethnicity and Education* 15, 1:5–21.

Waters, Mary. 1994. "Ethnic and Racial Identities of Second-Generation Black Immigrants in New York City." *International Migration Review* 28, 4:795–820.

Wei, Meifen, Kenneth Wang, Puncky Heppner, and Yi Du. 2012. "Ethnic and Mainstream Social Connectedness, Perceived Racial Discrimination, and Posttraumatic Stress Symptoms." *Journal of Counseling Psychology* 59, 3:486–493.

Wilton, Leo, and Madonna Constantine. 2003. "Length of Residence, Cultural Adjustment Difficulties, and Psychological Distress Symptoms in Asian and Latin American International College Students." *Journal of College Counseling* 6:177–186.

Yamamoto, Eric. 1997. "Critical Race Praxis: Race Theory and Political Lawyering Practice in Post-Civil Rights America." *Michigan Law Review* 95, 4:821–900.

Yan, Kun, and David Berliner. 2011. "An Examination of Individual Level Factors in Stress and Coping Processes: Perspectives of Chinese International Students in the United States." *Journal of College Student Development* 52, 5:523–542.

Yao, Christina. 2016. "'Better English is the Better Mind': Influence of Language Skills on Sense of Belonging in Chinese International Students." *Journal of College and University Student Housing* 43, 1:74–88.

Yao, Christina. 2018. "'They Don't Care About You': Chinese International Students' Experiences with Neo-Racism and Othering on a U.S. Campus." *Journal of the First-Year Experience and Students in Transition* 30, 1:87–101.

Endnote

[1] An earlier version of this chapter was published as a journal article in *Race, Ethnicity, and Education* in 2019.

Part III
Perspectives from the Field

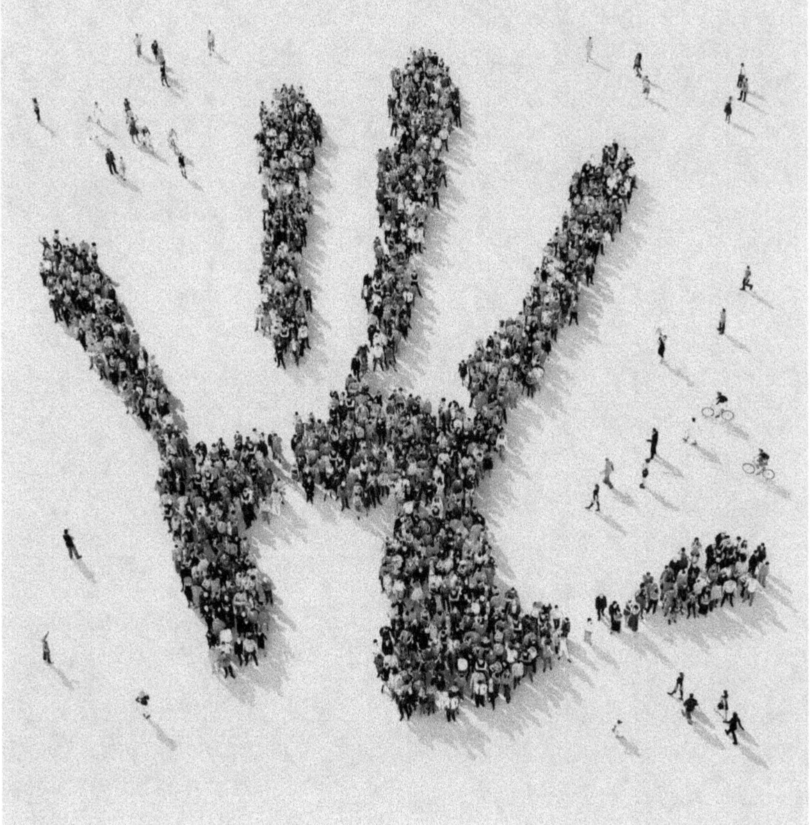

Building a Movement for Justice
Short-Term Programs Abroad

SHOSHANNA SUMKA, MAA

Shoshanna Sumka, MAA, is the executive director at ISEEN: Independent Schools Experiential Education Network.

The world needs students who are equipped with the skills to actively fight injustice and build community. International alternative breaks—short-term, student-led community engagement programs that enable participants to explore social justice and environmental issues at their root—focus students' altruistic desires on constructive and movement-building endeavors. As students learn from inspirational community leaders through direct engagement, they also learn to become active citizens in their communities, harnessing their energy, curiosity, and resources in ways that provide for deep learning, relationship building across borders, and continued action and social change.

To prepare for such international programs, students should spend time learning about relevant social justice issues, receiving orientation about the community they will visit, and completing training on necessary skills. Some schools may structure the learning around the United Nations's Sustainable Development Goals (including no poverty, zero hunger, quality education, gender equality, and climate action) or around commonly explored social issues such as the environment, homelessness, health, youth development, and disaster relief. In partnership with community-based organizations, the students can determine what they will be doing in the communities they visit.

While abroad, the participants may engage in stakeholder meetings and practice critical reflection each evening. I have witnessed student leaders sitting down with community activists in Colombia fighting for human rights, with women leaders in Haiti creating a better life through microfinance, and with

Indigenous leaders in Ecuador protecting their water and their land. None of these programs lasted more than 3 weeks, but all of them had a lasting and meaningful educational impact on the student participants.

Upon their return to their home schools and universities, student leaders may continue their involvement in the work conducted abroad. Some may create student clubs that address the issues they encountered during their travels, and others may even ultimately seek careers in human rights, social entrepreneurship, teaching, or government service.

The crucial piece is a focus on justice. A focus on justice means that each program has a strong learning component and a social issue theme to ground the inquiry and guide the direct service work. A focus on justice means acknowledging and addressing power disparities and systems of oppression. There are inherent power inequalities when students from the wealthy global north travel to the lower-income global south, given the histories of colonialism, racism, slavery, resource extraction, and exploitation of labor. Students are capable of learning about the darker sides of history. Suggest that they speak with individuals from their host countries before the program begins and open themselves to humility to recognize they have much to learn from the wise people they might otherwise think they are going to "help."

Ideally, students engage in truly immersive, solidarity-based learning that can be meaningful both for the students and the communities and partners with which they engage. We need a dramatic shift away from well-intentioned volunteerism in favor of critical service-learning that focuses on systems of oppression and underlying structures of inequality, with the aim of building global solidarity networks across borders. This is more sustainable and respectful of the communities that provide the locus for these important student learning experiences.

Alternative breaks or short-term community engagement programs rely on strong, mutually beneficial community partnerships with organizations embedded in the host communities. These partnerships must be collaborative, with the relationships defined in large part by the community, not by the visitors. Global service-learning may appropriately include activism, so long as the activism is initiated and led by the community. Some communities may simply request that students listen and learn and become allies and advocates by retelling stories of the community's struggle. An incredibly powerful reciprocal relationship can develop when students continue their engagement by bringing the learning back home. The deepest learning occurs when participants are encouraged to reframe the experience as a long-term commitment to global citizenship, education, and solidarity.

A unique aspect of alternative breaks is that they are student-run. With the right guidance, training, and oversight, student leaders have the maturity, determination, and energy to reach out to community-based organizations, to organize the logistics and safety components, to conduct outreach and orientation on campus, and to lead thoughtful and critical reflection practice before, during, and after the program. Student leadership does not preclude faculty or administrator support and academic engagement but enhances the experience, leadership, and ownership. Such global community engagement programs have the potential to create global citizens who are active in their communities and have the skills and knowledge to address the issues we all face. Students learn that communities are stronger when people work together.

Endnote

An extended version of this article was published in the May/June 2017 issue of *International Educator*.

Study Abroad
The Power of Finding your Place in the World

SALLY SCHWARTZ, MA

Sally Schwartz, MA, is executive director of Globalize DC.

People around the world know Washington, D.C., as a global capital and center for nonprofit organizations, government agencies, and universities engaged in the work of international education. But those who live here know that D.C. also suffers from deep divisions of race and class. For most of the young people growing up here, the global activity that is so central to the identity of the nation's capital often seems very remote indeed. The work of Globalize DC is to build connections between the two worlds of the global and the local, by leveraging the city's unique global resources to expand access for its public school students to global education, language learning, and study abroad opportunities. We have created and facilitated a range of programs that help students recognize and embrace this global identity as their own. We see this as an issue of social justice.

I began this work as a high school social studies teacher in the 1970s, when I organized my first study abroad program to the Caribbean. To this day, what I find most compelling about study abroad for the students with whom I work—mostly lower-income students of color—I learned in that first exchange experience more than 40 years ago. Quite simply, study abroad is transformational, life-altering work. For students coming from D.C.'s hyper-segregated communities and schools, often living lives that are narrowly constricted and lacking agency, study abroad experiences can be both mind-blowing and empowering. In my observation, it is not just what the students learn about other countries or cultures, or what skills they develop for future careers, but what they learn about themselves that creates the magic. For me, the essential questions for students during their study abroad are always: What does this new information and experience tell you about yourself? Your life? Your community? Your future?

The experience abroad creates context for students who have little knowledge of the wider world and helps them to reflect on their community. For example, a group of D.C. students traveled to Tanzania where they visited a number of UNICEF-sponsored projects. They returned to Washington, D.C., talking about the extreme poverty they had witnessed. Schools had nothing, they reported; students and parents even had to build their own desks and chairs! The experience challenged the way these D.C. students saw their own lives and schools. The most meaningful takeaway was their collective observation that poverty in East Africa hadn't taken the same kind of psychological toll that they witnessed in their own communities. The students remarked that Tanzanians even seemed to walk tall, with pride and joy. This subject prompted much reflection, historical analysis, and ongoing discussion within the group. Imagine the impact felt by these young people of widening the lens and finding hope in new possibilities, new ways of being in the world, and a new way of reflecting on their own lives.

Students find so much power and self-confidence in the realization that they actually can survive, thrive, and contribute on a global stage. As mostly first-time international travelers, many of our students leave home feeling some fear and dread, and then return weeks later bursting with pride and a new set of expectations for their own futures.

For example, for years, Globalize DC worked with Americans Promoting Study Abroad, an organization that hosted a summer Chinese language program in Beijing. Most of our students were studying Chinese for the first time, and because the challenge was so great, they felt awe and a deep sense of accomplishment in their ability to successfully function (even minimally) in a Chinese language environment. The program included a visit to a school serving migrant children, where our students taught English and otherwise engaged with the younger Chinese students. As with many service projects, this was a turning point for many of our students, who recognized, most for the first time, that they had something valuable to contribute. This can be such a novel concept when a student feels so little valued in his or her own community.

Now, after decades of work in global education and study abroad, my focus is increasingly drawn to the challenge of what to do with these students after they return from a meaningful study abroad experience. Too often, students return to schools that do not have the resources to support follow-up activities or help students take the next step on the career or life pathway they have begun. Most families in the underserved communities and schools from which many of our students come do not have the time, the networks, or the social capital to do this work themselves—as we see among their more privileged peers.

Study abroad opens a door for many students. But it is only with real supports in place, extending from high school to college and beyond, that students can turn a transformational, mind-altering initial study abroad experience into a career and life story that no one could have imagined, least of all the student.

Toward Family Diplomacy for a More Caring World

PAUL LACHELIER, PhD

Paul Lachelier, PhD, is the founder and director of Learning Life.

Nearly 3 years ago on a sunny spring day, I stepped out of a school with two children participating in our program, The Family Diplomacy Initiative. I had recently met the children's family and introduced them to our program. The girl, who I will call Sarah, was 8 years old, and the boy, Peter, was 11 years old. I looked at the clear, expansive view of the city before us and spontaneously quizzed them: "What's that big pointy monument over there?" Neither knew the answer. We stepped into my car, and within a couple of minutes, Sarah and Peter were singing along to a pop song they pulled up on my smartphone. They knew all of the lyrics.

This story is ordinary enough. Plenty of kids don't know monuments but do know pop songs. However, this was the Washington Monument, arguably the most conspicuous monument in Washington, D.C., and that was Peter and Sarah's school overlooking the monument, so they could see it in plain sight every time they stepped out of school.

All of us get lost in our own little worlds, especially kids. But our little worlds are inextricably bound with our larger world, for better and worse. Contemporary American philosopher Michael Sandel (1992, 92) once observed: "In our public life, we are more entangled, but less attached, than ever before." We are more entangled, in part, because increasingly, what we buy and see on our screens is made all over the world, because people travel and talk more across borders, and because more and more pressing issues, from terrorism to climate change, are transnational. Yet, we are simultaneously less attached because we don't see, feel, or speak much of such connections, let alone our obligations to this complicated world to which we are increasingly tethered. This is why what Sarah and Peter see, and don't see, matters.

Good schools do their best to nurture equal opportunity, even as their selection and tracking processes often create inequalities. But families and neighborhoods worldwide mostly produce inequality because of segregation. Segregation may not be written in law so much anymore, but it is inscribed in privileged parents' visceral desire for the best for their kids. From that powerful and understandable desire springs exclusive neighborhoods, networks, and schools to protect and advance privileged families, leading to the exclusion, frequently unintended, of their impoverished counterparts throughout the world. The poor and privileged often live within walking distance of each other, but dwell in radically different worlds with, commonly, very different outcomes.

How can we connect these worlds and address our pressing paradox of entangled detachment? Some will argue, rightly in my view, that the answer is political. We need governmental action to desegregate housing, raise minimum wages, expand public transport, provide low-cost and high-quality child care and education, and so on. But alongside those governmental solutions, there is a need for feeling solutions, or creative ways to extend that visceral desire to protect and promote our own kids to other people's kids, wherever they are in the world. I believe one such feeling solution is family diplomacy.

In summer 2016, Learning Life, the nonprofit I direct, launched its Family Diplomacy Initiative (learninglife.info/fdi). We began by connecting small numbers of lower-income families online via Skype to learn from each other about the world. We did so with the conviction that the internet can help open the world to those who cannot afford to travel. In 2017, we completed a community photo project engaging families in Jordan, Senegal, and the United States. In 2019, we completed a food culture and nutrition project involving families in El Salvador, Senegal, and the United States. We are now developing a Facebook group (facebook.com/groups/familydiplomacy) to engage thousands of families worldwide in sharing and learning from each other.

Family diplomacy is a novel form of citizen diplomacy and an accessible way to engage in global learning and citizenship. Across our globe, most people live in families and strongly value families. In our complicated world, people feel and understand the family better than any other institution. Families, at their best, are exemplars of caring in a world that needs far more caring. Families are also highly vulnerable and often directly impacted by world issues, from poverty to terrorism to climate change.

Families thus have the power to connect minds and hearts worldwide. Of course, families are never perfect, and some are downright oppressive. But we at Learning Life believe that by connecting people worldwide around family life and sharing the most tolerant and caring forms of family, we can help build a more just and caring world, a world in which we all become more attached to each other, a world in which Sarah and Peter see the monuments and more.

Reference

Sandel, Michael J. 1992. "The Procedural Republic and the Unencumbered Self." In *The Self and the Political Order,* ed. Tracy B. Strong. New York, NY: New York University Press.

Embracing Our Greater Purpose
The Role of International Education in Advancing Educational Equity

ANDREW J. GORDON

Andrew J. Gordon is CEO and founder of Diversity Abroad.

At its core, the goal of social justice is equitable access for all communities to the opportunities and privileges that our society affords. Given that international education is an integral part of higher education—a societal opportunity that continues to be a key factor impacting upward social mobility—it's imperative to examine the work of international educators through a social justice lens.

International education, whether at home or abroad, is an educational opportunity that, when properly administered, can be a high-impact practice that supports the academic success, interpersonal growth, and career readiness of students. Taking advantage of the benefits gained through international education positions students for success in our dynamic and interconnected world. Thus, the work of international educators can be instrumental in preparing students to thrive in the twenty-first century.

However, as with many societal opportunities, access to international education and its benefits are not equitably distributed among students. Participation in education abroad for students of color, first-generation college students, and those with high financial need, for example, is not representative of enrollment trends in higher education more broadly. Additionally, students from traditionally marginalized communities may face unique identity-related challenges once they decide to go abroad. These challenges have the potential to impede such students' ability to fully access the benefits of education abroad like their peers. Similarly, while certain countries have been successful in recruiting international students, there has been less success in building a culture of inclusion and belonging on campuses that would position international students to truly thrive academically and otherwise. Hence, in establishing that international education is an opportunity that supports student success, yet one within which traditionally marginalized communities are underrepresented and/or undersupported, the necessity to critically consider the central role of social justice in the international education sector becomes undeniable. What, then, does social justice look like in our field?

To me, social justice in the field of international education means that as individual professionals and as entities—institutions, organizations, and government agencies—we work to actively break down the structural barriers that have, in part, made our field complicit in contributing to educational inequities, primarily by denying all students equitable access to the benefits derived from international education. The question we must ask ourselves is whether we want our field to be one that perpetuates educational inequities or one that strives to democratize educational opportunity. What is our individual role in ensuring the latter?

Through my work as CEO of Diversity Abroad—a global consortium of educational institutions, government agencies, nonprofit organizations, and companies dedicated to supporting student success through advancing diversity, equity, and inclusion in global education—I work to advance social justice by championing the following: (1) equitable access to education abroad; (2) inclusive support for international students; (3) global engagement at home for all students; and (4) diversity, inclusion, and belonging among international educators. While these are four distinct components of our field, they are all interrelated and critical if our sector is to embody social justice principles.

Diversity Abroad's work in each of these areas is both strategic and practical. We firmly believe that a measure of passion for social justice is necessary to advance these principles in our work; however, passion in and of itself is not sufficient. In each of the four areas I've highlighted, our work focuses on structural solutions. First, through tools like the *AIDE Roadmap* and the *Global Equity & Inclusion Assessment*[TM], Diversity Abroad develops and disseminates diversity and inclusion good practice operational guidelines. These tools allow international education offices and organizations to assess their operations through an inclusive lens with respect to engagement with students, stakeholders, and the professionals who work in our offices and organizations.

Second, we work to empower educators. We do this primarily through hosting learning opportunities that help professionals in our sector develop the knowledge, skills, and competencies required to advance social justice principles in their work. Continued learning and development are essential for individual professionals to gain the ability and confidence required to advance practices and policies that support social justice within our field.

Finally, we connect students directly to relevant resources and opportunities. From our digital advising platform Abroad360° and scholarships to country-specific diversity insights and career readiness guides, we work to ensure students are empowered with the information, guidance, and inspiration needed to pursue global educational opportunities and then leverage such experiences to thrive academically, interpersonally, and professionally.

Advancing social justice principles in international education is not prescriptive. Each institution and organization will go about this work in slightly different ways. The important thing is action. I feel privileged to be at the forefront of diversity, equity, and inclusion work in international education through my role at Diversity Abroad. The passion I have for this work centers on my belief in the power of international education and its potential to position traditionally marginalized students for success. For our field to live up to its potential, we must never lose sight of the power of these opportunities and continually work to ensure our field embodies social justice principles in word and deed.

Afrophobia and International Education

KESHIA ABRAHAM, PhD

Keshia Abraham, PhD, is a seasoned scholar-educator bringing more than 25 years of international higher education experience to her role as founder of The Abraham Consulting Agency.

Afrophobia, the fear of Blackness, includes a range of negative attitudes toward Black people of African descent. Afrophobia is not the same as xenophobia, as it is not country specific and therefore transcends nationality. Afrophobia challenges Black students from around the world engaging in international education because it typically goes unacknowledged and unnamed. When students participating in international education share questions, experiences, or concerns about Afrophobia, they are often explored within the context of initiatives developed for broadly defined marginalized groups. If international educators do not name Afrophobia, how do we prepare students, faculty, and staff to address it when they encounter it at home and abroad?

One example of Afrophobia, with which I have personal experience, emerges from apartheid, the South African system based on racism and segregation that both the country of South Africa and the larger Southern African region have been transitioning out of since 1990. During apartheid, a White supremacist form of minority rule that lasted officially from 1948 to 1994, the all-White National Party enforced strict policies that made visiting or migrating to South Africa difficult for Black sub-Saharan Africans. During this time, African American, Black British, and Afro-Caribbean people who chose to visit or study in South Africa were granted "honorary White" status so they could enter the country without being subjected to apartheid's humiliating system of racial segregation but this exacerbated inequality between and among Black people—those granted "honorary Whiteness" and those not granted this status. For students like me, being assigned this status required embracing an identity responsible for establishing conditions of disenfranchisement in the very nations where the diaspora sought to belong. Students may not have been prepared to address this challenge—and even today, Black students may grapple with confusing or contentious issues of identity that stem from a country's history of Afrophobia.

While apartheid has officially ended, certain divides persist. When attacks against non-South Africans (namely, Zimbabweans and Nigerians) became a recurring theme in headline news in 2015 and again in 2019, people around the world were affected, prompting more complicated questions about advising Black international and study abroad students. Are we considering for example, what a "Black" student of Nigerian descent, born and raised in the United States, might be concerned about when considering studying abroad in South Africa? Blackness is not monolithic, so international students of African descent from different nations can experience Afrophobia very differently. Racial identities vary widely both within and across national boundaries. As such, Afrophobia is not only a fear of Blackness but also a fear of disempowerment and marginalization by other Black people.

As professionals committed to social justice, international educators must acknowledge that Afrophobia is rooted in racist, colonialist, and White supremacist ideologies designed to foster self-hatred, and we must work to counteract this worldview among our students. We must reframe historical relationships to recognize and talk about Europe's role in the global slave trade and colonization. We need to discuss and engage with postcolonial migration patterns that have shaped the diaspora so students experiencing colonial empires understand cultural influences and resonances; otherwise, international education programming runs the risk of inadvertently sustaining Afrophobia. Black lives are at stake when Afrophobia is ignored or dismissed.

The COVID-19 crisis in 2020 provides other examples of Afrophobia in action. For example, in the first half of 2020, the world became aware of a resurgence of Afrophobia in Guangzhou, China. The context for Afrophobia in China was highlighted prior to COVID-19, as referenced in Roberto Castillo's 2016 article "Claims of 'China's Afrophobia' Show We Need New

Ways to Think About Race and Racism," which opened with the question, "Is Afrophobia really on the rise in China?" The treatment of Africans of various origins during the COVID-19 pandemic provides an affirmative response to this question. The BBC published several articles within days of each other on the topic. One BBC headline read, "China McDonald's Apologizes for Guangzhou Ban on Black People," when a notice was posted on a McDonald's door stating that "from now on [B]lack people are not allowed to enter the restaurant." Three days later, in "Africans in China: We Face Coronavirus Discrimination," author Danny Vincent described blatant racism against African students forced out of their residences, kicked off campuses, and forced to sleep on the streets, despite no evidence they had any symptoms of COVID-19. As of the writing of this essay, there have been no articles posted or published that document similar treatment of White European or American people living in China. African students currently studying abroad in China are vulnerable to this form of Afrophobia, as are African American, Black British, and Afro Caribbean people living and working there, as their Blackness in this case supersedes their nationality. This is anti-Blackness at work. This modern-day iteration of Afrophobia emphasizes why international educators must be prepared to guide students through these challenging scenarios.

The question is, How do international educators address Afrophobia around the world? Afrophobia raises profound questions regarding social justice in international education: How does Afrophobia intersect with education abroad? How do we prepare international students for the Afrophobia they may face? What does preparing Black students mean in countries around the world when Afrophobia is acknowledged? How do we foster critical race consciousness within the African diaspora? And finally, how do we prepare students of African heritage or descent to be aware of their own biases toward Black identities when they travel abroad?

Because Afrophobia is also connected to intra-racial discrimination, concerns about Black students studying abroad in Africa are even more nuanced. Many students of color contemplating where to study have questions about their identity that their peers may have never considered, such as "Will I be considered Black there?" "If not, how will I feel about that?" and "Will I be welcomed?" Caring, insightful conversations as part of a holistic predeparture process can help students begin to think critically about these questions and others that may arise.

The process of fostering success begins in the initial stages of advising. Regardless of location, advising students of color necessitates a thorough understanding of who the students are and how Afrophobia in any given country may affect them. For example, when a student of African descent is advised about education abroad, faculty and staff should ask themselves, "What assumptions am I making about this student?" "What do I think I know about this student's family or cultural background?" "What are my cultural blind spots in advising this student?" and "How can I do this work through a social justice lens?" The goal is not to steer students of color away from studying in the country of their choosing; instead, aim to provide them with a framework for understanding identity in a new cultural context. Being aware of Afrophobia can help advisers address a student's academic and social concerns so the student will thrive in their host country.

We cannot continue to speak in generalizations about people of color without considering the specifics of what it is to be Black and of African descent in the world. Anywhere students go, it matters how Blackness has been there. We need to provide additional guidance and support to students, staff, and faculty to more fully realize the potential of international education as a platform for social change and a vehicle for transforming racial and social consciousness. To achieve these goals, we must diversify the field and our approach to meaningful, equitable international education.

Information About Afrophobia in South Africa

BLQ. 2019. "Afrophobia—Call It What It Is." April 4, 2019. https://blaque.co.za/afrophobia-call-it-what-it-is/.

Faul, Michelle. 2013. "What Life Was Like in South Africa During Apartheid." *Business Insider*. December 9, 2013. https://www.businessinsider.com/what-life-was-like-in-south-africa-during-apartheid-2013-12.

Pitts, Leonard. 2019. "Opinion: Honorary Whiteness Must Be One Powerful Drug." *The Salt Lake Tribune.* July 25, 2019. https://www.sltrib.com/opinion/commentary/2019/07/25/leonard-pitts-honorary/.

University of South Africa. 2016. "Afrophobia vs. Xenophobia in South Africa." November 15, 2019. https://www.unisa.ac.za/sites/corporate/default/News-&-Media/Articles/Afrophobia-versus-xenophobia-in-South-Africa.

Information About Afrophobia in China

BBC News. 2020. "China McDonald's Apologises for Guangzhou Ban on Black People." *BBC News.* April 14, 2020. https://www.bbc.com/news/world-asia-china-52274326.

Branigin, Anne. 2020. "Africans in China Say Police Have Told Them to Stop Sharing Stories About Racial Discrimination: Report." *The Root.* April 30, 2020. https://www.theroot.com/africans-in-china-say-police-have-told-them-to-stop-sha-1843179562?utm_medium=sharefromsite&utm_source=_facebook.

Castillo, Robert. 2016. "Claims of 'China's Afrophobia' Show We Need New Ways to Think About Race and Racism." *African Arguments.* August 12, 2016. https://africanarguments.org/2016/08/12/claims-of-chinas-afrophobia-show-we-need-new-ways-to-think-about-race-and-racism/.

Kuhn, Anthony. 2016. "For U.S. Minority Students in China, the Welcome Comes with Scrutiny." *NPR.* September 17, 2016. https://www.npr.org/sections/parallels/2016/09/17/491476036/for-u-s-minority-students-in-china-the-welcome-comes-with-scrutiny.

Small, Cy-Anne. 2018. "Black & Abroad: My Experience in Chengdu, China." *University Studies Abroad Consortium* (blog). October 26, 2018. https://blog.usac.edu/black-abroad-my-experience-in-chengdu-china/.

Vincent, Danny. 2020. "Africans in China: We Face Coronavirus Discrimination. *BBC News.* April 17, 2020. https://www.bbc.com/news/world-africa-52309414.

Information About Afrophobia in Europe

Atterberry, Arien. 2019. "Navigating Spain as a Black Person." *Diversity Abroad.* November 7, 2019. https://www.diversityabroad.com/articles/navigating-spain-black-person.

Giles, Gillian. 2019. "Being Black in Amsterdam." IES Abroad (blog). June 30, 2019. https://www.iesabroad.org/blogs/gillian-giles/being-black-amsterdam#sthash.lhZMK1HL.Kku7888F.dpbs.

Phillip, Nicole. 2018. "My Very Personal Taste of Racism Abroad." *The New York Times*. October 23, 2018. https://www.nytimes.com/2018/10/23/travel/racism-travel-italy-study-abroad.html.

The RED Network. 2011. "Afrophobia 'Staged Auction' at a University Student Party with a 'Jungle' Theme." *Monitoring Extremism*. April 18, 2011. http://www.red-network.eu/?i=red-network.en.items&id=645.

Street Law
Using the Law to Effect Social Justice

SEÁN ARTHURS, EdLD, AND JOHN LUNNEY, MSc

> Seán Arthurs, EdLD, was a clinical teaching fellow with the Street Law Clinic at Georgetown University Law Center and an adjunct professor with the Clinic. He is presently a principal at Arthurs & Associates.
>
> John Lunney, MSc, is a solicitor and course manager at Law School of the Law Society of Ireland and also leads its Street Law program.

During the 1960s and 1970s, as movements for social change and legal equality for women, minorities, and other traditionally marginalized or economically dispossessed groups gained strength and spread across geographic and political borders, law students, professors, and legal practitioners became increasingly interested in how the law could be used as a tool for effecting social change (Milstein 2001). In 1972, several innovative law students at Georgetown University Law Center seized the moment and decided that their skills could be best put to use by sharing their knowledge of the law with others, especially the law that affects our day-to-day lives. These students began by teaching Washington, D.C., public high school students a course in practical law and birthed a global Street Law movement, one that continues to build and grow internationally.

Street Law—where law students and lawyers teach about the law in local school, correctional, and community settings—is now the fastest growing and most popular type of experiential legal education in the world, and with good reason. The Street Law methodology of learner-centered, participatory education helps make the law more relevant, more accessible, and more understandable. In helping both law students and lay audiences understand their legal rights and opportunities, Street Law programs also help create informed, empowered, and aware citizens who are more likely to engage in all forms of civic action, from voting to volunteering, and from helping protect the rights of others to participating in efforts to make the law more just for all. Street Law programs now exist at more than 50 law schools in the United States, as well as dozens of international law schools, and are offered globally through local bar associations and state-related law organizations.

Though the Street Law program was originally keyed to the U.S. legal system, the model and its goals of improving access to justice and creating empowered youth are flexible enough to work in any country or context. Freda Grealy of the Law Society of Ireland recognized the universal applicability of Street Law during a visit to the United States in 2013 and knew the program would have a positive impact on both her law trainees and students from local secondary schools. Teams from the Law Society and Georgetown worked together to build an orientation weekend program that was hosted in Dublin, Ireland, staffed by Georgetown Street Law personnel, and welcomed 25 anxious but intrigued law trainees in fall 2013. From the outset, the Street Law partnership and program were huge successes. In addition to becoming one of the most popular opportunities for trainees and being featured in Irish newspapers and national television shows, the program organically spread to multiple other universities in Ireland and the United Kingdom. Today, the Law Society's program maintains its initial commitment to placing trainees in less advantaged schools, but also works with community groups, nongovernmental organizations, and incarcerated youth.

The collaborative work done by the U.S. and Irish teams to help Street Law "cross the pond" is one example of how international cooperation can help spread education models that grow and support social justice efforts. In addition to the immediate awareness and informational impact on the participants, the act of teaching Street Law creates a cadre of lawyers who are more interested and committed to public legal education and doing pro bono work, both now and in the future. The result of a public with increased levels of legal literacy and a more active and engaged legal profession is a more robust and accountable system of justice.

As Irish Chief Justice Frank Clarke highlighted shortly after his appointment, "there is little point in having a good court system, likely to produce fair results in accordance with law, if a great many people find it difficult or even impossible to access that system for practical reasons" (Phelan 2017). Street Law programs help lay audiences understand how the law works and prepares them to be more effective advocates for themselves and others. Street Law also helps participants and trainees understand how to change the law and the importance of working within existing structures and systems to effect lasting change.

The Law Society now trains more than 40 trainee solicitors annually, beginning with the fall orientation program that is still staffed by Street Law practitioners from the United States. The partnership between the Georgetown Street Law clinic and the Law Society of Ireland has created a program that not only promotes social justice in the local community but has also developed a community of practicing solicitors who are committed to continuing with this work through their legal careers.

References

Milstein, Elliot S. 2001. "Clinical Legal Education in the United States: In-House Clinics, Externships, and Simulations." *Journal of Legal Education* 51, 3:375–381.

Phelan, Shane. 2017. "Most People Cannot Afford to Pursue a Court Case, Says the New Chief Justice." *Irish Independent*. September 27, 2017. https://www.independent.ie/irish-news/courts/most-people-cannot-afford-to-pursue-a-court-case-says-the-new-chief-justice-36172754.html.

Perspectives on the Intersections of Social Justice and International Education

JESSICA BLACK SANDBERG, MA

Jessica Black Sandberg, MA, is dean of international enrollment management at Duke Kunshan University.

World peace seemed like a simple goal at the time. In the late 1990s, international education was a niche field that tended to attract people like me: buoyant idealists with voracious wanderlust. The ideals I'd gathered from my personal travels and my political science education rolled effortlessly into my new profession. As a student, I'd become a true believer in Woodrow Wilson's people-to-people diplomacy and was equally inspired by Senator William Fulbright's pivotal role in pioneering international student exchange. "Educational exchange," he said, "is not merely one of those nice but marginal activities in which we engage in international affairs, but rather, from the standpoint of future world peace and order, probably the most important and potentially rewarding of our foreign-policy activities" (Fulbright 1989). I believed that my work could bring young people together and bridge cultural divides. I believed I could help fulfill Fulbright's foreign policy vision. It felt like a calling. These forefathers of international education lured me into my career and, soon after, I met the living heroes. David Larsen of Arcadia University (then Beaver College), Allen Goodman of the Institute of International Education, and Marlene M. Johnson of NAFSA held up the lanterns, and I was eager to follow.

Many of us, and certainly those who came before me, entered the field in this manner. They were Peace Corps alumni, dual citizens, global nomads, former expatriates, first- or second-generation immigrants, children from military families, and so forth. As a group, we faced the crisis of September 11, 2001, alongside our students and immediately understood the new vulnerability and urgent necessity that the tragedy thrust upon our work. The industry sagged in the early 2000s under visa delays, xenophobia, and the sudden weight of monitoring requirements under SEVIS. I remember attending the first annual NAFSA conference after 9/11 in San Antonio, Texas, with 7,000 to 8,000 others. It was, at the time, the largest attendance the conference had ever seen. I remember impassioned speeches, loud voices, and trembling soliloquies. The open sessions with the Department of Homeland Security (then Immigration and Naturalization Services) were tense and raw. The mandate was always the same, though, and always obvious to us: *open doors*.

Soon after, there was a rapid creep of years in which universities, affected by various fiscal and demographic shifts, placed new interest, then focus, then priority, on international enrollment. Globalization became a regular feature in university mission statements. Those lofty ideals of the early days appeared to yield to an unapologetic commodification of international education. The pendulum had made its full swing back, and the industry surged. The ranks of administrators swelled. A new C-Level of senior international officers developed. An agency business boomed. Marketing, recruiting, and tech firms entered the scene. International education became big business. The idealistic abstract was not lost, but the drumbeat of the bottom line sometimes drowned it out. During those heady years, it was easy to forget the political nature of our work, until late 2016, when politics hit us square in the collective face.

The months of heated anti-immigration rhetoric surrounding the 2016 U.S. presidential election were further inflamed by the January 2017 executive order barring travel to the United States for citizens of seven countries. In worried conversations across social media, on calls, and surrounding the watercooler, the collective panic among colleagues was palpable. *Would students still come?* Movements are formed, not from a new idea, but from a common need.

When I came across the #YouAreWelcomeHere (YAWH) phrase, I recognized it as the message already on the tips of thousands of tongues in our professional community. I launched it and watched it catch fire (www.youarewelcomehereusa.org). It was a unifying and electrifying moment. Individual interests were cast off for the greater good. Colleagues rallied together. Even profit management played a critical role in the movement's rapid adoption. The fear of international student tuition revenue loss provided the necessary justification for many professionals to put resources into the campaign and, later, the associated scholarship program. Anyone who questions the true motivation of the campaign need only view a handful of #YAWH videos to feel the overwhelming spirit of its advocates. YAWH supporters were fighting for the meaning of their work, for intercultural understanding, and for open doors. World peace was back on the to-do list.

On a personal level, the YAWH movement has been the most gratifying experience of my career. It gave me renewed hope for our profession, our country, and our planet. I still firmly believe that education, for all the flaws within it and all the barriers that surround it, is the single greatest vehicle for improving the circumstances of the individual and forging understanding among the masses. International education may not resolve the divisiveness that has permeated so much of the globe, but it is a crucial part of the antidote.

Reference

Fulbright, James William. 1989. *The Price of Empire*. New York, NY: Pantheon.

Social Justice Through the Eyes of an International Educator

RODOLFO "RUDIE" ALTAMIRANO, PhD

Rodolfo "Rudie" Altamirano, PhD, is director of international student and scholar services and director of immigration and integration services at the University of Pennsylvania.

As a young boy, I yearned to study in the United States. This desire sprang from my perception of what an American education could offer: top-notch universities, a myriad of rich and diverse academic disciplines, access to trailblazing researchers and professors, and the opportunity to realize my American dream! In 1983, after a nerve-racking visa interview and an exhausting plane ride, I finally set foot in the United States as an international student.

Although I had braced myself for culture shock, I was not prepared for the unconscious biases, microaggressions, and instances of racism that would mark my entry into the revered experience of higher education in the United States. Back then, though social justice was a foreign concept to me, I felt the impact of its absence. Today, I have made it my mission to integrate the principles of social justice, including integration, inclusion, and intercultural competence, into every aspect of my work as an international educator.

As a student, I had my fair share of encounters with social *injustice*. I will never forget how a professor avoided eye contact with me for the entire semester and treated me differently from my American classmates. In another incident that still haunts me, a group of young men screamed at me from their convertible, "Hey, chink! Go back to your boat." When I applied for an on-campus job, I was told that the university did not hire international students because we did not speak English like natives.

Now, as the director of an international office at an Ivy League university, the stories shared by my students bring back these painful memories. Today, however, the stakes are much higher, and my commitment remains unbreakable. The United States is losing its luster as a top destination for the world's best and brightest students. The U.S. immigration landscape has shifted dramatically, creating an unwelcoming climate for international students. The refrain "You are NOT welcome here!" echoes across the skies and oceans.

When I came to the University of Pennsylvania (Penn) 13 years ago, I was adamant that the role of international offices should extend far beyond immigration. Even though I did not have a crystal ball to foresee the deterioration in the climate for international students, I was determined to promote their successful integration into this country and our universities. I was convinced that U.S. universities must *proactively* develop the infrastructure for successful integration and social justice in international education to remain the destination of choice for international students.

My new vision for international student integration at Penn prioritizes promoting intercultural competence and social justice across all constituencies, including but not limited to international students. Research has demonstrated that the positive outcomes of integration include enhanced well-being and retention (Andrade 2006). Integration instills a sense of global awareness and citizenship in all members of the university community. It affirms that every member of the Penn community, international and domestic students alike, should have the opportunity to be part of and benefit from a truly global campus.

Successful international student integration demands that intercultural competence and social justice be embedded in every one of our interactions with students, and it requires seamless cross-campus collaboration. This high-touch approach is the most effective way to ensure student success and wellness, produce global citizens, enrich the university's cultural and academic fabric, and promote a lasting culture of integration.

During my time at Penn, I have established a diverse array of programming to empower individuals as active bystanders and to recognize and cope with microaggressions and unconscious biases. I have striven to create a warmer, more welcoming and respectful climate for international students and scholars that recognizes and acknowledges their enormous contributions to the campus community.

Thirty-six years ago, I came to America as a young man committed to higher education but who felt helpless in the face of attacks on my sense of dignity and self-worth. Today, I am carrying the torch to cultivate an environment where international students thrive, where their presence is reaffirmed, and where their contributions are celebrated.

Reference

Andrade, Maureen S. 2006. "International Student Persistence: Integration or Cultural Integrity?" *Journal of College Student Retention: Research, Theory & Practice* 8, 1:57–81.

Social Justice and International Education
Where Are the Voices of International Students and Scholars?

LING G. LeBEAU, PhD

Ling G. LeBeau, PhD, is associate director of international student success at Syracuse University.

The call for social justice has become louder in the past decade, and the term "social justice" has become prevalent in the field of higher education. For example, a number of graduate programs in higher education include an aim to "promote social justice" in their mission statement. Terms such as "diversity," "inclusion," and "multiculturalism" are used interchangeably by institutions and stakeholders. However, in society as a whole—and higher education institutions in the United States specifically—students, faculty, staff, and administrators from underrepresented communities and cultures are still marginalized. Applying a social justice lens for our daily work could help us view students' and other campus stakeholders' success through diverse lenses and ensure they feel valued in our community.

Social justice efforts strive to address inequality and oppression. Within higher education institutions, social justice initiatives often aim to enhance students' understanding of social and political diversity and improve their critical thinking skills. Few initiatives, however, have focused on helping faculty, staff, and administrators reflect on real social justice issues in their administrative work or teaching. Addressing and promoting social justice issues in higher education administration and teaching could help us develop a welcoming, safe, and inclusive environment and cultivate responsible citizenry for a more peaceful and accepting world. For example, in a class that includes both domestic and international students, the instructor could create an inclusive classroom by intentionally facilitating communication among students, developing ways for students with different cultural backgrounds and learning styles to learn from each other, encouraging international students to share diverse perspectives, and designing activities for comparative analysis in class.

It is of interest, however, that diversity and inclusion initiatives at higher education institutions rarely reference global education or international students, scholars, and faculty. Issues regarding international student and scholar populations are often excluded from the agendas for meetings and forums related to diversity, inclusion, and social justice. For example, international students and scholars from non-English-speaking countries are often not included in governance bodies such as student government. Isn't it ironic that even as higher education institutions advocate for inclusion, they intentionally exclude certain groups of people because they are not "American" and they do not "fit" within the context?

To advance social justice in international education, higher education institutions must continue to promote international education as a means toward achieving greater diversity and inclusion in the world and strive to ensure that social justice policies and initiatives include all students, faculty, staff, and administrators, regardless of their country of origin. The success of higher education internationalization depends on the diversity, equity, and inclusivity of international education.

Finally, how have U.S. higher education institutions engaged international faculty in university governance and discussions of major university issues? What percentage of university leaders come from other countries? Are university leaders open to the different communication styles of international faculty, or do those faculty members not "fit" in either? International students and scholars should be included and integrated into social justice initiatives and strategies. Diversity and internationalization should not exist as silos but should be interconnected with all aspects of institutional life. Diversity must be viewed holistically from local and global perspectives. For example, a university's office of diversity should not target only domestically diverse populations but should be open-minded to include international populations in strategies and initiatives. Both domestic students of color and international students often feel marginalized on campus, and those developing diversity strategies and initiatives should keep both groups in mind to address these students' needs.

The social justice movement is reshaping the landscape of higher education and will continue to evolve with the demographic changes of students, faculty, staff, and administrators. As international education advocates, we should keep abreast of these focuses and challenges and ensure that the international populations on campus have their voices represented.

The Sustainable Development Goals, Social Justice, and Global Learning

JOE WARREN, MPHIL

Joe Warren, MPhil, is program manager and lecturer of global learning in the Global Education Centre at Stellenbosch University International.

I am the program manager of global learning at Stellenbosch University (SU) in South Africa. I live and work in one of the most unequal towns in one of the most unequal countries in the world. This inequality is largely rooted in South Africa's apartheid history, in which SU, as an Afrikaans language university, has played a significant part. This gives SU, and all staff, the enormous responsibility of driving positive transformation in our local, national, and international contexts and encouraging our students, both local and international, to do the same. Given that the United Nations's Sustainable Development Goal (SDG) 10 is to "reduce inequality within and among countries," this problem is clearly not ours alone (United Nations 2015). Global inequality is just one of the many interconnected, complex problems facing the world in our pursuit of social and environmental justice.

I believe very strongly that effective global learning would equip students to face, and tackle, problems such as the one sketched above. Global learning encourages students to think about the issue in a complex and systemic way, to work collaboratively and in a participatory manner to address issues, and to be critically self-reflective in assessing the efficacy and suitability of their actions. In short: global learning is a powerful tool to assist students in addressing the major problems of social and environmental justice.

There are a multitude of ways to try to define "social justice," and I won't try here. However, it is evident that the SDGs provide an excellent starting point for developing international education programs that are aligned with social justice. In my role at SU, I oversee the internationalization-at-home team and teach some of our global- and service-learning courses, among other things. I will expand on an example of each to illustrate how global learning, international students, and social justice can, or ought to, intersect here at SU.

International Student Organization of Stellenbosch

The International Student Organization of Stellenbosch (ISOS) started out as an organization to help orient international students on campus and provide cultural excursions and events. While these are both useful components of any abroad experience, we have recently focused efforts on redesigning the excursions to be more explicitly aligned with global learning and social justice. For example, our introductory Cape Town tour includes a stop at the infamous Rhodes Memorial, a monument built in memory of Cecil John Rhodes, the British businessman, politician, and imperialist. Rhodes is a controversial figure in South Africa because for many people, he symbolizes a terrible colonial past, while for a few, he is a generous benefactor.

In South Africa, many of our most pressing social justice problems—including SDGs 1 (No Poverty), 4 (Quality Education), 8 (Decent Work and Economic Growth), and 10 (Reduced Inequalities)—are, to some extent, rooted in colonial practices (United Nations 2015). At SU, we realized that we needed to include more local students in our excursions and facilitate discussions between the local and international students in thinking through how those practices still affect contemporary South Africa. We have therefore expanded our local cultural partner "Matie Buddy" system to include training for facilitating social justice discussions. These local Matie Buddies then facilitate discussions with our international students during this Cape Town tour and other excursions. This type of learning and engagement is in line with our internationalization-at-home, global learning, and social justice objectives.

Global Service Learning

The Global Service Learning (GSL) program is a development education program that encourages students to critically assess dominant paradigms of, and practices in, development. South Africa, as a "developing country," is naturally a beneficiary of all kinds of development assistance and aid. One of the most pressing development issues in South Africa, for example, is education (SDG 4); our mathematical and reading literacy levels are among the lowest in the world. The GSL program seeks to educate international students on the various reasons why this is the case, how South Africa and other countries approach the problem, and how to actively engage in addressing the issue.

For the active engagement part, our students are placed in a school that services learners from lower socioeconomic ranges. There, our students work in multinational groups with a local teacher to practice participatory development principles in a safe space (i.e., where they are closely guided by the teachers and GSL staff). The program requires students to spend significant time practicing reflective speaking and writing to encourage principles of lifelong learning and self-evaluation. For the fall 2020 cohort, we will be able to add South African students into the classroom, which will further strengthen the program.

Though these are two small examples, they illustrate firm principles. No single course or excursion could adequately provide global learning all on its own; it will take a network of intentionally designed activities over the course of the (co)curriculum to achieve this.

While I am proud of the work we have been doing, the principles of global learning are important for us as educators and practitioners, too. It is only in our own efforts to learn and employ more diverse perspectives that we can encourage our students to do the same. We need to think beyond the university, further than our disciplinary or professional boundaries, and more broadly than what we currently believe. This may lead to some discomfort, but *that* is a precursor for growth.

Reference

United Nations. 2015. *Transforming Our World: The 2030 Agenda for Sustainable Development*. United Nations. https://sustainabledevelopment.un.org/post2015/transformingourworld.

The Fight for Refugee Children's Education

ZAMA NEFF, JD

Zama Neff, JD, is executive director of the children's rights division of Human Rights Watch.

The schoolyard at night was hot and dark. Buses pulled in, but they weren't bringing children to class. In Sri Lanka, in the middle of the civil war, tens of thousands of people were fleeing rebel-held areas being attacked by government forces, walking into government-held territory, and being transported to makeshift camps set up in schools. I spoke briefly with mothers and grandmothers collapsing into hastily erected white A-framed tents. In the midst of this crisis, their questions surprised me. Government exams were coming up, and the women kept asking: How could their children take them and not miss their chance to continue schooling?

My experience that night fueled in me a passion for the fight for education. Since then, I have spoken with children who risked recruitment, kidnapping, and forced marriage to go to school in Mogadishu, Somalia; Afghan refugees who refused to return children to home villages without schools; and Rohingya refugee children who wept as they described being kicked out of classes in Bangladesh the day before. Syrian families landing in Europe have told my colleagues at Human Rights Watch that they embarked on the perilous journey of crossing the Mediterranean Sea because there was no education for their children in Syria's neighboring countries.

Far too often in the midst of protracted war and displacement, education is treated as a secondary priority or used as a political bargaining chip—with lifelong harm to boys and girls. The numbers are inexcusable: More than half of school-aged refugee children were not in school in 2018, according to the

United Nations High Commissioner for Refugees (2018); less than a quarter were enrolled at the secondary level.

This failure is even more stark when posed against the promises of the United Nations (UN)'s (2018, 13) "Global Compact on Refugees," which aspires to provide forcibly displaced children with schooling "a maximum of three months after arrival," integration in national education systems, and "access to…primary, secondary and tertiary education," including for girls.

There are plenty of reasons for this shortfall, not the least of which is chronic underfunding of education in emergencies. But the lack of funding is far from the only problem. Too often, host governments obstruct refugee children's education. According to our research at Human Rights Watch (Van Esveld 2019), the Bangladesh government not only bars hundreds of thousands of Rohingya refugees from enrolling in local schools but also has blocked UN humanitarian agencies and nongovernmental organizations (NGOs) funded by international donors from providing Rohingya children with any formal, accredited education.

Other countries have imposed bureaucratic requirements that prevent refugee children from enrolling in or physically reaching schools, costing them years of education. In Lebanon, Human Rights Watch found that prohibitive residency fees and documentary requirements imposed in January 2015 prevented many Syrian children over the age of 14 from crossing checkpoints to reach secondary schools, leaving internationally funded school placements unfilled (Khawaja 2016). The restrictions were lifted only in mid-2018.

Education is not a luxury or a bonus. Formal education, including secondary education, is a right that children are entitled to enjoy without discrimination. "We have a saying," a Rohingya teacher living in a Bangladesh refugee camp told my colleague, "if you want to destroy a community, you don't have to kill the people, just prevent them from studying." At Human Rights Watch, my colleagues and I are using our research not only to expose where the right to education is violated but also to advocate for change.

Donors, host countries, UN agencies, and NGOs should adhere to the "Global Compact on Refugees," which includes a three-month deadline for getting children into school, and governments should be held to account for blocking education for refugees.

Treating education as a right means that refugee boys and girls deserve formal, accredited education, not solely "child-friendly spaces" or "informal" school programs. Humanitarian groups that provide education may fear that speaking out against abuses will endanger their funding or antagonize the host government, but they should recognize when staying silent or providing services that camouflage but do not fix government abuses contributes to a discriminatory system that prevents children from getting an education. Donors, including governments and international funding mechanisms that have raised critical money for emergency education, should ensure that their funding goes to the kind of education to which all children, including refugees, have a right.

References

Khawaja, Bassam. 2016. *"Growing Up Without an Education": Barriers to Education for Syrian Refugee Children in Lebanon.* New York, NY: Human Rights Watch. https://www.hrw.org/report/2016/07/19/growing-without-education/barriers-education-syrian-refugee-children-lebanon.

United Nations. 2018. *Report of the United Nations High Commissioner for Refugees "Global Compact on Refugees."* https://www.unhcr.org/en-us/excom/unhcrannual/5ba3a5d44/report-united-nations-high-commissioner-refugees-part-ii-global-compact.html.

United Nations High Commissioner for Refugees. 2018. *Turn the Tide: Refugee Education in Crisis.* Geneva, Switzerland: UNHCR. https://www.unhcr.org/5b852f8e4.pdf.

Van Esveld, Bill. 2019 *"Losing Their Golden Time for Learning": Denial of Education for Rohingya Refugee Children in Bangladesh.* New York, NY: Human Rights Watch.

over&over

PÁDRAIG Ó TUAMA, MTH

Pádraig Ó Tuama, MTh, is a poet and theologian.

Here's the thing: What is past is never past.

And what happened before will happen again.

Remember Augustine? He went to the theater over and over and over. He finished the theater and he stayed to see another show. He lost himself in the losing of himself. He binged. It was over 1,500 years ago in North Africa, but he was Netflix binging anyway.

Nothing's new: The past is never the past and neither is the present. What has happened before is happening again.

History isn't history, it's urgency and it's now.

One hundred years ago, something happened that's still happening. What is it? A border? An annihilation? The answer is yes. The arc of history is long and it bends toward repetitionrepetitionrepetitionrepetitionrepetitionrepetitionrepetitionrepetition.

(When I was writing this, my computer corrected *repetition* to *reputation*, and then when I tried to correct that, it changed it to *reparation*. The truth is written on the walls—and if not the walls, then on the screens.)

Ten years ago, there was a man I worked for and I thought I'd never meet someone as incompetent as him ever again.

Twenty years ago, I found myself finally feeling free from a demon that plagued me.

Thirty years ago, I found myself saying a brave thing, thinking it would be the last brave thing I would need to say.

There is a place—I don't know where it is—where stories are written that repeat themselves.

over&over&over&over&over&over&over&over&over&

All of this is to say that history isn't history. And that because history isn't history, it's worthwhile learning that history isn't history. To look at the eugenics movement in Australia in the early twentieth century is to look at the way that things were repeating. "Be more subtle" the devils say, "hide your hatred in POLICY! . . . they'll *never* notice."

Yaaaaaayyy, the devils say.

> There is a place where evil stories go to be reborn.
>
> That place is ignorance.

I don't mean stupidity. I suppose I don't believe in stupidity. I mean ignorance, which means *not knowing*. Sometimes it might have an element of ignoring in it, but often we aren't avoiding knowing what we don't know; we just don't know what we don't know.

When my friend Marie wants to teach Emily Dickinson, she doesn't open the book. She creates a narrative connection.

Who has had a panic attack? she asks.

And they answer. It doesn't matter who they are. I know that you know you can imagine.

They raise hands, or nod, or say *Mmm mmm*. Or they hide their eyes. All of it is a response to a truth that isolates us in a story of isolation.

(Isolated comes from Insola, meaning Island, meaning we aren't connected to anything, meaning we are in the middle of a large sea. *Lord help me*, the Bretons prayed, *The Sea is so Large and my Boat is So Small.*)

Marie asks them what metaphors they use. Being buried alive, someone will say. Being suffocated, someone will say.

All of this has happened before, Marie says, and all of this is happening again.

I felt a Funeral, in my Brain

Emily Dickinson said. More than one hundred and fifty years ago she said that. Soon it'll be two hundred years. And it still happens. But little rescues occur when we tell ourselves that it has happened before.

And islands become joined. And borders become crossed. And people meet people. And history might change when we learn lessons of courage. And justice now doesn't need to be made from things unknown. It can be made anew from old and changed stories.

There is a place where things go to be reborn; reborn better. Maybe not brilliant. But better.

That place is learning. It is truth. It is beautiful because it sets us freer than we've been.

About the Authors

Becca AbuRakia-Einhorn, MPA, is the manager of education abroad and international fellowships at Gallaudet University, the world's first and only university designed to be barrier free for the deaf and hard of hearing. She is a graduate of the NAFSA Academy of International Education program and was named the 2019 NAFSA Rising Star Young Leader and the 2019 Diversity Abroad Rising Star. AbuRakia-Einhorn holds a BA from Pomona College and an MA in international affairs and an MPA from American University. She is working toward her doctorate in higher education administration at The George Washington University. She is proficient in English, Spanish, Portuguese, American Sign Language, Arabic, and Hebrew.

Supriya Baily, PhD, is a researcher, activist, and educator with more than 25 years of experience working on social justice issues around the world. Her work before joining the academy focused on refugees, youth, and women on issues related to agency and community transformation. As associate professor of education at George Mason University, Baily teaches courses in international and comparative education, gender and education, qualitative research methods, and teacher education. Her research interests focus on gender, education and empowerment, the role of teacher agency to support social justice issues, and theorizing qualitative research methods. She has coedited four books and has written numerous articles and book chapters.

LaNitra M. Berger, PhD, is the senior director of the Office of Fellowships in the Honors College at George Mason University. Her work focuses on preparing and supporting students, particularly those from disadvantaged backgrounds, in applying for nationally competitive awards such as Fulbright, Truman, Boren, and the Critical Language Scholarship. Berger serves on the NAFSA Board of Directors as the vice president for public policy and practice. She received the Spirit of King Award in 2015 and the Margaret C. Howell Award in 2018 for her work with underrepresented students. Prior, Berger served as director of leadership and international programs at the National Association for Equal Opportunity in Higher Education, where she organized three national dialogues on diversity in international education. She received a PhD in art history from Duke University and a BA in art and international relations from Stanford University.

Aaron Clevenger, EdD, assistant provost and dean of international programs, serves as the senior international officer at Embry-Riddle Aeronautical University and an adjunct professor in the Department of Security Studies & International Affairs. Clevenger holds an EdD in higher education and organizational change from Benedictine University. He earned an MA in educational leadership from the University of Central Florida and an MS in human security and resilience from ERAU. Clevenger is a graduate of the NAFSA Academy of International Education, Class 16, and currently serves as NAFSA Region VII's International Education Leadership and Teaching, Learning, and Scholarship liaison.

Eduardo Contreras Jr., EdD, is the assistant provost for international education, diversity, and inclusion at the University of Portland, where he also teaches courses in higher education and intercultural understanding and serves on the Provost Council and the President's Leadership Cabinet. He is the 2020–21 chair of the NAFSA Education Abroad Knowledge Community. With nearly 2 decades in public and private U.S. postsecondary education, Contreras has a long-term commitment to equity and comprehensive internationalization in higher education. In addition to an EdM and EdD from

Harvard, he has a BA in history and an MA in Asian cultures and languages from the University of Texas at Austin.

Shontay Delalue, PhD, is vice president of institutional equity and diversity at Brown University, where she also holds an adjunct assistant professorship in American studies. She completed her PhD in education through a joint program between the University of Rhode Island and Rhode Island College, where her dissertation research focused on the experiences of African and Caribbean international students studying in the United States. She received her bachelor's of arts in communication and master's of education from the University of Maine. Delalue has served as a partner in NAFSA's Global Dialogue Fellowship Program.

Chrystal A. George Mwangi, PhD, is an associate professor of higher education at the University of Massachusetts-Amherst. Her scholarship emphasizes structures of opportunity impacting diverse students going into and throughout college; the internationalization of higher education and higher education as a mechanism for international mobility; and African and African Diaspora populations in higher education. She has received NAFSA's Teaching, Learning, and Scholarship Knowledge Community (TLS KC) Innovative Research in International Education Award. George Mwangi received her master's degree in higher education and student affairs from Florida State University and her PhD in higher education administration from the University of Maryland-College Park.

Bryce Loo, MA, is research manager for World Education Services (WES). He has conducted research in the fields of international higher education, student mobility, and skilled immigration and has published and presented on numerous topics, most notably on credential assessment for refugees and career services for international students. Loo holds a master's degree in international education development from Teachers College, Columbia University, and a bachelor's degree in history from California State University-Bakersfield.

From 2011 to 2013, he served as a U.S. Peace Corps volunteer in Mongolia, where he taught English at a provincial teaching college.

Victoria K. Malaney Brown, PhD, recently earned her PhD in higher education from the College of Education at the University of Massachusetts-Amherst. Her qualitative dissertation explored critical consciousness in the narratives of multiracial collegians at a predominantly White institution. A scholar-practitioner, Malaney Brown's research interests focus on the racialized experiences of undergraduate students in higher education, intergroup dialogue, and college student activism. She currently serves as the inaugural director of academic integrity for undergraduates at Columbia University. She earned her BA in English and Spanish with minors in dance and Latin American studies from Skidmore College.

Tonija Hope Navas, MA, is director of the Ralph J. Bunche International Affairs Center at Howard University, where she oversees study abroad, global programming, and the comprehensive internationalization process across the institution. She is a graduate of Macalester College, where she received her BA in Spanish/Latin American studies, and The George Washington University, where she received her master's degree in tourism administration. Currently, Navas is working on her PhD in higher education leadership at Howard University. For more than 20 years, she has worked to increase access and opportunities in international education for students of color. She is fluent in Spanish and Portuguese.

Yecid Ortega, MA, is a PhD candidate in the Language and Literacies Education program and the collaborative specialization program in comparative, international, and development education at Ontario Institute for Studies in Education of the University of Toronto. He has more than 15 years of experience in the field of language teaching in Canada, Colombia, and the United States and has worked with teachers in curriculum design and action-oriented pedagogies. His general research interests are within decolonial critical ethnographic and case study approaches in international contexts. Ortega explores how globalization, capitalism, and neoliberalism influence language policy decisionmaking processes and their effects on classroom practices and students' lived experiences.

Malaika Marable Serrano, MA, is vice president for diversity and inclusion at WorldStrides—Higher Education. She has been engaged in international education for nearly 20 years. Prior to joining WorldStrides/ISA, she served as executive director for academic and field programs with Semester at Sea, associate director for global communities living-learning program at the University of Maryland, outreach and alumni officer for the U.S. Department of State's Critical Language Scholarship Program, and associate director for education abroad and international enrollment management at NAFSA: Association of International Educators. Serrano received a BA in sociology from the University of Southern California and an MA in college student personnel from the University of Maryland.

David Wick, EdD, is an assistant professor of international education management at the Middlebury Institute of International Studies at Monterey (MIIS). Wick's teaching, scholarship, and service are at the intersection of equity, diversity, and inclusion and international education. Prior to joining the faculty at MIIS, Wick served in education abroad leadership roles at Arkansas State, San Francisco State, and Santa Clara universities. He holds a master's of science in education and a doctorate in education leadership for equity and social justice. Wick is a recipient of NAFSA's Advocate of the Year and Lily von Klemperer Awards.

Tasha Willis, EdD, is an associate professor of social work and faculty director for internationalization at California State University-Los Angeles. She teaches courses on diversity, intersectionality, racism, and cultural humility and researches educational equity issues in both domestic and international contexts. She has led or supported multiple programs abroad since 2007 and works closely with campus constituents to create access and equity in international offerings. Willis earned her doctorate in higher educational leadership at

California State University-Long Beach and her master's degree in social work at the University of Chicago. She cofounded Social Work Abroad Program, a 501(c)3.

Christina W. Yao, PhD, is an assistant professor of higher education and a program coordinator for the higher education and student affairs master's program at the University of South Carolina. She is a qualitative researcher who primarily studies student engagement and learning in higher education. She operationalizes her research focus through three connected topical areas, including international/comparative education, teaching and learning, and graduate education. Some of her current projects include a collaborative study on graduate students' international scholar-practitioner development, graduate student teaching and learning in Vietnam, and the college transition process for international students of color.

www.ingramcontent.com/pod-product-compliance
Lightning Source LLC
Chambersburg PA
CBHW072121290426
44111CB00012B/1733